# Finding
# Normal

# Finding Normal

SEX, LOVE, AND
TABOO IN OUR
HYPERCONNECTED
WORLD

# Alexa Tsoulis-Reay

ST. MARTIN'S PRESS
NEW YORK

Library of Congress Cataloging-in-Publication Data

Names: Tsoulis-Reay, Alexis, author.
Title: Finding normal : sex, love, and taboo in our hyperconnected world /
    Alexis Tsoulis-Reay.
Description: First edition. | New York : St. Martin's Press, 2022. | Includes
    bibliographical references and index.
Identifiers: LCCN 2021037794 | ISBN 9781250140937 (hardcover) |
    ISBN 9781250278012 (ebook)
Subjects: LCSH: Sex. | Sex customs. | Social norms. | Online sex—Social
    aspects. | Online identities. | Online social networks.
Classification: LCC HQ21 .T88 2022 | DDC 306.7—dc23
LC record available at https://lccn.loc.gov/2021037794

# Contents

Some names have been changed to protect
the privacy of individuals.

# Introduction

My interest in the way people use the internet to challenge the boundaries of what's normal began in 2014 when my editor at *New York* magazine noticed the considerable buzz generated by a Reddit "Ask Me Anything" with a man who has two penises.[1] He suggested I write an interview column in the spirit of that candid Q&A: it would be based on in-depth conversations with people living lives unfamiliar to the typical reader of *New York* magazine. The resulting column, "What It's Like," was featured on the magazine's online human behavior vertical the *Science of Us*. It wasn't long before I realized I was onto something: it was regularly the top-performing piece across our website, and it was often picked up by other outlets. One interview, "What It's Like to Date a Horse," became the most read article, and for months I received messages or emails from readers, and hundreds more went online to leave feedback.[2]

"What It's Like" connected powerfully with readers because it gave ordinary people space in a mainstream publication to speak freely about things that they (and others) often did not feel safe sharing even with those closest to them. The brief was simple: I was to talk to people whose experiences weren't readily reflected in the world around me, and instead of editorializing, diagnosing, or judging, I'd listen while people told me about what it's really like to be them.

In retrospect I have to acknowledge that as much as the series was meant to provide an empathetic space for people to talk about difference, it could fairly be accused of problematically lumping together sexual identities with medical and psychological conditions, physical disabilities, and illegal behavior. I talked to a woman with a debilitating phobia of vomiting, a man plagued by the desire to amputate a limb, and someone who elected to undergo chemical castration because he couldn't stop cheating on his wife. There were interviews with people who couldn't recognize faces, who were slowly losing their eyesight, who had excessive amounts of body hair, or who had a very small penis. I also talked to mature aged people who had never had sex and, arguably most troubling, people who claimed to be in consensual sexual relationships with family members.

As a reporter I found the lack of coherence liberating: whom I spoke to and what we talked about were largely up to me, so I was free to explore anything I was curious about. It was a science publication, but I had a background in media and cultural studies, which definitely influenced my more qualitative approach to human behavior. I found most of my interview participants online. I signed up for mailing lists and Facebook groups, I used Google to locate blogs and virtual communities, and I browsed forums like Reddit where users from around the world gather to anonymously discuss very specific experiences.

The subjects covered represented my own perspective at the time about what would be both interesting and provocative for a general readership. Of course, I wanted the series to be widely read, but I was mostly looking for experiences that even in a very confessional epoch still weren't openly talked about.

I'd run ideas past my editors and then go on a search for people who were willing to confide in a stranger and have their story shared.

For about two years, from my office in lower Manhattan, I immersed myself in conversations between people from a range of backgrounds and generations. Then I identified myself as a reporter, made connections, and arranged to talk on the phone. When they'd adjusted to my accent (I lived in New York for a decade, but I grew up in New Zealand), we would become familiar with each other and talk for hours.

The conversations were confessional, raw, and intimate. We discussed their bodies, their sex lives, their deepest shames and desires. I was struck by how intimate our conversations were and the rapport we were able to build from a distance in a relatively short amount of time. People were usually equally nervous about sharing their private life with a reporter and excited to have the opportunity to candidly talk to someone at length, without the pressure of a face-to-face encounter. I often felt a heavy weight of responsibility for being the one who would eventually communicate their very private experiences to a public audience.

My interviews about sexuality and relationships invariably attracted the most interest and often went viral. On the one hand, readers were surprisingly generous and open-minded; many saw themselves reflected in the experiences of others and relished the boldness of those who talked to me without a filter. But others responded angrily, condemning me for writing about taboo experiences, accusing me of "normalizing" undesirable thoughts and behavior. As far as conservatives were concerned, I was a sick enabler assisting in this country's moral decline. As one blogger put it, "By asking some of the most detailed, graphic, and disturbing questions, that no one . . . would be comfortable reading about," I "put Howard Stern to shame."³ In liberal publications I was a dangerous normalizer. The accusation was that allowing certain people to speak in depth about taboo experiences would result in their behavior being copied or become a guidebook for anyone who might stumble upon them online.

What was striking, though, as I discovered when I was researching people to participate in the series, was the normalizing that some feared I was contributing to was happening online without my help. When people gathered and shared experiences and ideas, new support systems, identities, and ways of being in the world were created and became known, including to journalists like me. During interviews almost everyone said the exact same phrase, that after failing to find themselves in real life among peers and role models or on film or TV, they went online, where they were relieved to discover "I am not alone." I became focused on the internet's power to allow people who might otherwise feel invisible or isolated or even truly demonized to connect with others, share ideas, get information, and find a place where they could be "normal"—a word that was routinely used by those I spoke to as a sort of shorthand for locating their place in the world, finding community, support, and happiness, and knowing who they are.

When I conducted this virtual ethnography for "What It's Like," three things became clear. The first was the extent to which the internet was helping people who might have once lived closeted lives find community and come of age. This wasn't just a case of young people exploring new identities: coming-of-age could come at any age. I'd listen to the details of their journey, often a long self-directed search, and find myself in awe, marveling at how, against the odds, they'd managed to find peace.

The second was how normal people become, even those living outside the bounds of what might be "normal" to you, after you spend some time listening to them and understanding their world, their choices, and their courage to embrace who they are without a clear map. It occurred to me that this experience of finding normal mimicked the normalization that happens when people discover themselves online.

The third was how much the pressure to appear "normal" shapes the lives of everyone, including people who appear to be living quite far outside its bounds. While we might have found new ways to live, normality still governs how we see ourselves in the world; it's a relentless search from which it's difficult to opt out.

Another layer emerged when the interviews went viral. While many participants had been representing themselves online in closed supportive spaces for years, when their stories were picked up by an outlet like *USA Today* or the *Daily Mail*, they were exposed to a totally different audience. They were read by people across the country, and the world, and a conversation—or an argument—about boundaries and tolerance played out in real time as their experiences were shared, reposted, discussed, commented upon, and dissected online, on TV, and on radio.

As noted above, with virality came a mix of hate mail from people who worried that I was normalizing problematic behavior (with great variation on what was viewed as problematic). And in truth, behind the scenes, my own sense of normal *was* being shaken up. As you will see in the final two chapters, I spent a lot of time in online communities where experiences that were previously abstract became familiar or "normal" to me. In some cases this led me toward a radical empathy; in other cases it was almost as if my own sense of normal were dangerously compromised. And in one case, it made me question the limits of my tolerance in a way I still haven't reconciled.

The project also made me question my role as a reporter involved in creating content for an online publication. When my interviews were shared, they were often summarized, reduced to bullet points, reposted with a brief opinion, or simply reported as headlines. A good example of the way they were commonly repackaged by other publications is that when readers write to me, they often think the pieces are personal essays. And what about the practice of relying on a single source (whom I had often only met online or on the phone) without any context or supplementary reporting? Was I producing decontextualized clickbait?

I wanted to learn more about the less sensational ways that people use media technologies to find themselves as normal. I also wanted to consider in depth some of the more sensational experiences I'd only scratched the surface of for "What It's Like," especially those that were so taboo they went viral and received so much backlash. I wanted to celebrate the liberating, connective power of the current media landscape, which I call the "hyper-connected media era," while also exploring its potential dangers.

There has always been an "us" and a "them" that is exploited for mass consumption. In the nineteenth century, the great showman P. T. Barnum paraded biological anomalies like conjoined twins and dwarves—as well as fabricated "never-before-seens" like the Feejee Mermaid—before paying crowds of middle-class spectators as a form of entertainment. Part of the ticket holders' pleasure derived from the unconscious, comforting reminder that they were superior to those on display. The popularizing and dramatizing of the divide between us and them, or "normal" and "abnormal," was rebooted in the late 1980s and early 1990s on talk shows. At the heyday of their ratings, shows like *Donahue, Sally Jessy Raphael,* and *The Jerry Springer Show* were bemoaned for signaling social decay, exploiting the lower class, and promoting a breakdown of privacy. They were slammed by critics on both sides of the political divide for exploiting their vulnerable guests and sensationalizing complex experiences and identities.

But they had their defenders who urged critics to appreciate how they functioned as a radical public forum: audience members and guests could finally share their stories using their own voice. With the talk-show revolution and the concurrent explosion of tabloid news, we began to watch real people, people we didn't know, grapple with very personal problems, all manner of sexualities, and experiences traditionally excluded from the mainstream.

The shows were popular because of their Barnum effect, of course. They were also successful because they triggered their audience with base emotions like outrage, shock, and disgust (talk to anyone who works in online journalism, and they'll confirm that these are still some of the main ingredients for success). But they were also revolutionary. It can't be understated how much it mattered that they resonated with those who saw their own secrets, problems, desires, or relationship structures reflected in the media from the lips of flesh-and-blood humans often for the very first time in their lives. They became part of the media landscape that offered what could be called "templates for normality," scripts for knowing who you are.

Our fascination and concern with unraveling the private lives of "real" people went prime time in the early years of the twenty-first century with the reality TV boom. Mainstream media became obsessed with how real people lived their lives. Serial adulterers, incestuous families, women addicted to pregnancy, restless homemakers transforming into dominatrices, people in unorthodox relationships. These "real" depictions were sensational and salaciously edited, exploitative, and often literally scripted, but once the world began to hear stories of pain and struggle directly from individuals, unrelatable experiences were humanized, even if it was in hyperbolic form.

This allowed for empathy. Experiences that were once abstract became understandable, perhaps even relatable, and shared. And we knew the characters at the heart of the drama were real people who continued to exist when the camera was turned off, even if they were acting a certain way because of the camera in the first place. There's still plenty of reason to critique the ways that people were edited and scripted, but these were not fictional characters invented by a few individual elites who were lucky enough to work in media production; they were real people who exist in the world, and that mattered a lot.

But the biggest shift came when kids who are now adults we call millennials were being born or coming of age—that is, with the internet. Early adopters at colleges and in labs and home offices began to "connect" with each other online. Even before the World Wide Web was made public in the early nineties, people were creating chat rooms and communicating with one another anonymously across state lines and national borders. First came BBS services, then Usenet, and later chat rooms on AOL or Yahoo Groups. This made it easier for people to trade pornographic pictures or for fans to offer their own readings of *Star Trek*, but it was also, crucially, a way for people who for various reasons could not connect well in real life (IRL, as we say now) to form communities.

As more and more people went online and internet technology advanced its bandwidth and its accessibility went wireless, it became a force responsible for both shaping and reflecting our identities. Communities grew, populations that were already marginal joined forces, and new identities were born. The internet interrupted the prime position of TV, film, and print media as the vessels that impart scripts for normality. But it didn't replace them; it joined them, which brings us to the final shift that brought us to this moment: the rise of social networking and the blurring of the boundary between producer and consumer. While that boundary was already slowly being eroded by the impact of the internet, with the rise in social networking and app culture we all became media producers: from small, private audiences on Instagram or Facebook, using text and a pseudonym on Reddit, to larger audiences on YouTube or Twitter when content went viral.

In this country at least, media technology is now fully embedded in our everyday lives—on a phone in our pocket or on a laptop that lies next to us when we fall asleep at night. We are all both producers and consumers of media at once, at the same time. The technology has become more intimate and so have our ways of using it. We turn to the internet to manage everything from birth to death; we meet each other there for sex, to date, to marry. The sender-receiver model has been dismantled. It's a two-way street, and everyone is traveling on it: this is the hyperconnected media era, our current moment.

The hyperconnected media era is defined by an increased ability to connect with others we might never have encountered in our everyday lives, share information, form community, and give birth to new identities or templates for normality. In the hyperconnected era, media is connected to everyday life. The virtual and the real are intertwined in such an intimate way that it's impossible to disentangle them, but we are still bound by the social structures that govern our IRL circumstances. This is important.

With so many new ways of being swirling around us, the limits of our tolerance are being tested. There are more ways to be normal, but does that also mean that we are more aware of, and focused on, being normal in the first place? What are the limits? Can anything become normal? What stops something from becoming normal? What is normal, anyway? How do we find it? Why are we looking?

Normality is the unspoken set of rules that govern acceptable behavior. These rules are often so taken for granted they have become invisible: we hardly think about it when we put clothes on before leaving the house or brush our hair. In many ways, the normal gains its power by being so inconspicuous. But normal is not neutral; when we say normal, we often mean acceptable, good, sane, or reasonable, as opposed to its opposite.

As the philosopher Ian Hacking has put it, the normal "uses a power as old as Aristotle to bridge the fact/value distinction, whispering in your ear that what is normal is also right." Or as Peter Cryle and Elizabeth Stephens write in the introduction to their critical genealogy of normality, the word "normal" has a "dull charm," which is the source of its "unspectacular strength," the power of normal is "persistent but elusive." They quote Hacking, who importantly said, "the benign and sterile-sounding word 'normal' has become one of the most powerful ideological tools of the twentieth century."[4]

We look around us—to our family, our peers, institutions like health and education systems, film, TV, and social media—to find our sense of normal; we breathe it in, internalize it, and allow it to govern our lives even if that means rejecting it. Consider the last time you did something new and challenging (say, having a child, getting married, starting college). How much of what you expected from that experience was drawn from what you've seen on film or TV? How often did you find yourself asking friends what they did in your situation, or googling it to see if what you were going through aligned with the experience of others?

But if we are honest, none of us ever feels normal, because the normal is an ideal. Normal is the bond we imagine other people have with their parents. The perfect relationship our neighbor has with their partner. Or the dreamy lives we see our friends living on Instagram as we toil through loneliness or depression or just the drudgery of everyday life.

From the superficial (like our height or the size of our breasts or feet) to the more important biological hardware that lays the foundation for how the world sees us (the color of our skin, the number of limbs we have, our genitals) to the way we live our lives (what we do for a living, what our family looks like, whom we love or have sex with, how, when, or whether we conceive children), most of us will deviate from the norm in some way.

Normal is defined in relation to its opposite. It's only through labeling another person different that we come to know ourselves as normal: "heterosexuality" (as a word in the English language) did not come into existence until the coinage of its opposite, "homosexuality," in the late nineteenth century. Or as the writer Peter Kurth has observed while reviewing Michael Warner's *The Trouble with Normal: Sex, Politics, and the Ethics of Queer Life*, normality "is a hallucination, a mixture of statistics, concealment and received 'common sense,' bearing none but a comparative and usually intimidating relation to any individual's actual life."[5] Normality may be a hallucination, but it's a collective trip, and it takes a lot of energy to come down. While a culture's conception of being "normal" may change, and change for the better by becoming more inclusive and flexible, the concept itself remains: it is one of life's certainties.

As a culture, we've become more aware of, and very sensitive to, the ways that things are normalized. The phrase "the new normal" has become news-media shorthand for how people adapt their behavior to deal with change—from a personal tragedy to a global pandemic. But there's also a preoccupation with worrying about what might become normal. The fear is that if something is shared, repeated, and discussed enough, it will become taken for granted and normal. There's a sort of cultural Tourette's where the word "normalization" is used when people worry that something they don't like is becoming normal.

Concerns about normalization come from conservatives and liberals alike; normal doesn't necessarily care about your politics. When the United States legalized same-sex marriage in 2015, those who were against the revision of this supposedly sacred institution were horrified about what it would lead to, just as Democrats were worried about the impact of President Trump's normalizing sexism, racism, or xenophobia via Tweet. This preoccupation with the bounds of normal behavior is a sign of a culture confronting cultural change that can feel overwhelming or out of control.

Norms can be useful. We depend on them to create social order and protect the vulnerable. For example, most would agree that pedophilia and sexual assault should be illegal and that having sex with children or with someone who doesn't consent is not normal in any sense. However, things that are illegal can be normalized; "rape culture" is a good example of that. And things that are legal may violate cultural norms; in many parts of America it is legal to marry a first cousin, but in this country marrying relatives is certainly not normal.

Normalization can be scary. Some worry that young men's use of the internet for pornography will normalize the more violent and nonconsensual fantasies and practices they find there. Or that young people with eating disorders will go online and find support in pro-anorexia chat rooms or on websites where their damaging behavior is applauded. Or that the online normalization of things like misogyny, terrorism, and white supremacy will cause them to spread uncontrollably.

This awareness of, and obsession with, how, why, and what might become normal has come in tandem with the hyperconnected media era where there is a constant tension between what's normal (the limits imposed by our legal system, medical and educational institutions, the government, our city, our neighborhood, our family) and what *could* be normal (the stories, experiences, images, and communities we engage with online). This means that we are finding ourselves increasingly confronted by new ways of being in the world. How will we find ourselves in the hyperconnected media era? The boundaries between both are slippery, but when we are talking about the future of normal, it's important to always keep in mind those real-world constraints. Everyone must step away from the computer at some point (even if those computers are almost a part of us now). The real world matters, and the stories in *Finding Normal* show that face-to-face community, conversation, and role models are key ingredients in how something might become normal.

In the stories that follow, "normal" is used to mean locating yourself on a map, discovering language, role models, and a name for who or what you are. They at once celebrate the power of the hyperconnected era for rewriting the ways that people go about finding what's normal and warn about the dangerous side of that seemingly limitless freedom. These stories show us that normal has its limits; there are some things that we will never accept as normal. They also show us that humans have always wanted to connect, discover who they are, find community and a place in the world. Yes, that essential human search has been shaken up in the hyperconnected era, but we have always been looking for normal.

My reporting process mimics the way that the people you'll read about have come to know themselves and find a "normal" place in the world. From New York, I met people who lived in other cities and countries. My relationships were built over phone, email, text, and instant messenger, and then there was a journey and a face-to-face encounter, or series of encounters. I am not an invisible, objective narrator. Each story is an encounter between me and the people I write about, and that's by design because I want you to think about my role as a reporter, and by extension the role of media gatekeepers more generally, in creating content that contributes to the cultural fabric of what's normal.

The stories in part 1 are about people who have come of age in the hyperconnected era and found themselves as normal in exciting new ways. These three chapters did not originate as interviews for "What It's Like"; they tell the stories of a range of people who have used the internet to make a life-changing connection related to their sexuality. To some readers, the idea that they ever *weren't* normal to the wider society may seem strange. Everyone has their own sense of what's normal, and while some of the experiences covered in part 1 may be very familiar to you, others may be well outside the bounds of what you think is normal. Reflecting on the limits of your tolerance—your sense of normal—is part of the project of the book.

The stories in part 2 are based on the most viral, and controversial, interviews from "What It's Like." They confront what for me were more troubling taboos and questions of consent. As was the case for the readers of my column, they may make you feel that I am listening too empathetically and, in the process, normalizing behavior that shouldn't be normalized. In fact, for me, they had the opposite effect—forcing me to think hard about the limits of my generally open and permissive views about what is and should be normal.

Part 2 takes a more critical approach to the hyperconnected era and asks if finding like minds to share a taboo experience with means that experience will be normalized. What are the forces that stop something from becoming normal? What are the dangers of normalization? The stories in part 2 delve into areas that will be upsetting to many people, so much so that they need their own space in the book, which is what unites them as a pair.

Readers should be warned that chapter 4 contains themes and descriptions of incest and sexual assault that may be distressing or traumatizing.

I must acknowledge that by featuring certain experiences alongside each other, I may appear to be drawing a parallel between them or comparing them somehow, and I'm aware that might be the outcome when people talk about the book. To be clear, that is not my intention. The stories in *Finding Normal* share only the fact that the people in them have used the connective power of the internet and new media technologies to connect with others and find communities in which they are normal. If there's any point to be made by the presentation of these people alongside each other, it's that they all exist together in the hyperconnected era. If you look, you can find them; that's how I came across them after all.

The stories that follow ask some big questions about how we date, relate, love, and have sex (or don't have sex) through the small and intimate experiences of real people for whom the answers aren't thought experiments, people who are dealing with the same issues faced by previous generations—the quest to know who they are—but in a world in which constant connection has opened exposure to countless new ways of being. There are so many new ways to find normal. But that doesn't mean that normality has been abandoned as a goal; we will always be finding normal. The search is never ending, for humans and society; it will never be resolved. Like happiness or life purpose, finding normal is perhaps the definitive human struggle.

Part I

# Becoming Normal

# Ken, Russ, Emily, and Kathy

It was early fall and I was in a heavily air-conditioned room on a sprawling university campus surrounded by block-size frat houses and foraging squirrels, when I was sent back in time to what it was like to try to bypass the teachings of your immediate environment, find community, and "connect" with like-minded people about thirty years ago, before ubiquitous internet. More specifically, I was looking through the polyamory collection in the archives at the Kinsey Institute on a mission to find out when and how the concept of consensual non-monogamy, or "open marriage," came to be known in the mainstream. I knew that the internet had given this relationship template a much wider reach, but I wanted to know how people outside coastal cities, or college towns, in Middle America, rural locations, and Bible Belts got information and made connections before chat rooms, meetup groups, and online dating apps.

"Consensual non-monogamy" is an umbrella term used to describe a spectrum that challenges the idea that a romantic or sexual relationship should be strictly between two people. It incorporates polyamory, which literally means "many loves," and usually describes people in open and approved emotional or sexual relationships with more than one person. But there are many ways to be consensually nonmonogamous. People might say they're "monogamish"—a term coined by the sex columnist Dan Savage to refer to couples who might allow for occasional extramarital sex or have some sort of "open marriage."[1] You could be into swinging, or the "lifestyle," which usually refers to couples who enjoy having extramarital sex but aren't so much drawn to emotional or romantic relationships. The basic premise of consensual non-monogamy is that intimacy with other people is permissible if discussed and talked about openly—that it's unfair to expect one partner to fulfill all your romantic or sexual needs, and the idea of true love with a soul mate who can complete you is a cultural script that society expects everyone to blindly follow.

I searched through the boxes of material curated by Ken Haslam, a retired anesthesiologist and enthusiastic consensual non-monogamy advocate. He'd photocopied material on the subject from textbooks and encyclopedias in case one day all the books in the world disappeared. *The Continuum Complete International Encyclopedia of Sexuality* charts the history of the term "open marriage" and references the 1972 best seller *Open Marriage: A New Life Style for Couples*, which brought the concept of non-monogamy into the mainstream.[2] So in the early 1970s it was paper and ink that disseminated the information to households across America. Open marriage was covered in mainstream media back then, fueled by the sexual revolution with its cries of free love.

The word "polyamory" wasn't used, though. Next, I found a DVD of an interview Haslam did with a woman named Jennifer L. Wesp who is credited by *The Oxford English Dictionary*, which included the word in its 2006 edition, as the first to use the term. She explains how she was a college student in 1992, online, having a flame war (an online fight) about open relationships on the alt-sex newsgroup when she typed the word for the very first time ("non-monogamy" was too long, and she wanted to use more positive language).[3]

There were boxes of information about *The Ethical Slut: A Guide to Infinite Sexual Possibilities*. It was published in 1997 and came to be known as the bible of polyamory. The authors, Janet Hardy (who used a pseudonym for the book's first edition) and Dossie Easton, turned on their head myths about jealousy, true love, and sexual desire. Their mission: to shatter the fundamental idea that the ideal relationship is long term and monogamous and that true love is the result of a lifelong "connection" between just two people who forsake interest in anyone else, forever. They rejected the idea promoted by romantic songs and film and TV that "true love" conquers all, and they laughed at one of the central components of the myth of monogamy: that there's one perfect person out there who can complete us. For Hardy and Easton, our culture is "monogamy-centrist"; in fact monogamy is a cultural construct that had led us to assume that any relationship not geared toward lifetime bonding has failed.[4] The human capacity for love, sex, and connection is infinite, but most people have been schooled so hard in monogamy that they "submerge" their identities in relationships, which is "psychological suicide."[5] The "ethical" part of their name meant that abundant love should be practiced responsibly—with openness and communication.

Hardy and Easton's book was revolutionary stuff, using the tone of a pair of fed-up "sluts" who were possibly writing from bed in a postcoital daze ("I'm in the bedroom right now. My life partner is in the bathroom, showering another woman's juices off his skin," they write in one early chapter).[6] They were on a mission to normalize sexuality and introduce the people of mainstream America to a concept called "sex positivity," which was first used by educators at the National Sex Forum in the 1960s.[7] Sex positivity is a commitment to the belief that sex is a positive force in our lives. Someone who is sex positive is open-minded and nonjudgmental about consensual sexuality whatever form it may take.

The *Encyclopedia of Sexuality* also referred to a psychologist named Deborah Anapol as a leader of the "contemporary polyamory movement" that emerged in the 1990s.[8] Her book *Love Without Limits*, a guide to managing open marriages, got widespread media coverage when it was first published in 1992.[9] She also helped found an alternative magazine about polyamory and ran an early online resource network for people interested in opening up their marriage. I found piles of 1990s magazines with cover stories about consensual non-monogamy, or open marriage. It was as if editors at all the glossies had a meeting and decided they must all have a take on this "new" phenomenon, and frankly you'd be forgiven for thinking that there was a virus threatening marriages across the nation. In the summer of 1990, *Glamour* magazine asked, "Can lovers cheat and still be faithful?"[10] A few years later *Cosmopolitan* covered it in sensational, woman-shaming fashion with the cover line "Married . . . with lover (who is someone else's husband)."[11] Consensual non-monogamy was having another media moment, but just like in the 1970s it was firmly seen as a threat to that omnipresent relationship model: monogamous marriage.

Talk shows were also thirsty for this sort of material. They embraced the conversation about consensual non-monogamy, but largely with a sneer, presenting those in open relationships as abnormal or, to be more specific, deviant, oversexed, and possibly insane. They usually featured Deborah Anapol and her colleagues Barry Northrop and Ryam Nearing before a horrified audience, who stood in for the viewers at home. It was easy to imagine the producer's thought process: Anapol and company were white, professional, well dressed, and articulate heterosexual men and women. These weren't unrelatable bearded and shaggy free-love hippies shacked up in yurts somewhere in California. They were maybe even people whom magazine editors and TV producers would socialize with.

On her talk show in 1992, the comedian Joan Rivers plays the jaded single who can't imagine why anyone would jeopardize their marriage by having sex with other people.[12] On this show the nonmonogamous are oversexed and greedy; they hoard lovers. "I'm dating," she says, amid a performative dry retch, "and I don't even want a man to say another woman is attractive." She lists all the problems: jealousy, the impact on kids, what the neighbors will think, laundry ("Two men? That's a lot of dirty jockstraps"). "How do you keep your calendar straight?" But despite the shtick, she asks some sensible questions and seems intrigued by the arrangement. "I know I sound stupid, but I loved when I was married that I could really trust this person." To which Anapol replies, "Why can't you trust two people?" Anapol explains that when she opened up her marriage, she charted a journey without a map; she didn't have any models: "Until my book came out, there really was no other source to read about these things and understand there are other options."

On *Donahue*, one of the most popular talk shows of the period, a more sensitive host does not make the reception any less brutal.[13] A twenty-two-year-old woman is especially outraged: "I think these people are a little too old to be playing these games." *Diseases! Kids! Grow up!* The show ends with a man grumbling, "That you haven't been able to find the beauty in a monogamous relationship, there's some deficiency in your personality."

I went back to the piles of paper and magazines and found a whole box dedicated to Anapol. I paused on the letters that had come in response to her talk-show appearances; there were so many that she'd even recorded the number of letters she received each time she appeared on a different show. After

*Donahue* she got at least one letter each day, but on busy days it was more like ten.

The letters weren't full of outrage like those audience members cherry-picked on TV. Instead, people from across North America and even abroad offered moving, confessional, and sometimes desperate pleas for information about this script for a new way to be in the world. They were riddled with intimate details, often pages long, sometimes accompanied by Polaroid photos. The correspondents related to her, and when she spoke, they saw themselves, or at least their ideas, reflected back on TV maybe for the very first time. A man from Texas wrote, "I should express the respect I have for you having the confidence to allow yourselves to be subjected to the public scrutiny which you faced by appearing on *Donahue*. Listening to you touched my heart."[14] Those talk shows might have been sensational and hostile, but when people across the country watched this woman speak on their TV screens, they saw themselves for the very first time, and they reached out, eager to connect with a like mind. In a typewritten letter, a man from California wrote, "I am pleased to find that someone else exists who believes as I do."[15]

They wanted connection. They wanted community. They wanted information, and they wanted to thank her for having the strength and courage to break a taboo and become the face of a new way of being normal. People told their life stories and offered details about their romantic and sexual histories, interests, and lifestyles as if she were a matchmaker. Maybe indicating a need to confess and be seen, many sent photographs. "I am a red headed empath, I love children and do not smoke or drink," wrote a postal worker who also provided two glossy self-portraits.[16] A thirty-six-year-old from rural Mississippi wrote about the trouble he and his wife had finding someone with whom they could "develop a discreet relationship" owing to their professional reputations and the fact that they live in the Bible Belt.[17] They included photos because they wanted to meet sex partners, but the pictures also showed Anapol that the letter writers—these anonymous men and women writing from afar—were upstanding, respectable, "normal" people.

For some, the challenge of connecting with like minds—and sexual partners—was the most frustrating. Even finding Anapol's name and address was an odyssey. "I was glad to see your representatives on the *Donahue* show several months ago but I did not write to you then . . . because I wasn't prepared to deal with another disappointment about connecting with people," wrote one.[18] There were many apologies for misspelling the organization's name, usually blaming it on the brief window of time they had to write the information down.

A retired couple from Wyoming went on a hell of a quest for a connection with a third person to bring into their marriage; they'd placed advertisements in magazines and newspapers, but they were unsuccessful. The woman who wrote the letter first saw Anapol on *The Jerry Springer Show* a year before her 1992 *Sally Jessy Raphael* appearance and made numerous calls to the network asking to connect with Anapol, but they were never passed on. It was sheer luck when, twelve months later, her husband came back from the kitchen and saw her name and address flash on the TV screen. But it was a surprise, so they weren't prepared with a pen and paper. The intrepid couple didn't give up. Next, they contacted the network and paid for transcripts. When they got them a few weeks later, they combed through them to find an address for Anapol's organization. Back in the polyamory archives, I looked at the photos of a smiling elderly pair with matching cropped curls posing in a studio against a backdrop of sky and clouds, and marveled at their determination.[19] This really was a way of being in the world without an easily identifiable script.

While some lived in locations that provided ways to connect—newsletters, community organizations, and alternative bookstores—many who wrote to Anapol didn't have access to anything of the kind. They also lacked internet resources where these themes were being discussed—like that Usenet group where the word "polyamory" was first used. But more than that, they couldn't even find her book. There was no Amazon at the time, and many letter writers complained that it wasn't on the shelves at their local bookstore or library; some had trolled the region searching for a copy. Requests came from Richmond, Virginia; Albuquerque, New Mexico; Milwaukee, Wisconsin; West Liberty, Kentucky; and Muncie, Indiana. A woman from rural California wrote on hot-pink paper, saying how happy she was to see two very intelligent people who shared her views on monogamy. She explained that she and her husband have considered opening their marriage, or engaging in swinging, but have had trouble knowing how to find like-minded couples. "My thanks to you both for appearing on nationwide TV to discuss the subject. I hope there are lots more out there like you,"[20] she wrote.

At the top of each letter Anapol indicated which of three main themes it hit on: a desire for *community* with like-minded people, a *connection* (or in many cases a sex partner to bring into a marriage), and requests for *information*. After reading all the letters, I'd add a fourth: a desire to compliment Anapol for having the courage to speak up and become the face of what was then considered a very taboo lifestyle. She was the human face of a set of ideas that might have previously been abstract, and people were desperate to thank her for that. When she was beamed into living rooms across the country, she showed viewers who felt the same way she did that they were not alone. By being visible and talking about this alternative path, she let people know about a shared experience for which there may even be a template to help them discover who they are. She made it normal.

Three decades after the publication of Anapol's book, polyamory, consensual non-monogamy, and the idea of "open marriage" are everywhere. Ethical non-monogamy is a concept that people have heard of; it's a phrase that's known. Open marriages are the subject of sympathetic features in *The New York Times Magazine* and *Rolling Stone* as well as women's magazines like *Marie Claire* and *Elle*.[21] And there are countless ways to get information and connect with other people who are questioning monogamy: many dating websites and apps have the option to indicate that you are open to non-monogamy, and there are a range of non-monogamy-focused websites for connecting with partners. There are discussion groups, newsletters, subreddits, and Facebook groups devoted to the entire spectrum of non-monogamy, from swinging to polyamorous triads or alternative family structures. In 2018, *New York* magazine's *The Cut* asked me to write a Thanksgiving piece about consensually nonmonogamous people coming out to their families.[22]

Most often, history is erased in media conversations about current consensual non-monogamy. It's described as a brand-new template; young people who are growing up in a more sexually permissive era than their boomer parents have access to the internet, which indoctrinates them into open relationships. A 2014 feature in *Rolling Stone*, "Tales from the Millennials' Sexual Revolution," distills that take. The writer argues that there's a new brand of non-monogamy sweeping the country that's young and hot and "cool." She heralds millennials as "pioneers" navigating a limitless "sexual terrain" that no previous generation had felt comfortable exploring.[23]

But despite all this, in the mainstream monogamy is still the norm—as both an ideal and a relationship model. The only thing more sacred than traditionalists holding that marriage is between a man and a woman is the underlying assumption of monogamy. While marriage rates have decreased by about 8 percent since the 1990s, and the median age for marriage has increased (people are staying single longer), marriage as an institution hasn't really been threatened.[24] In fact by 2017, half of American adults were married.[25]

When Dr. Heath Schechinger, a Bay Area psychologist, started practicing in 2016, he was shocked at both the monogamy-centric nature of the industry and the near absence of studies looking at the outcomes of nonmonogamous relationships. "About one in five of the U.S. adult population have engaged in consensual non-monogamy—it's as common as owning a cat," he said to me on the phone—but despite the community being so large, those who practice psychology know very little about it and unfortunately propagate the same myths about consensual non-monogamy that are still found in the media: that it's something immature, damaged, or otherwise dysfunctional people are drawn to; that it's unstable and certain to fail. People try it because they were unsuccessful in normal "monogamous" relationships; they're over-sexed, harming children, and ruining families. According to this normative logic, it's just a stage. Once they have all that sex out of their system, they'll calm down.

Why does monogamy remain the most "normal" and accepted template for relationships? Dr. Schechinger says that while some individual attitudes might have shifted, our cultural laws and regulations were created under a paradigm of religious fundamentalism. But more than that, unlike some other markers of difference—say, race—sex is easily hidden. The best way to destigmatize something is to show it to people. It's only through "exposure" that things become normal. The human impulse to fit in is very powerful. The pressure to fall in line with the status quo—even if only for appearance's sake—is relentless. As he

put it, "Nobody wants to be weird." And there lies the dilemma
when it comes to consensual non-monogamy: it becomes a self-
fulfilling loop; many people who practice it keep it hidden because of the stigma, and it never becomes normal.

Kinsey's polyamory collection was put together by Ken Haslam,
an eighty-seven-year-old polyamory advocate who lives in a re-
tirement village in North Carolina. About a year before my visit,
I'd heard him talk on a podcast discussing his involvement in
nonmonogamous communities in the 1990s, and I emailed asking him to talk to me about his history with the movement.[26]
He'd responded quickly and enthusiastically, and we'd begun
a series of Skype conversations. Each time, I found him smiling, wearing the same rainbow suspenders and a plaid shirt that
made him look like a cross between an Amish farmer and an
aging hippie. His current partner—a "nonpracticing bisexual"
with whom he says he's "85 percent happy"—was often milling
around behind him folding socks or getting tea.

Because of his age, and his reputation as a sort of poly-
godfather figure, I was expecting Ken to tell me an analog story of
discovery before the days of apps like FetLife or the polyamorous
option on OkCupid, but he didn't discover polyamory or ethical
non-monogamy until he was in his early sixties. A retired anesthesiologist who'd grown tired of his mostly conservative profession,
he'd had his midlife crisis, gone through a "nasty court divorce,"
and decided that he was done with marriage. This disillusion-
ment put him in a dark place; he ended up living on a farm, with
a cat and some goats, where he thought he'd be forever a recluse.
He had dial-up internet, though, and something he read online
led him to believe that society was telling him something that, as
he puts it (he likes to refer to himself in the third person), "just
didn't work for Ken Haslam." He was online when he discovered a
word for what he was: "polyamorous." It was a sea change in how

he thought about the world: "I essentially said, fuck you, society, I'm going to try it my way."

. Like that couple from Wyoming, he was intrepid. But unlike them he had the internet. So, starting with some scraps of information he found online, he worked the phone and wrote letters. He joined as many poly or consensual non-monogamy-focused communities as he could. When he heard about Deborah Anapol's research network, he got in touch and learned that there were local meetings across the country. Someone recommended *The Ethical Slut*; so he sat down and read it over the course of a few days. He visited chat rooms; he even tried to set up his own listserv called "poly geezers" to connect with people his age who were identifying the same way he did.

But he was at a meeting for members of Loving More, a polyfidelitous education and research group, when he heard about a local community of open-minded people who gathered to have picnics and dinners, go bowling or dancing, and occasionally have what Ken referred to as "extracurricular sex." It was an adult "social club" called Delaware Valley Synergy that started in the 1970s, inspired by communes in California, and at its peak in 2000 had over four hundred members. Ken's new contact said he'd try to score him a spot. He did, and Ken made connections that have lasted to this day.

He described Synergy as like an extended family. There was sex, a lot of it, but that wasn't the main appeal. When he joined, he found a tight-knit community of like-minded people who all saw themselves outside the mainstream of "proper," normal behavior when it came to their attitude toward sex. They formed deep, long-lasting friendships while they went on a journey together rejecting the norms that governed their own sexual coming-of-age and learning a new template for how to be in the world.

Ken asked his old friends whether they'd be willing to talk

to me. Many were worried that after all these years of keeping their participation in Synergy secret, they'd be outed. But his core group were keen to relive the early days. My first conversation was with then sixty-two-year-old Emily, a retired insurance worker, and her eighty-year-old husband, Russ, a retired teacher from Pennsylvania, former members of the Synergy steering committee. Occasionally talking over each other on speakerphone, like Ken they were brimming with memories about the community that changed their life. They told me about the lack of sex education they'd had growing up in the 1940s and 1960s and the long-lasting friendships they made in Synergy. They discussed the sex. "Do you know what a puppy pile is?" was one of the first questions Russ asked me. I didn't, but not wanting to come across as naive, I said "of course," and quickly typed the words into my computer to run Google image search, where I saw pictures of heaps of semi-naked bodies intertwined like a litter of newborn pups.

They organized a reunion at their house in Chester County, Pennsylvania, just outside Philadelphia, and invited me to join. They lured Ken from Durham with the promise of a king-size bed and Kathy, a retired teacher from New Jersey who was also part of their original crew. Two other couples would come for a dinner party. They don't have sex much these days, I was told, but they are still the best of friends, and they were keen to finally share this history with someone from outside the community.

I was struck by their openness and sense of social adventure; I probably wouldn't invite a stranger to stay for the weekend. Of course it did cross my mind: Would they have sex with each other while I was there? Maybe, I thought, when Emily left me a very direct voice mail informing me that they may all get in the Jacuzzi and I may be more comfortable in a swimsuit so I'd really better pack one (as it turned out, nobody was in the mood). Then I reasoned, if that is what they're planning, that was a code to let me know I wasn't obliged to join in.

Emily and Russ kept in constant touch leading up to the event, asking me about my taste in food and drink, giving me detailed information about train schedules. On the day I arrived, I was curious about what they'd be like in person, and given how open they'd been about sex and their alternative relationship structures, I was taken aback by their gender normativity when Emily texted me saying that she'd be sending the men to pick me up from the train station while she and Kathy finished preparing dinner.

Russ was waiting for me on the platform. He's five feet ten and skinny at about 155 pounds. With his bald head and puffer vest he looked closer to fifty than eighty; in fact the only thing that gave away his age was a flip phone the size of a brick bulging in his pocket. Ken was having a snooze in the car. He'd flown in from Durham earlier that morning and was zonked from the journey, but I instantly recognized his plaid shirt and suspenders and his gray hair pulled back in a ponytail. I'd gotten to know Ken so well, albeit virtually, that it felt more as if I were visiting a friend. Maybe the combination of frank, open conversation about sexuality and video calls had fast-tracked an intimacy that might have otherwise taken much longer? But also, it was as if I could sense how hospitable and socially competent the whole group was, even from afar.

Emily and Kathy waved at us from the balcony as we pulled up to their two-story house, set on six acres. Emily is tiny, five feet tall with waist-length brown hair; she looks like a streetwise Sissy Spacek and has the energy of a windup doll. Kathy, then seventy-six, is more laid back and reminds me of a character from *The Simpsons* with her large glasses, blond shoulder-length hair, simple T-shirt, and shorts. Emily led me inside and gave me a quick tour of the house, once a Delaware Valley Synergy party HQ, hosting sleepovers that sometimes included as many as thirty people, before taking me upstairs to a table set with silverware and cloth napkins. Kathy and Russ had spent the afternoon preparing a salad that was dressed with Russ's special mix of seeds and grains; he's into healthy food and can't remember the last time he ate red meat. In fact, that was a point of contention when he met Emily, whom he calls a "hamburger person." Like other stumbling blocks in their relationship, they got through it with compromise and conversation, but he still won't allow junk food in the house, so Emily indulges when she's on dates with other men. Russ's girlfriends were thankful when Emily moved in because she stocked the fridge with milk and butter.

Emily was first introduced to Synergy in 1997, a few years before Russ. She was in her early forties and had spent decades unhappily married to a man she met when she was fifteen. It was the same year that *The Ethical Slut* was published, but she'd never heard anything at all about this thing called "consensual non-monogamy." All she knew was monogamous marriage or cheating—no other option. She was cleaning the house when she found her husband had an entire drawer devoted to his decidedly *unethical* non-monogamy. He'd placed a classified advertisement in *Philadelphia* magazine posing as a single man and even had a secret P.O. box and phone line and bundles of letters from other women (it was the analog equivalent of discovering your partner's OkCupid account). She was devastated. They had two children, and she was financially dependent on him; she couldn't leave. When she confronted him about his secret cheating drawer, his solution was for her to come with him to this club he'd discovered. Why did she go? I asked when we first talked on the phone: "I'd always liked to dance and he never wanted to. I saw that there was dancing, and I thought, well, maybe someone would be willing to dance with me."

He didn't last long. He wasn't really interested in ethical non-monogamy; he just wanted to replace Emily, which he did. But he'd unwittingly introduced her to a place that became home. She still remembers how she felt during her orientation when she looked around the room and realized she was in the company of people she might never have encountered in her day-to-day life as a mother and insurance worker; it was like the unifying and connective power of the internet. There was a judge, teachers and nurses, doctors, a physicist, even an airline pilot. "He danced for Disney on Ice; he had a beautiful Australian accent," she said. "He could have been a model, what a body," weighed in Russ, who remembered him too. And like every other member of Synergy I talked to, her first thought as she surveyed this crowd of open-minded and sexually open adults was "Everyone looks so normal."

Her relationship with Russ began at a Synergy New Year's Eve party in 2002. On the drive there, her husband had told her he wanted a divorce; emotionally intelligent Russ saw the pain on Emily's face. They got married at home in 2009 and then they had what they call a "normal traditional reception" at a Holiday Inn with eighty guests, followed by a party for fifty of their "horizontal" friends, meaning friends they have sex with; all of those "horizontal" guests had been lovers of either both or one of them at some time.

It took me a while to understand that Synergy was first and foremost a social club. While of course there were some, like Emily's husband, who were just looking for sex, the majority were there to connect with interesting adults who also wanted to expand their horizons, challenge the sexual puritanism of their communities, and encounter new people and ideas. Many members were women who had recently divorced or spent their early adulthood focused on their career or studies when they found their social circles were full of the same types of people—married couples or colleagues from work.

It fell into place for me on my second night in Pennsylvania when Russ presented me with a stack of Synergy newsletters he'd saved from his time as a member. We were preparing dinner, Emily had assigned everyone tasks, and while my hosts sat around chopping apples and peeling root vegetables, I busied myself looking through the newsletters, which were printed on colored paper and illustrated with cartoon graphics of things like love hearts and turtles wearing spectacles. As a member wrote in a letter to the editor, "DVS is a friendship based group, the sex is merely an extension of the friendship and support."[27]

There was bowling, canoe trips, dancing, outings to art galleries and museums, family picnics, dinner parties, and trips to the beach. I paused on a listing for a "non-permissive" Victorian-themed event at a house near Princeton, New Jersey. Guests were asked to bring a swimsuit and warned that "children and dogs will be home."[28] "What does 'permissive' mean?" I asked the group when Emily was laying out predinner snacks. "Fucking," said Ken, who was dunking a blue corn chip in hummus. During orientations it was always stressed that it was a place to make friends; as Kathy put it, you couldn't just "close your eyes to whoever you are with." Even if the event was permissive, the sex was always optional and never expected.

Membership was strictly regulated. You had to have sponsors and prove yourself during an introductory period, which included attending a minimum of four nonpermissive events where the hosts would observe how potential members behaved and report back to the steering committee. Potential members were taught the group's rules and history, and during interviews their character was assessed. When they became members, they spent six months matched to a mentor who had the same relationship status (for example, single women with single women). Mentors fielded questions about things like clothing and etiquette. During parties and events she'd keep an eye on the new recruit or otherwise be available for support. After each party, the host would report back to the steering committee, and if a provisional member misbehaved, news traveled fast. It was a tight-knit community rather than a meat market.

In addition to social activities, there was a lot of education in the form of seminars, book clubs, reading groups, and workshops. There was a feminist sensibility; they were exposed to radical new ways of thinking about sex and gender. This was perhaps most evident in discussion groups. Every Wednesday for ten years Emily and Kathy would meet with the other women of DVS for a women's group. They were in their element around women their age, some of whom had recently divorced and were coming into their own in their thirties and forties. They were schooled in feminist ideas about sexuality and relationships, and that was where they learned about consensual non-monogamy.

Emily, who didn't go to college, had never been exposed to such ways of thinking: "The music, the culture, the era I grew up in, was all that love and romance and one person always and forever." Kathy, who graduated from Swarthmore in the 1960s and came from a relatively liberal Quaker family, also says that when she learned about it, it was as if she'd been given a language for a set of feelings that were inside her but didn't know how to come out. She'd always been uncomfortable with the taken-for-granted conditions of monogamous marriage, especially the expectation that women give up their independence and that couples seal themselves off in a bubble. When she learned about ethical non-monogamy, she came to believe that there's nothing inherently normal about monogamy; it's just that the culture pushes you in that direction.

There was nowhere else in life that they could talk freely

about sex. Synergy gave them the tools for that, as well as a supportive group of peers to listen. They were literally given new language: there were brochures with glossaries including terms like "abundant love" (the belief that it's possible to love more than one person at a time), "ambiguousweetie" (a colloquial term for a partner whose official role is not defined), "body fluid monogamy" (where extramarital sexual activity must not involve the exchange of body fluid), "candaulism" (when you're sexually aroused watching your partner and somebody else have sex), and "compersion" (a feeling of joy when your partner gets pleasure from another sexual relationship). They read *Sex at Dawn* and *The Ethical Slut* and were schooled in sex positivity. All of this information gave them words for what they'd always felt but didn't know how to discuss, or live by. Such naming was powerful: it validated who they had become; it made them feel normal.

The men were also radicalized. In men-only groups they deconstructed traditional masculinity and were encouraged to express their emotions, insecurities, and fears—like the pressure to make money, stay strong for their families, hide their emotions, or climax during sex. Then the genders would mingle in couples discussion groups, which were often candid conversations about sex. One was called "the fishbowl." The women sat in a circle, and the men sat on the outside; the men had to keep completely quiet for an hour and listen to the women. Well, that's how Russ remembers it. According to Emily, the women had prewritten anonymous questions: like on Reddit or another online forum, they could communicate anonymously and crowdsource answers; everyone would weigh in.

Emily recalled a man confessing to the group that he'd fake orgasms. When she raised this now, almost twenty years later, it generated a frank conversation as if they were back in a couples discussion group. "If you're using a condom, it's easy," said Ken.

"Also if you're really wet, or there's lots of lube, it can be hard to tell," Emily offered. "Why would you do that?" I asked, realizing I'd never, ever heard a man admit to that. They listened thoughtfully while Ken gave the group an earnest explanation. "I didn't know how to stop and not hurt her feelings. Now, as an old man, I can say, 'This is not working. I am not going to orgasm. Let's stop.' But I wasn't comfortable doing that when I was younger," he said. Emily was sympathetic: "Growing up in our culture, in our generation we were taught that the event wasn't over until the man came."

During the weekend I was struck by Russ's version of masculinity; it was hard to believe he was born in 1939. He's in charge of the dishes and grows his own vegetables. One afternoon when Emily and I returned from a walk, we found him on the couch with his friend—a man in his forties—who'd come by to talk to Russ about some problems he was having with his wife. According to Russ, one of the most important things he learned at Synergy was how to deal with other people's emotions; it was during a men's group that he learned the art of listening rather than trying to fix people's problems.

Of course they didn't just share information and feelings; they also shared their bodies.

So you have all seen each other have sex, and you have all had sex with each other? I asked the room just as Emily was dishing out seconds. Emily looked at everyone at the table one by one. "That's correct," she said. Fixing her eyes on Ken, she said, "One of my best sexual experiences was with you." How exactly did it work? Did they go on double dates? Did they swap partners? Were there orgies? All of the above? There was no set script. Creating your own boundaries and guidelines was encouraged; Ken calls them "designer relationships." You could have a play partner—someone you'd look for at parties but not date. Or you could be in an official secondary relationship. There was also casual sex, or "hooking up," as we'd call it today, and yes, orgies, and three-somes or those puppy piles Russ had referred to on the phone.

But Russ and Emily and company mostly formed deep connections with their sex partners who supplemented their primary relationships. None of them expected their husband or wife to be their "everything"; they accepted that different people fulfill different needs—sexual, social, emotional, and intellectual. Their version of ethical non-monogamy allowed them both stability and variety. Russ would travel to Manhattan to visit his girlfriend Maggie, a neurologist. They'd lounge together in bed in her West Village apartment reading *The Wall Street Journal,* which didn't threaten Emily. In fact, she was relieved: "I don't want to be talking about stocks or Greek philosophy or all that intellectual stuff." In turn, Emily would go wine tasting with her boyfriend Dave, whom she still sees regularly. Russ is a home body, so he's happy to stay in and watch the History Channel while Emily is on dates. Russ and Kathy both enjoy nudism, and they still go away to retreats and camps together. After Russ and Emily had been married for a few years, Emily started dating a truck driver. Russ encouraged her to go on an overnight trip with him so she could stay in the sleeper, saying, "You'll learn what it's like!" He was excited for his wife to have an adventure. Kathy and Emily have shared Russ and Kathy's late husband, Doug. A guy called Rob would drive to spend the weekend with Emily and then leave for Kathy's on Monday morning before heading to New York to see Maggie. Rob was also "fucking Millie," Ken's ex, whom Emily is still very good friends with. "That plant came from her," she said, pointing to a succulent on the windowsill. They'd discovered a way to relieve each other of having to be the sole charge of happiness in their partners' lives.

I thought of one of the judgments commonly thrown at the consensually nonmonogamous: that it's greedy and selfish, which

seemed such a gross distortion; these people were fully committed to sharing. They had veto power but rarely used it because the
loving friendship bonds that were created when they socialized
with their friends in Synergy minimized the threat (incidentally,
for many contemporary polyamorists such arrangements, which
privilege a "primary" partner, are considered out of date and
unethical). They knew what was happening and whom it was
happening with. There was trust and accountability. Everything
was open. They had their husband or wife, and then they had
"partners." They got used to their spouses sleeping with other
people, and it became normal through exposure and openness.
The more open they were about sex, the less power it had. As
Ken put it, "You eventually say so what? Why is this thing about
penises and vaginas such a big deal? We need to learn not to am-
plify it so much."

For people who are familiar only with monogamy, this setup is
likely very confounding. Why don't they feel jealous? Are certain
people drawn to open marriages, or could anyone adapt? People
like Ken would argue that it's innate: either you're monogamous,
or you're not. Others, like the Ethical Sluts, would say that nobody
is truly monogamous; it's a cultural construct. Russ, Kathy, and
Emily are less concerned with theories; they just know that for
them it works. That doesn't mean that they didn't occasionally
experience jealousy or, as Emily put it, feel "fussed." It was by no
means a free-for-all; they all had their boundaries. Emily became
so uninterested in what Russ does sexually with other women she
stopped asking, but a line is crossed if another woman comes into
her home and fails to respect her status as Russ's wife. Once a girlfriend of his spent the weekend at their house. They were cozied
up in the living room, fireplace roaring, when she asked if she
could give Russ a massage. If this woman had been alone with
Russ, or if the logistics had been different, Emily wouldn't have
cared, but they were already in the living room, which is where

she'd usually retreat, put headphones on, and watch TV while Russ was having sex. Then the woman stayed longer than scheduled; there was a snowstorm, and Russ had to spend the morning shoveling her car out. But the nail in the coffin was when she called and left a message thanking Russ for a wonderful weekend. She'd disrespected Emily's hospitality, and that was a huge no-no.

Kathy was slightly put out when Doug told one of his girlfriends that he loved her. I was curious about that: Do they love their lovers? "It's pretty rare, but it does happen," said Kathy. "It depends how you define love," Emily added, noting that she loves Ken, "but am I in love with him? No. Three nights and three days, that's about all I can take." In discussion groups they talked through emotions like jealousy and envy and how to separate them. They learned that jealousy is the fear of losing; envy is when you want something that you can't have. They were taught how to give each emotion space without letting either one dominate.

In a 2017 story for *The New York Times Magazine*, Susan Dominus, who spent about a year interviewing couples who opened up their marriages, wrote that she found consensual non-monogamy isn't just suited to people who are especially interested in sex; it's for people who are especially interested in people.[29] I was struck by how intimately the Synergy crew knew each other, the depth of their connection, which spanned two decades. They knew about each other's medical histories and food allergies. They were sensitive to each other's insecurities: Ken knows that health-conscious Russ was upset when he polished off half a bottle of scotch and snuck an after-dinner cigarette. Emily and Kathy know that Ken is sensitive about his stomach and stop themselves from making "dick-to-belly ratio" jokes when he's around. They know the intricacies of each other's career and work lives, their past relationships, their dynamics with their children and spouses, and they often step in as chosen family. Ken recently spent Christmas with Russ and Emily because his partner's family doesn't approve of their relationship. Kathy's Synergy friends were so supportive when her husband, Doug, passed away—taking her on vacation, having her over for holidays—that she doesn't know how she would have coped on her own. On my first night there when Kathy went to the bathroom, Emily came up to me with tears in her eyes and handed me an envelope of photos and pointed at a man in a suit, whispering, "That was him." One morning I heard Kathy and Ken's pillow talk from my bedroom. After laughing about how Kathy checked if he had a pulse when she crept into bed with him the night before, he comforted her when she said how much she missed Doug. They know who is particular about how their vegetables are sliced and who can't even make a cup of coffee.

They also know what it takes to make one another have an orgasm, who is a voyeur, who has a fantasy about being a prisoner of war "forced" to endure endless blow jobs. They know who has a weakness for small breasts, short men, soft bodies, or hairy backs. They know what they all look and sound like when they have sex; Emily says you could walk into a house and know who was there based on the moans. When Russ has an orgasm, his whole body vibrates; "it's very intense," Russ and Emily agree. "I don't want to get too graphic," Kathy said, staring at me, before explaining that Russ knows exactly how to make *her* ejaculate, right as Emily came in, sweaty from the heat of the oven, her scarf pulled down across her head, clutching a basket of apples. "You know I think I should bake them in the other tray," Emily said.

They know which men were comfortable with male intimacy during threesomes. Kathy's husband, Doug, wasn't; as Ken put it, he was "a bit of a homophobe." "He'd always yell, 'Get on the other side of the bed. I don't want to touch you!'" Russ agreed, groaning at the memory. They know that Ken is heterosexual but he'll have sex with a man if the mood is right. In Ken's words, "If there's female essence in the room, I can suck a dick. But I would never pick up a guy in a bar and suck his dick. In a threesome? Guilty." Ken has a mantra, "When you're turned on, the rules change."

They all know that Kathy only likes to be sexual with women when she's with another man; that's when she craves something soft. She usually doesn't perform oral sex on women, but will happily oblige if they want to do it to her. "It's a lot more work than sucking a cock," Emily agreed, scrolling her phone, looking weary. Kathy and Emily have, in Emily's words, "interacted," but only in a group-sex situation; as Emily put it, "I probably wouldn't take Kathy by the hand and say, 'Let's go.'" They were connected by sex, in a powerful way, both through having it and through discussing it openly. As Kathy put it, "There's some sort of intimacy with us that's not the same as a monogamous couple's; it's different." Like the bonds created during war, there was an us-and-them dynamic constructed; it was only in the horizontal world that they could be their true selves.

Most of the group are romantics, especially the men. Ken needs to have an intellectual connection with his sex partners; he's drawn to the former schoolteacher Kathy because she has a varied vocabulary and they share an interest in reading. He refers to sex without an emotional connection as "vaginal masturbation." Russ finds sex and love hard to disentangle. "I get attached," he admitted. Russ has written love poems to Emily that hang on the living room wall ("one by one as the years wandered by, we melded together like fruits in a pie").

He refers to the passion he feels for his sex friends as "love feelings." During sex, he looks at his partner and thinks, "I am in your body and that overwhelms me." Part of me was terrified when he found a sex diary detailing his time in Synergy. But it was hardly a book of conquests. He had sections for location, personality traits, and "emotional" details about his partner; each encounter really mattered to him. Once, Emily went on a date with a man who didn't call her back, and Russ was so upset he got in touch and suggested that a bunch of flowers would be nice.

I asked Russ when he looks back over his long life, what are those relationships? Is there language for what they are? He described them as "loving relationships." "I cry when they hurt," he said. Many of his Synergy friends have passed away in recent years; when Kathy lost Doug, he "felt it too."

With the exception of Ken, all of them kept their non-monogamy secret from the "vertical" world. Russ was a teacher. He says if they knew about sex parties and multiple lovers, they would have assumed he was a pedophile and kicked him out. But also, when he was younger, he cared more about fitting in and being normal; he'd internalized the adage "what will the neighbors think?" When he moved to Chester County, he'd registered as a Republican just so he didn't stand out. Kathy kept Synergy completely sealed off from her life as a teacher in suburban New Jersey; she also recalls people being outed and fired. She confided in a few female friends, and their reaction was as brutal as a talk-show audience member's, so she went underground and hasn't talked about it since.

Russ is no longer so concerned with blending in; these days he wants to be open. But Emily doesn't. She has to stop him from mentioning it at their Unitarian church. She's concerned about their judgments, especially that people will think they're thirsty for casual sex partners. But mostly she worries that if they discover the "truth," they won't feel comfortable being their friends. Kathy still doesn't want most of her "vertical" friends to know; even today she thinks she'd lose them. In more than twenty years their attitudes haven't shifted. On my first night at Russ and

Emily's, we had a long discussion about the merits of naming Synergy because Kathy is still so worried about being recognized. Ken is always challenging her to "come out," but the stakes are still too high for her. She's resigned to the split. "I have been in two worlds for as long as I can remember," she said. An added complication is that she's gearing up to think about dating again: What will potential boyfriends make of her past?

Of course the advocate Ken firmly believes that consensual non-monogamy should be normalized by being discussed, visible, and out in the open, even with children. As he put it, "Kids don't care who Mommy fucks. Security is what matters to them." If it's known and transparent from the outset, it will be normal for them, and he thinks that consensually nonmonogamous people have a responsibility to future generations to be open so they can show them a different path. "I have never been afraid to stick out my neck and let things hang out; that's how social change happens. If you don't talk about it openly, it still has a stigma attached to it," he said to Kathy.

Synergy still exists on Facebook, but it's largely dormant. Ken, who teaches sex-ed classes to the elderly using videos from YouTube (his favorite is a teenage boy unsuccessfully trying to draw a vagina), celebrates the internet for making the sorts of ideas he learned in Synergy widely accessible and facilitating connections that might not have been possible in previous eras. But he thinks the myriad websites and apps and ways to connect have destroyed rich community structures that were built before its arrival. As he bemoans, "Synergy is 'dead'" because of "Tinder, swipe right swipe left." Russ is much less technologically deterministic, linking the aging and death of core members to Synergy's demise. "People got old, people died," he said to Emily, irritated, when she gave an impassioned speech about the internet killing Synergy.

But one of Kathy's former lovers, who was head of Synergy's

steering committee for much of the first decade of the twenty-first century, confirms that when non-monogamy-friendly dating websites and apps were introduced around 2007, Synergy membership started to decline. They even tried advertising for members, as they did in the 1990s, when membership dipped during the HIV crisis. These days Synergy parties are irregular, have a rotating cast of new faces, and are poorly attended. When people do show up, they "come in, screw, and leave," he says. He's adamant that it's the fault of technology: "It's this instant gratification people have grown up with over the last thirty years."

While Kathy drove me and Ken to the airport, Ken entertained us with stories about his past monogamous relationships, including his days married to a woman who flew airplanes. The discussion about the internet displacing the importance of Synergy left me thinking about how similar it was to online communities. Synergy brought together people from different walks of life in a community where they could connect, share ideas and information, and create a language, and it gave them tools that allowed them to feel normal.

Something Ken said stuck with me as I boarded the plane and made my way home: "If I have learned anything about humans, it's that we are all fucking different . . . but I want you to be like me." While they were an open-minded group, they still had their limits—for example, casual sex without that deep friendship connection or the contemporary non-monogamy landscape where people meet online. Ken and company were audacious for challenging the norms of their social worlds and the eras in which they came of age. How are older adults doing that today? I had an invite to a sex party in St. Louis where I was hoping to find out.

It had been a very secretive couple who first told me about being in the "lifestyle." "Dave" and "Felicia" had seen my call for people who had opened up their marriage or had discovered consensual non-monogamy later in life via a tweet from an NYU adjunct professor and sex researcher named Dr. Zhana Vrangalova. The pair, who are in their sixties, discovered the lifestyle in 2016, and they were keen to tell their story, on the firm condition that they remained anonymous.

On the one hand the "lifestyle" is the contemporary, politically correct word for what used to be known as "swinging"—the form of consensual non-monogamy that doesn't really excite the Synergy crew. According to a recent literature review, most who have studied it agree that "swinging" as a subculture began to be referred to during World War II, when fighter pilots would swap partners as a sort of bonding ritual, and that demographically speaking its participants are usually socially conforming, white, heterosexual, and cisgender.[30] But the lifestyle doesn't just refer to sharing partners; it's an umbrella term that is often a code for being interested in group sex, open relationships, or sex parties. Some use the term simply to indicate that they are consensually nonmonogamous or that they like to engage in extramarital homosexual sex.

The lifestyle is not a "product" of the internet; in fact, according to Terry Gould, an investigative journalist who reported on the scene for his 1999 book, *The Lifestyle*, the term was adopted by the community in the 1980s and 1990s, when they got sick of the media demonization of swinging.[31] But the internet has certainly rewired lifestyle communities that might have migrated online and were harder to access in previous eras. In this sense, the lifestyle brings together a range of online and off-line communities or groups, and because it can be easily searched for, many lifestylers discovered it on social media and use social networks to meet people and connect.

Dave and Felicia, the secretive couple, gave me an overview of the subculture and introduced me to some of its language, which was very different from the terms distributed in those Synergy meetings; you could say it was more coded. Unlike the language explored in Synergy, which was primarily used in IRL conversation to assert an identity, they are euphemisms used online as keywords to search for specific types of connections or sex acts, or as a secret handshake to discreetly convey membership in this "club." For example, "play" generally means sex or sexual activity. "Unicorn" refers to an unattached, bisexual woman (or a woman who is happy to have sex with both men and women). "Full swap" refers to penis-in-vagina sex. Then there are symbols, like the pineapple, a traditional icon for hospitality, which can be used to signify being part of the lifestyle, and black wedding bands, which are a code for an interest in ethical non-monogamy. I learned that to many in the lifestyle the term "swinger" is a slur that implies a sexist form of "wife swapping" and excludes unattached people, who are a very important part of the scene.

Dave and Felicia said that if it weren't for the internet, they wouldn't be consensually nonmonogamous; logistically, it would be too hard. They have a military-like protocol in place to keep a lid on their double life. They mostly meet people on websites like Kasidie, a popular social network that connects people who are, as the website puts it, "sexually social."[32] Dave likes Kasidie because "it has functionality like Facebook." They also use Swing Life Style, another popular social network for matching with people for sex dates, or Kik, an anonymous mobile messaging app that doesn't store phone numbers. He's in charge of technical operations, and he carefully manages their online profiles and burner email addresses to make sure that nobody can track them down. I couldn't; I tried.

They have an emergency plan in case of sudden illness or death. That's how concerned they are about social judgment. They've given a very close lifestyle friend a key to their house and a list of their computer and social media passwords. If anything happens to both of them at the same time, their children have been instructed to call the man Dave referred to as "Mr. X." Officially, he's their accountant, and he knows where their wills and financial information are stored. But the truth is he knows how to make those sex messages, chats, and online profiles disappear. As soon as he gets the alert, he'll come in and do a cleanup job so that their children and families never, ever find out the truth.

After establishing that I was "Vanilla," meaning that I am not part of the lifestyle (Russ and Emily and company would have called me "vertical"), Dave read me a sort of taxonomy he'd prepared for our conversation. For some lifestylers, it's sport ("they treat it as an activity or competition"). There's "social lifestylers," who especially enjoy meeting and connecting with new people (which is where they say they sit on the spectrum). There's the "vacationers," or as Dave calls them the "one and done living out a fantasy" lifestylers, who will indulge on special occasions (when they're abroad, for instance). I was stuck on the last type he described, the "notch in the bedpost hard-core lifestyler," those who are driven by sex. I was on speakerphone, listening to the couple talk over each other and could imagine them keeping in touch with their children that way.

I knew that the crew in Delaware Valley Synergy were skeptical of the contemporary consensual non-monogamy universe, or the idea of anonymous sex with strangers. They tried not to judge, but for them this form of sex was too transactional and impersonal. When I first talked to Russ and Emily, they stressed that they aren't "swingers" and would hate to be characterized in that way. The subject came up a lot during the weekend I spent with them. Russ and Ken said they'd make terrible swingers; remember Ken calls sex without an emotional connection "vaginal masturbation." While it's not for him, he really doesn't judge; in fact he coined the term "swolly" to refer to polyamorous people who also enjoy casual sex.

Dave and Felicia wouldn't risk an IRL meeting, so I tried a few more people who had contacted me after seeing Dr. Vrangalova's tweet. I began emailing with a forty-nine-year-old man named Joe, a scientist living in St. Louis who was very excited to talk about how this alternative to monogamy changed his life. "I LOVE sex . . . we've got a great community here in St. Louis and they are some of our greatest friends. It's great to be able to be ourselves completely around them," he wrote. We began emailing and talking on the phone, and it became clear that Joe was more of a hard-core lifestyler; most of his weekends and free time are spent at sex parties or clubs. Unlike those in Synergy, where community and friendship were a key appeal, Joe was clear that it's "sexual," not "emotional," consensual non-monogamy that changed his life. He feels as if he's discovered a secret—a relationship model that feels natural and normal and completely right. I was struck by how powerful and yet mundane his life-changing "discovery" was. It took place at home, on a Wednesday afternoon when he was using Facebook.

Joe is a fun dad. That's his brand. His Instagram feed is full of playful photos of his teenage daughter and son. They keep him up to date with the latest filters or animation apps, and he posts videos of them vomiting computer-generated rainbows or playing golf in their living room on a simulated island. When he turned forty-nine, they gave him a cake, and he posted a photo of it on Instagram. It said "Happy Birthday, Dad!" in gilded frosting, alongside candles spelling out "you're old." When he and his wife got divorced, he was adamant that custody would be shared and that his open, close relationship with his kids wouldn't be damaged by their failure to stay connected as a couple.

If you met him at a bar or during school pickup, you'd probably describe him as "normal." By normal, I mean inconspicuous. In the context of white middle-class suburban St. Louis, there's nothing about him that stands out. He's a middle-aged dad, a standard guy. Given his usual style of dress—polo shirts, button-downs, and nice slacks—you could easily mistake him for a Republican, or at least very socially conforming.

He loves organized communal celebrations like Cinco de Mayo, St. Patrick's Day, and Pride, where he joyfully nurses a craft beer or vodka soda, and if he had a favorite adjective, it would probably be "crazy" or "fun." He loves data and facts and keeps lists and records of the most important events in his life, like the date and time his kids were born, the moment he learned his PhD dissertation had been accepted, or the number of people he's had sex with. When he met his ex-wife, his count was fifty, but when they divorced (after seventeen years of monogamy), that number quickly reached a hundred. He also has a list of personal "records," like the number of sex partners he's had in one day (it's currently ten thanks to an eventful party in Chicago).

He was divorced and living in a bachelor pad, swiping on Tinder, when one of his dates mentioned that she used to be a "swinger" and that she still maintained a secret Facebook group for local people who were interested in what she referred to as an "open minded community" of adults who enjoyed "playing" with each other. He'd adopted monogamy by "default"; it was the prescription for relationships society wrote for him growing up Catholic in Atlanta in the 1970s. He had absolutely zero exposure to an alternative model. Discovering this new community was as simple as a conversation and the click of a few buttons. Facebook was accessible, and he knew how to use it; he went from sharing links about football to finding local sex partners and parties. Two years after his divorce was finalized he was a member of about five groups that are all private and dedicated to people in his local area; there's between two hundred and a thousand members in each.

On Facebook, it was as if this world had been hiding in plain sight, and he'd been living in the same city for about twenty years. He emailed the moderator, and after a few questions and references from some mutual friends he was invited to his first event. What he thought was an impenetrable fortress was only a few Facebook invites away. He learned that on certain nights bars in his neighborhood would have private events where more than three hundred lifestylers would gather. There was even a sex-positive library and café not far from where he lived; he went and peered around the space adorned with Barbie dolls in handcuffs and wall-size infographics showing the spectrum of non-monogamy, and borrowed books about masculinity, feminism, and gender.

His first lifestyle event was a meet and greet at a local bar. During these events people from Facebook groups gather IRL for a few hours so they can get to know each other in the flesh. He was dizzy thinking that he'd never been in a room where the types of relationships were so diverse: "single guys, single girls, poly couples . . . couples where you have no idea that this person is their husband because they spent the whole night with this other guy." He was being adventurous, approaching strangers, when an older woman asked how long he'd been in the lifestyle. He looked at his watch and said, "About forty-five hours." It was her designated "play night." Her husband had a woman coming over, would Joe like to join them? Back at her house there was pizza, more drinks, and eventually a hot tub, which is where they all removed their clothes before they paired off and went to separate rooms.

He became friends with a pair of unicorns, and together they created their own Facebook group, "St. Louis Blunicorns," exclusively for singles in the lifestyle, which quickly got fifty members. (He was what midwestern lifestylers call a "bluefish," which means a single man or the male version of a unicorn, which doesn't have a similar regional label.) He geeked out planning the event, stamping his Facebook group logo on coffee mugs: a pink unicorn with a blue fish. He ordered condoms in bulk from Amazon, made sure he had waterproof mattress protectors. "What for?" I asked him, given that he'd just stocked up on condoms. "The squirters," he said, without skipping a beat.

Sex was the glue that connected Joe and his fiancée, Susie, as a couple. When Susie told me about the night they first met, there was no story about some instant "across the room" love-at-first-sight connection that revealed itself like magic. When I asked what she liked about him, what she was drawn to, she looked at me, smiled, grabbed Joe's arm, and said that when she arrived at his party, it took her about fifteen minutes before she "fucked him." Later, they told me that first time they had sex—a threesome with another man—was the first double penetration for them both. For their first official date Joe invited her to a winery with a bisexual woman he'd met the previous weekend.

After a few months of playing together, Joe and Susie had become an official consensually nonmonogamous couple. They started listening to Dan Savage's podcast, which often discussed non-monogamy, and read *The Ethical Slut*; they established ground rules for what Ken Haslam would call their "designer relationship"[33] and decided they'd be full swap (which means they have sexual intercourse with their other sex partners) and would always play together in the same room, with some exceptions, which are always agreed to beforehand. They browsed lifestyle dating websites so they could meet people when they were on vacation or traveling for work and landed on c4p (Club Foreplay), a Midwest/southern lifestyle dating site, and settled on the moniker the BigBangCouple in homage to Joe's job as a scientist. They prefer using Facebook, though. It's transparent, there are fewer creepy faceless profile photos, it's easier to organize subgroups and keep up with messages and conversations. Setting up events doesn't come with a barrage of porn or solicitations. On Sundays they wake up early and go to spin class, followed by brunch; if they have a few too many drinks, they might start messaging their Facebook friends to see if anyone wants to come by.

They observed and tried things out slowly, learning what they did and didn't like through trial and error. They tried the "dating experience," but private texts and calls with other people felt like cheating, and neither of them especially enjoyed it when their phone blew up with dick or vagina footage at work in the middle of the day. Joe enjoys group text flirting, which means being on a chain with another couple and sharing naked photos or describing what they'd like to do to each other later, but that doesn't excite Susie at all. Texting on a closed chain feels like cheating, but sex doesn't—as long as they're together in the same room.

They were on an adventure together. It was so easy to tap into the lifestyle's national and global network. Joe went online and found a list of lifestyle websites, ordered by what's most popular in major cities in every single state (in Anchorage it's SLS, but the people of Des Moines prefer Swing Village). According to Joe, there are sex clubs "all over the country." Without the Facebook network, events are harder to access when you travel, but there aren't that many hoops to jump through. They listed the various parties and clubs they've been to as if they were monuments or theme parks: Chicago; Atlanta; Florida; Vegas; New Orleans (where they go to an event called Naughty N'Awlins). Joe messaged me a meme of Willy Wonka's face with the text "so much fucking" before he set off on that year's hotel and bar takeover.

There were threesomes, foursomes, and that was when Susie discovered how much it excited her to watch Joe having sex with someone else; I thought of the term "candaulism" Emily had learned in Synergy. How exactly does that work? She's turned on by watching him please someone else, while she's also being pleasured by someone else; then that rebounds into their sex life when they're alone. She described it as a three-step process. First, they'll have what's called "reclamation sex." They are alone enjoying the contrast of intimacy after sex with other people. They'll have sex again the next day, and this time they'll recall the group sex. They describe what they saw, what they did, and anticipate doing it again; they're still talking about a threesome from a year and a half ago.

When she's watching Joe have sex with another woman, Susie feels powerful. It's as if her association with Joe were somehow charging that other woman's pleasure. Susie can separate sex and love, but love is still important to her (she's very much in love with Joe). In fact, she doesn't believe in polyamory, because she doesn't think you can be in love with two people at once. For her sex is "animal." Like Joe, her non-monogamy is sexual, not emotional. I asked Joe what I learned was a pretty normative question: "Do you prefer sex when there's an emotional connection?" Joe struggled to answer because sex with other people emotionally connects him to Susie.

How should I dress for a sex pool party? I rummaged through my bag, which seemed to contain only the same black fabric in different shapes: an oversize jumpsuit; a long dress that outside New York City, in the sticky heat of a St. Louis summer, carried the energy of a Greek widow—definitely not appropriate. Knowing my limits, I decided on a sleeveless slip dress and threw my modest two-piece swimsuit in my bag, just in case.

I'd arrived in St. Louis to meet Susie and Joe the night before; they'd taken me to dinner at Susie's favorite French bistro. Her blond hair extra bouncy in the humidity, Susie was wearing glasses and a summer dress as she nursed a bottle of wine between her thighs in the front seat next to a clean-cut Joe, who followed the GPS to our destination. At dinner I watched as Joe let her take the lead, ordering bone marrow and champagne cocktails. Occasionally she'd point out women she found attractive or speculate about how other couples met. "I think they're on a first Match.com date," she said, snickering at an elderly man in a suit and toupee who was awkwardly dining with a younger woman. "That chick is hot," she said, pointing toward a young couple in formal wear waiting for their table. I felt as if I were with close female friends rather than lovers. But the big event was happening on Sunday afternoon.

Susie had called ahead to get permission to bring me to the pool party. "Will there be sex?" I asked. "It's family friendly during the day, then adult after dark," she said, with a glint in her eye. On the drive to the suburb on the outskirts of St. Louis, which took about an hour (people in the lifestyle joke that's the average distance they'll commute to an event), they speculated about who would show up. One downside to blocking people on Facebook is you can't scan the guest list to see if your enemies will be there (Joe has a system: if it shows more guests than names, he can usually guess by process of elimination). "That creep might come," said Susie, referring to a man she finds racist. He'd recently blocked Joe on Facebook after Joe called him out for posting a photoshopped picture of Obama. I was nervous.

When I'd arrived at their house and saw Joe in his polo shirt and khakis, I'd relaxed about my clothing, but I felt a rare anticipation. I was trying to put my finger on it. I thought about a story Ken had told me about a sociologist who once came to observe Synergy; later they'd made fun of how he'd awkwardly lowered his pale body into the Jacuzzi, clutching his notebook. As we approached a detached suburban home, parked, unpacked our cooler and fold-out chairs, and went through a side gate, I realized what it was: I'd never been to a sex party before, so I had no idea what to expect, how to fit in and act normal. The idea I was basing it on was a stereotype: deliriously feminine women and jacked men in Speedos lounging by the pool, a version I knew only from Hollywood movies or porn.

We entered the yard, clutching our gear. Women were tucked into bikinis and men were in shorts, standing in the sun chatting, while kids and dogs mulled around a large fenced-off pool. I looked over to a table of young men and women drinking beers. A kid clambered around wet next to a plastic Minnie Mouse baby bouncer. Visually, Susie in her bikini, faded tattoos and mesh cover-up, fit in, but Joe, unpacking his premixed Skinnygirl Margarita with his cleanly shaved face and tattoo-and-piercing-free skin, was a bit of an outlier. I thought about how unlikely it was that Joe would ever have ended up here if he hadn't joined that group on Facebook and was relying on his IRL social network of dads and scientists.

Pineapples were everywhere. They were on towels, swimming costumes, paper plates, in bottles of flavored alcohol water Joe had brought in his cooler. A large wooden etching of a pineapple hung over the pool with a sign reading, "Sunday funday." There was even a traditional pineapple "welcome" sign on the host's front door and a giant decorative pineapple sitting on a deck chair as if it were a person. "Why, hello, Miss Alexa. Make yourself at home, my house is your house, my wife is your wife," said Hammer, who looked like Greg Kinnear in saggy board shorts. He took my hand and held it in both of his, performing a mock bow.

Susie had described me as a "Vanilla" reporter writing about the lifestyle (and of course, when she'd got approval, it was to bring a Vanilla reporter to the event). That was where I learned who I was to them: Vanilla. Talking to Hammer, I was aware of my feet sinking down into the soil, which was wet from all the pool traffic. I kept flicking mud off my sandals, which made me feel even more uptight than my black dress, and this all seemed to be working together to clearly mark me as other, as Vanilla. I looked at Hammer's hand and noticed he had a heart tattoo on his finger as a wedding ring. He lives with his children and a woman named Nicole; they aren't married, but he calls her his wife. "My wife's boyfriend is back there somewhere," he said, pointing to the pool, where one of his sons was also flipping about on an inflatable slice of watermelon.

Noticing how close the neighboring houses were, I asked Hammer, who'd begun laying a tray with burgers and hot dogs, what happens when the family-friendly portion is over. He pointed to two long pieces of rope stretching from each side of the house to the fenced-off pool, upon which he'd hung a series of plastic shower curtains to seal off the yard from his neighbors. It was quite the setup. "Do you think they know?" I asked, considering how curious I'd be if I looked out my window and saw that my neighbors had given their pool a modesty curtain. "Oh, they know. They can either join me or not give a shit," he said.

I found Susie inside the kitchen assembling a plate of chips and dip and asked, "Are you looking at everyone, deciding who you'd want to have sex with?" There was nobody she was especially interested in. "Maybe him," she corrected herself, pointing to a bald man in Stars and Stripes board shorts. Finding a couple they both mesh with isn't easy. Susie calls herself sexually—but not romantically—bisexual, so their perfect match is another straight couple. She has tougher requirements for her sex partners than Joe does: intelligence and politics. She's the kind of woman who has a pro-choice sign in the trunk of her car just in case she has to infiltrate an antiabortion protest. In life and sex she avoids getting too close to Republicans.

Hammer had joined a picnic table of men and women in bikinis and shorts, smoking, eating, and laughing. I was reluctant to approach them. I was worried they'd think I wasn't Vanilla—that I was into the lifestyle, which would mean that they could all look at me and judge me as a potential sexual partner, or as a lifestyler who is bad at the lifestyle and failing to fit in.

A woman in her twenties was standing in a black two-piece loudly talking about her hopes and dreams. She described the complications she had during her pregnancy, giving birth, and how she recently made a switch from unfulfilling bar work to child education. At the other end of the table, a pair of women embraced and traded compliments about each other's weight loss and grief-coping mechanisms (one had just returned from her father's funeral). When a smiley middle-aged woman in a bikini decorated with half-eaten cherries accosted Joe, who asked after her husband, she launched into an involved story about their recent divorce. There was no small talk.

After about five minutes at the table, I relaxed. It was almost as if I were in a couples rap session somewhere in Philadelphia in the early years of the twenty-first century. The men were discussing the logistics of an orgy, specifically how they deal with same-sex contact. "I roll with the punches when I find myself in an awkward situation," Hammer said. When I asked him to define "awkward," he described a situation where he and another man were having sex with a woman: "The other man grabs my dick and starts shoving it in her mouth. I'm like, okay, that's kinda hot. Next thing I know, he pulls my dick out of her mouth and puts it in his." The group listened, nodding thoughtfully. They all agreed that there's nothing worse than homophobic panic at a sex party. Body parts touch; things can get messy and confused. As Ken said, "When you're turned on, the rules change."

If a guy flips out because he accidentally makes contact with another man, it kills the vibe, and vibes are contagious. What else ruins the vibe? I asked (hoping they didn't say Vanilla reporters with muddy sandals). Small talk about family doesn't go down so well (as Hammer put it, "If someone is all, How are your kids doing? It's really hard to fuck").

Everyone at the table, who were aged between twenty-five and their early fifties, had discovered the lifestyle online. I thought back to Ken's Kinsey polyamory archive and those letters to Anapol. The breadth and depth of each writer's search. Even though I grew up in a relatively isolated country before the advent of the internet, from today's spoiled perspective the difference in speed was overwhelming. Yes, there were networks and ways to connect and get information before our entry into our current media moment, but the journey was much longer. The path wasn't fully lit; in many cases it might not have even existed. There weren't the myriad different templates that we now bathe in every day. It took that one woman from Wyoming twelve months to get the information she needed to even *begin* to connect with a like mind.

But it also struck me again how the norm hasn't really shifted much. Each member of the St. Louis crowd had their own relationship with privacy. Some, like Hammer, were totally open, while others were more careful about whom they shared the information with; the consensus was you never know how people will react, and non-monogamy is still a taboo in most of their social worlds. While ethical non-monogamy might be more accessible and easier to explore, the stigma is almost the same as that experienced by the Delaware crew twenty years ago.

One of the judgments I had about people in open marriages was that they were hypocrites who ran around in the shadows, having casual sex, then posed for family portraits, contributing to the myth that a monogamous marriage with kids is best for all of us. It wasn't the non-monogamy that I judged; it was the secrecy. My logic was this: you're too scared to own your identity in public, so you appear to adhere to a norm that sets a standard that impacts us all. When I talked to Dr. Heath Schechinger, the psychologist who initiated an APA consensual non-monogamy task force that aims to educate practitioners about this relationship type, he emphasized that while the more people are open, the more the behavior will become normalized, but there shouldn't be a drive to push consensually nonmonogamous people out of the closet. Certain people who have marginalized, intersecting identities aren't as privileged when it comes to the risks of coming out. And coming out often means outing your partner, or partners, too. But he encourages people who are safe to do so to be more public to reduce the stigma. When the press reported that the APA task force had been established, he got emails from people thanking him, saying that it gave them the confidence to come out because this institutional acknowledgment made them feel normal. But he agrees that real-life human examples are just as important.

If it were up to Joe, he'd tell everyone, including his kids. After he'd been dating Susie a few weeks, he went home to Atlanta on a high. He told his childhood best friend. He told his sister, and he was poised to tell his Baptist mother when Susie reminded him that would mean outing her, too. She knows how much people judge non-monogamy and feels that at the end of the day it's just nobody's business. I felt judgment creeping in: he's operating from a base masculine desire to parade his conquests.

However, that was unfair. He wants to be open about his new lifestyle because he wants to offer the next generation a real-life template for a different way of being in the world, which was something he only discovered when he reached middle age. Joe has a problem with the secrecy of the lifestyle precisely because he wants sex to be open, he wants it to be normal. You hide things that you're ashamed of, and he's not ashamed of his relationship model; he's proud of it. That pride is why he talked to me in the first place. He wants his children to know so that if they're like him, they won't spend their lives forcing themselves into a monogamous mold. He wants to be like Ken or Deborah Anapol, an inspiration and a template for others to look at and know what could be normal.

# 2

# Julia and Eileen, Andrew and Jane

Sometimes Eileen jokes to her wife, Julia, that they need to call animal control because there's a cougar in their flat. The wild cat? Britney, a kitten named for the pop star Julia grew up idolizing. Britney the cat is usually very well behaved. She prowls around pawing empty Amazon packages and nudging her nose against curling irons or hunting false eyelashes that lie on the floor like dead spiders. Sometimes, she'll sit purring on the windowsill with a side eye down to the merry Chelsea high street with its black cabs and busy Londoners in heels and suits. Occasionally she gets rough and she'll scratch and paw her mistresses, like a miniature panther. The last time that happened, Julia quickly found the first aid kit and tenderly dressed her wife's wounds. Britney was their first shared responsibility as a couple. "I'm sure kids are wonderful, but I have Britney and I love her to pieces," said Eileen when she introduced me to her for the first time.

Julia and Eileen have been together three years, and they're inseparable. They march together up the King's Road, go on dates to the movies (Eileen loves to sing along with the credits, making her more introverted wife sink down in her seat) and in summer they swim together in the lake in Hyde Park; "by swimming, I mean paddling around and hugging, like puppies," says Eileen. Recently they were trudging up the stairs after a day running errands when Julia turned to her wife and said, "I really love doing anything with you. I just love being with you."

Despite their social media feeds with endless footage of them at parties and fashion shows, they're mostly homebodies. Their main shared interest is probably social media. They love it, all of it. Instagram and YouTube are their oxygen. When they're updating their status or monitoring "likes," Eileen slips on a pair of spectacles and holds her leather phone case up close, as if she were reading a book. When Julia has her furry pink phone in her hands, it looks as if she were holding cotton candy. Then they'll both cross over into a trancelike glossy-eyeball state while they gauge how popular they are in the form of clicks and likes and shares.

I first saw Julia and Eileen online when a feature about them in a British tabloid went viral.[1] The story, and accompanying video, were pegged to the "news" that their relationship exists. The fact that they are living together as a romantic, sexual couple and were at that time engaged to be married is quite literally the story: it's the "OMG you will not believe your eyes" variety of clickbait that depends on shocking visuals and an attention-grabbing headline to make its point.

In a living room scene Julia feeds Eileen cake with her whole body pressed up against her. There's also photos of them outside their London flat locked in a very passionate kiss and a picture of the pair with Julia's mother, who looks like Eileen's peer, awkwardly smiling as the three lean in for a photo on Julia's phone. The story appears under the headline "Woman, 24, with Girlfriend, 61, Says 37-Year Age Gap Doesn't Affect Relationship."

I searched their names online, where I came across Julia's YouTube channel, which she started in 2014, when she was twenty. I settled down to watch some clips. She mostly posts "story time" videos—intimate, diary-like monologues. In a video of the pair meeting Julia's mother in Brazil, Julia, who is dressed in a bikini, jumps into a swimming pool and into the arms of Eileen, who is wearing a one-piece (with modesty skirt). She strokes her arms and kisses her neck. Eileen kicks about in a rubber ring while Julia coos: "Look at my gorgeous girlfriend. She's so beautiful, I love her so much."[2] Both visually and conversationally, Julia is like one of those exploding text messages bursting with glitter and hearts and "awww bless" and "baby." Her long hair looks like a puddle of runoff from a kid's party: crimson at the roots, lavender at the ends. Eileen is striking with a long bob and oxblood lips, with a splash of age spots on her décolletage.

There's no sex in the videos; they are just going about their everyday life. They go away to the country for a weekend together where they check into an Airbnb, dance at a music festival, and eat hot chips.[3] They film their morning routine, during which they eat breakfast in bed and wash their faces.[4] They renovate their flat together and unpack boxes.[5]

While I watched these everyday scenes of the pair, I was looking for loopholes—cycling through all the clichés I'd absorbed about relationships with a large age difference. They live together in London, but Julia is from Brazil and Eileen's American, so maybe visas are involved? What does Eileen actually do for work, anyway? I searched around online and discovered that she had been a writer who occasionally does commentary about American politics on the radio. She doesn't have a "real" job, I thought, which made me suspicious; she's probably living off inherited wealth, so maybe Julia is after her money. Or, because Julia is a YouTube influencer with hundreds of thousands of subscribers, they're capitalizing on the shock factor of their relationship for media attention: they aren't in love; it's just an act to make money. On the one hand, it was as if I refused to believe that this relationship wasn't sustained by the trading of some secret currency. On the other hand, I was pathologizing all of them and wondering what sort of a mother is comfortable with her twenty-four-year-old daughter living in a sexual and romantic relationship with a woman in her sixties.

My response, which I'm not proud of, was typical. When Eileen began to appear in Julia's videos, shortly after they got together, they went viral (that's how the tabloids discovered them). Julia's audience is usually a closed circle of supportive, mostly female subscribers, but in this case millions of people ended up on her YouTube channel, many leaving disgusted comments:

> That old woman is a pedophile!
> Julia has mommy issues!
> She's sleeping with grandma!
> She's kissing a dirty old lady, ew ew ew!

But it wasn't just anonymous trolls who were horrified. Walking in public, they feel the eyes of strangers on them. It's as if the air were thick with the unspoken: Are they in a relationship? What's going on? And even people who know them judge them. When they first got together, one of Eileen's oldest friends alluded to power and consent when she mentioned that the human brain is not fully formed until you're twenty-five. The most common criticism among those who know them was "why is this young woman exploiting her?," as if Julia were a contemporary P. T. Barnum parading her fake girlfriend to get more likes and followers and that their relationship can't possibly be real.

When I considered where my own preconceptions about relationships with a large age difference come from, I realized I didn't really know any IRL. In fact all of my ideas came from film or TV and tabloid headlines and were based on heterosexual relationships, usually between older men and younger women. The most common trope is the lecherous older man showering his indifferent trophy lover (who is waiting for him to die) with Versace and diamonds. In the 1990s there was the Playboy Playmate Anna Nicole Smith's marriage to a wheelchair-bound eighty-nine-year-old billionaire. In the first decade of the twenty-first century, mainstream media liked to discuss the female version, known as "the cougar." The term was reportedly first published in 2001 on a Canadian dating site, cougardate.com—one of the founders had overheard her nephew use the word when he was talking about her dating habits—before that the slang (which may have originally been used to describe women who hung around hockey teams) referred to women who picked up younger men in bars. The founders of cougardate.com were featured in newspapers and did the talk-show circuit, and as the human geographer Rosemary-Claire Collard has argued, once the media started circulating the term, its postfeminist thrust—a celebration of the power of older female sexuality—was diluted.[6]

The cougar's sexuality came to be seen as suspicious and aggressive, as if she were perpetually covered in sweat lounging somewhere in crushed velvet pleasuring herself, like a giant cat, on the leg of a vulnerable young man. In 2005 forty-two-year-old Demi Moore married twenty-seven-year-old Ashton Kutcher and became the first celebrity cougar. She was savaged by the tabloids as unstable and morally questionable for exposing her young kids to such an arrangement. Then came TV drama series like *Cougar Town* where Courteney Cox plays a comical cougar who is recently divorced and just having fun. When the cougar isn't aggressive and gross, she's a joke, going through a regressive phase and using a younger lover to rewire her sexuality. If, like me, you're relying on the mainstream media to shape your perceptions of these types of relationships, it's little wonder you're suspicious.

In a 2001 study conducted at the University of Manchester, the authors surveyed 122 people about their attitudes toward various heterosexual relationships with a large age gap and found that negative perceptions increased with larger age gaps and that older female partners received stronger opposition than their male counterparts. Among the assumptions held by those surveyed were that age-disparate relationships were not likely to last, the participants have little in common, and they are looking for a mother or a father figure.[7]

The small amount of research that's looked at age-disparate relationships shows that they are a minority. Judgments about relationships between people who have a large age gap might be explained by the fact that they really aren't that common. The most recent data from the United States shows that of the heterosexual married couples sampled, only 8 percent of men were ten or more years older than their wife; only 2 percent of women were ten or more years older than their husbands.[8]

But age gaps in same-sex relationships are more common. In 2014 the Williams Institute at UCLA School of Law found that 31 percent of married, female same-sex couples have a gap of five to ten years and 16 percent have gaps of ten years or more compared with 21 percent and 8 percent of their married straight peers.[9] Theories about why there are more of these unions in gay relationships are endless, like the small dating pool or an already complicated relationship to traditional markers of "normal" development like child rearing and marriage. In an online article about lesbian age-gap relationships, the writer Butch Wonders argues that age gaps are more accepted in the queer community because they are already embarking on relationships that challenge the norm: "An age difference on top of it is just icing on the deviance cake."[10] But gay women judge Julia and Eileen, too. Behind their backs at a dinner party a friend who is herself in her mid-fifties and has a thirtysomething girlfriend got heated when she tried to convince the room that Julia and Eileen are pretending to be in love. Her judgments were coming so hard and fast the polite British host had to call her a hypocrite.

I asked some relationship therapists who work with age-disparate couples for their observations about power but also the stigma. Dr. Gail Saltz, a psychiatrist based in New York, worked through the list of common assumptions. The search for a secret currency, a "transaction" like a visa, or money, can be explained by jealousy; "unhappy people bring their own baggage when they judge any relationship." According to this logic, where the couple seem happy (and people in age-gap relationships are often very happy, or at least have to project that image because their love is subject to so much scrutiny and stigma), it's human nature to want to know: What's in it? What about the tendency to pathologize older people, especially women, who are attracted to younger partners? Dr. Saltz suggests that aside from cultural discomfort with the idea that older women are sexual beings, it could be because we are uncomfortable with older people having sex, period. When a person is older, sex is no longer about procreation, and that's still a cultural taboo. "As a culture we see age as decrepitude, sex is life affirming, so the idea of having sex with decrepitude is yucky . . . like being pulled into the grave."

For the clinical social worker Karen Osterle, from Washington, D.C., the main hurdle to acceptance is that people project a parent-child relationship onto them and read them as incestuous. We often see the younger partner as a victim and incapable of giving consent. Of course, power is a concern in any relationship, and the power balance can be wildly off in a relationship with a large age gap because with age often comes wealth, status, and life experience, which all equal power. But we can't assume a power dynamic based solely on age. Power can be present in a range of ways, and assuming the older partner always has more power is as flawed as the assumption that older people always know better. And power isn't steady throughout the course of a relationship; an obvious way that's reversed in age-gap relationships is that the older partner will eventually lose power through aging or illness.

Dr. Saltz thinks that given the intensity of the social taboo, people who enter a relationship with a large age gap are often acting on a very strong desire, and while staying together through social judgment can threaten their bond, it's just as likely to strengthen it. In fact, learning skills to cope with the social stigma is one of the main reasons that people in age-gap relationships seek her help. Ken Page, an "out gay male" social worker and psychotherapist, agrees with Dr. Saltz that like other sexual minorities, people in an age-gap relationship are bonded by the social stigma; they often have to cope with shame caused by other people's projections, which take the form of cruel judgments: The younger partner is a gold digger, has a granny fetish. The older partner is a superficial loser plugging into youth to validate their relevance, as if they were fooling someone young and naive because they aren't good enough for a peer. Additionally, they are "mavericks" charting a path without societal support, which parallels the queer experience. Based on the clients they've seen, what usually causes age-gap relationships to implode? The same thing that causes most breakups: poor communication. Dr. Saltz agrees that the most important thing in any relationship is that you have similar values, morals, and goals and you can communicate properly.

In one of the only qualitative surveys of age-diverse relationships—a self-help book written by Jill Pitkeathley and David Emerson, based on interviews with a hundred people—the authors found that these connections often occur when people are away from their "normal" pattern of life, like on vacation.[11] Writing in 1995, before social media or online dating, they noted a "rise" of age-disparate relationships as more and more dating agency services connected people who might not have otherwise crossed paths.[12] Are these relationships more likely to occur in the hyperconnected era where people from different walks of life can more easily meet?

Online I discovered the term "age-gap relationship," which has been adopted by people in age-disparate relationships as a sort of identity. There's no founder of a single age-gap "movement": they are real people who are in these relationships connecting with each other and making themselves known in various online communities. Like the "lifestyle," this meta-community is typical of the hyperconnected media era. It's united by common language and even a hashtag (#agegaplove), but there's no formal society or club; instead, a range of groups are spread out on public and private social networks. On more public spaces like the May December Society (a social network founded by a couple with a large age gap) or YouTube and Instagram, the aim is usually activism and visibility: people join a community or go online to represent themselves because they want the support and acceptance of other people who share their experience, and they want to make their unique relationship model visible. They want to be seen.

I searched #agegaplove on Instagram and found thousands of tags. There's nearly thirty years' difference between twenty-two-year-old Lisa and her fifty-year-old boyfriend, Marc. I scrolled further through their feed, looking at pictures where she uses a floral-encased iPhone to take pictures of them in a graffiti-splashed mirror. They're both wearing sneakers. Melanie and Paul, who are twenty-eight and forty-nine, respectively, posted a portrait of themselves clutching each other in front of a white stretch limo the night they got engaged. They also share inspirational quotations: "True love has no expiration date"; "When you really love someone, age, distance, height, weight are just a number"; "Some people are old at 18, and some are young at 90. Time is a concept humans created"—Yoko Ono.

I lurked on the May December Society website, exploring some of the members' profiles. Everyone seemed drunk on love and very keen to show off their relationship to a supportive audience. Some proudly used their full names; others included pictures but only gave their first names. There's almost thirty years between Jill Carpenter and Eric Langley. Jill doesn't write much but shares photos of her and the twenty-three-year-old man she met online and married on her fifty-second birthday. Their wedding photo is a selfie of the pair with their tongues poking out.[13]

There was a picture of a sixtysomething woman named Jane Beckman with her thirtysomething husband, Andrew Crockett, holding each other in a tight embrace. Jane and Andrew are out and very proud. There's long posts about how they met and their everyday life and a range of photos showcasing them as a couple: at a Nightwish concert, campaigning for the Democrats, and on vacation in a field of poppies.[14] Jane describes herself as a "free spirit" who identifies more as a millennial than a boomer. She shares long posts about her family history; like her, many of her family members are in age-gap relationships. She tells her virtual friends that she's there to help normalize their unique relationships: "I'm going to establish my family as the new normal. That way, you can have a benchmark to point to and say 'See, compared to Jane's family, we aren't so different.'"[15]

There were a handful of women in same-sex relationships. Sixty-one-year-old Ailene and her female partner, nineteen-year-old Taylor, from South Florida, have a forty-two-year age gap. It looked as if Taylor were responsible for the selfies decorated with cartoon mouse ears and tiaras that say "love."[16] They regularly post diary-like photo entries updating the community about their relationship, which they have to keep secret from Taylor's conservative, religious family. On their second anniver-

sary they shared a post announcing they were engaged and after a long separation thanked the community for letting them
"share their love . . . it's almost the only place that we can be
proud of who we are."[17]

The website's founder, Joe Leon, who at the time was in a
relationship with Angela Di Pasquo, who is thirty-nine years
younger, told me the idea for the community came about when
he was musing that he never sees ordinary people in age-gap
relationships in the media; he was curious what would happen if
there was a website where they could all meet and connect. He
watched in awe as his tech-savvy partner sat down and created
the page that same afternoon. While some of the six thousand
members use it like a dating site, it mostly functions as a safe
space where people go to meet others who will be supportive of
their relationship. The most common admin request he gets is
from people wanting to update their profile picture to include
their partner; they are proud of their relationship but often
shunned in their real-life community. "Who else do they get to
show them off to?" Behind the scenes, he does a lot of counseling. Concerned relatives want advice about how to cope, and he
hears many sad stories about estrangements, secrets, and double
lives. When we spoke, he'd just finished talking to a woman who
was excluded from her brother's wedding because she's in a relationship with a much older man.

He also hears from a lot of journalists or reality TV producers
who want subjects for their stories. He explained that there's a
real suspicion when it comes to the media, which typically ex-
ploits these couples, hoping that they'll trap them into catering to
stereotypes. Joe's had bad experiences himself. When he appeared
on a reality TV show with Angela, he complains that they were
instructed to throw things at each other, and says the footage was
edited to make it seem as if Angela were on an endless shopping
trip at the mall. When I put out a call for interview participants

on their forum, I got a reply from a longtime member warning me about the trouble people have had with reporters: "Even reporters who claim to want to be sympathetic end up writing stories that make us look crazy; people have been harassed at their work, got demeaning emails, etc." When nobody got in touch with me, I reached out to a few people directly. Jill and her partner said they didn't want to talk to me because they wanted to stay in control of their story. When I emailed Jane Beckman and Taylor and Ailene, I didn't hear back.

There are also chat rooms and closed or more private spaces on Reddit or Facebook where visibility is less important; instead, people go there to find support and get advice from understanding peers. On Reddit, I joined r/AgeGap and spent hours reading through posts where I found engaged discussion about these relationship models that are regarded with suspicion. The stigma and dismissal they faced were based on a refusal to accept those they love. People talked about coming out and shared tips for managing judgment from therapists or other health professionals. There were conversations about the impact of being told that their love is amoral and perverted, and people offered support about how to cope with social judgment, including from friends and family.

There was debate about living out in the open versus hiding, and I learned that a common complaint is being kept a secret from their partner's social and professional worlds. Many stressed that despite major differences in age and life experience, they were drawn together by an unrelenting connection. In many cases this connection occurred despite their own reservations about the large age gap. They talked about how they personally came to terms with stepping outside dating age norms. There were conversations about health and differing energy levels, conflicting attitudes toward children or the desire to build a family, and of course the ever-present weight that impacts these unions, especially those with a very large age gap: that one partner will almost certainly get sick or die before the other.

When I talked to the r/AgeGap moderator (a man from the U.K. who has been in a number of relationships with younger women and insisted on anonymity because he's worried about stigma), he told me that critical discussion is fine as long as there's no trotting out of stereotypes or cliché arguments against age-gap relationships like that the brain is not properly formed when you are under twenty-five, that people who date older people have an unresolved relationship with their parents (a.k.a. as mommy or daddy issues), or that older people who date those over eighteen are pedophiles. He's happy to let contributors debate issues like power and consent, because, as he put it, "sometimes people who post saying their relationship is wonderful when it isn't really need to hear the warning bells," or as a moderator wrote on a recent thread, the space is not designed to be an age gap "circle jerk."

The responses came fast when I put out a call for people to talk to me, but all of the twenty who replied wanted to remain completely anonymous because they hadn't told their family or friends about their relationships. We communicated over the phone and email. Like Pitkeathley and Emerson over twenty years ago, I found a commonality to how they met, either online—through a dating or hookup app or age-gap community forum—or in a social situation that took them outside their usual demographic (a community college course, a social or charity event, or on vacation).

The redditors I spoke to had in common the fact that they were concerned about the judgments people make about the older partner in the relationship—that their interest in youth is predatory and evidence of an abuse of power. This is one of the strongest critiques of age-gap relationships and the basis of age normativity, that age necessarily equals power. Nina, a twenty-seven-year-old woman who is in a relationship with a fifty-five-year-old man, told me that she's not worried about what people will think of her, but she fears the judgments people will make about her partner's interest in a much younger woman. Another woman, who is twenty-nine and has a sixty-year-old boyfriend, begged me not to include their names because as far as her family is concerned, he's just a close friend; like Nina, she fears what they'll think of her boyfriend, who is only two years younger than her dad. The assumptions that bother her the most are the idea that there must be a secret transaction that justifies their love—the sugar daddy stereotype—and that she lacks power in the relationship. She went online for support when she felt isolated being in a relationship that doesn't resemble those of her close girlfriends: "I was hoping to find support from people who aren't just giving it because they know and love me, but because they actually understand what it's like."

I was looking through the list of May December Society followers on Instagram when I came across an eighteen-year-old woman from Texas named Jordan who moderates a Facebook group for lesbian age-gap relationships. The page used a picture of Julia and Eileen—smiling together dressed for a night out—as its logo. Jordan started that Facebook group when her forty-nine-year-old partner, who had more trouble with the stigma than Jordan, said that finding community might help her feel more comfortable about their transgressive relationship. She searched for local meetup groups, but there weren't any. As Jordan put it, "We shouldn't be looking for approval from others, but it is nice to have support . . . To see other people out there going through the same things makes it a bit easier."

The aspiring poet met her forty-nine-year-old girlfriend on Match.com. Her girlfriend, who has a corporate job at a large bank, was reluctant to get involved, but they struck up a conversation, met in real life, and started a relationship. Jordan says that older women are her preference; that's just whom she's attracted to. She waited until she could legally pursue her interests with the help of the internet before she acted on her feelings. As she says, "In real life nobody has a sign over her head saying, 'I like younger girls.'" They can and do online, though.

When she was making sense of her preference, Julia and Eileen's YouTube videos and Instagram posts were comforting; not only did it make her feel less alone to see another gay couple with a large age gap, but she found the supportive comments they got from their subscribers reassuring. She wanted her Facebook group to get more people talking about age-gap relationships, to make them more "normal." "That will only happen if people come out and start telling their stories. At the moment people just look at these relationships and think the younger one is using the older one for money and the older one is just using the younger one for sex, but that's not the case whatsoever."

The second time Jordan and I talked on the phone, she was upset; her girlfriend had just broken up with her. She couldn't cope with the stigma, fearing the judgment of her friends and family: "It feels right to her, but she knows the way that society perceives age-gap relationships, and she doesn't want to have to stand out or deal with the judgments that are put on us. It doesn't feel wrong to her, but the way other people see it makes her feel like it is." Jordan thinks that discrimination against age-gap relationships is no different from homophobia and that like homophobia it stems from ignorance: "It makes people feel better when they hate people who are different; they're usually just going along with what other people say. At the end of the day, homosexual couples, heterosexual couples, age-gap couples, we are all the same; there's no difference other than physical appearance. It's judging based on what you see, not what you know." That's when I realized the power of Julia and Eileen's self-representation: by being out in the world and aggressively coveting media attention, they are attempting to normalize their unique relationship type.

I wrote Julia and Eileen an email, asking if they'd be interested in talking, and received an immediate response from Eileen: "Being on the presumed vanguard of this 'new' form of love, we're grateful for the opportunity to normalize what for us is, really, just another way to experience the intimate grace known as romantic love."

When they connected on Tinder, the first thing Eileen noticed about Julia was that she wasn't using a standard posed and glamorous dating site photo. She was making a face, with one eye closed. This, and Julia's brief bio (vegetarian, music student, bright hair, Brazilian, twenty-four), suggested to Eileen that there was something authentic about this woman, who, she reasoned, must have a lot of confidence to defy online dating conventions with an imperfect photo. She did what any single person does when they are online looking for sex or love or both and feel that pinch of possible connection: swiped right and put her phone down.

It would be two weeks before she received an alert indicating a match. Eileen describes their initial connection as "unrelenting." "It was as if the planets aligned. I am not prone to that level of corniness," she says. "She seems so wonderfully unjaded," she thought to herself, and they broke the ice with flirty banter. They spent their days chatting, graduating from text messages to voice calls; it never felt as if they had to force it, the conversation flowed.

Neither was looking for love. Julia had recently ended a relationship and wanted to distract herself with a new, casual interest. Eileen, who had just come out of a long sexually dormant period, joined Tinder because she wanted to have sex and she'd heard its reputation as a hookup app. She'd put on a significant amount of weight and had been alone for so long she thinks she probably wouldn't have been able to make the leap if she'd had to go out and meet someone IRL. She didn't have the energy or confidence for bars or clubs, and even after she established an online relationship, the thought of meeting a stranger was daunting. Tinder was a laboratory that allowed her to connect with someone and explore her sexuality.

While she wanted sex, intimacy without an emotional or intellectual connection doesn't really do it for her, so establishing that rapport was important to Eileen. She connected with a few women who were closer to her in age but found it was difficult to relate. There were political differences, like a hairdresser from just outside London whom she chatted with for a while but was too conservative, so they never met. Many were back in the dating pool having recently come out and either had left long unhappy marriages to men, had spent their lives in the suburbs, were preoccupied with adult children and grandkids, or had lapsed into a middle-aged rut. It was hard to find people who had lived the same sort of varied life she had, in multiple cities and countries; as much as she tried, she just couldn't "connect."

Connecting sexually wasn't always easy, either. There was a woman from France who came to spend the weekend with her, but in real life wasn't attracted to Eileen's larger body (later, when she was getting to know Julia, Eileen sent a message saying, "I must warn you, I'm a little porky"). Another woman turned out to be heavily into feet: "I try not to judge anybody, and I love a good foot massage, but it just became the focus that was obsessive and that put me off." Eileen was up-front about her aims with all the women she communicated with, so during her early conversations with Julia after they'd flirted, made jokes, and learned about each other's lives, they quickly established what Eileen describes as an "erotically intimate" series of exchanges, initiated by Eileen but enthusiastically embraced by Julia.

Anxiety about their age difference was built into their relationship from the outset. Eileen insists that it wasn't a problem when it came to their actual dynamic, but she was concerned about what others would make of it. She's "hyperaware" of people's perceptions: "I don't mean that in a way to imply that I am insecure about it, just that I know [that to accept it] people will have to cross over when it comes to their immediate thinking of it." In fact, she lied about her age on her profile, saying she was in her early fifties. She told Julia the truth before they met, though; their virtual relationship had escalated so quickly she felt an obligation to be completely honest. When Julia got Eileen's message saying she had a confession, she held her breath and waited for Eileen's follow-up text: "I'm 60 and I am sorry I didn't tell you . . . I just didn't want to be judged and people judge women over 60—a lot." Julia's previous girlfriend was in her fifties, so she wasn't concerned about the extra years. She'd set her age preferences wide open from eighteen to a hundred. Her last girlfriend was closeted when they met on a dating website, and while she eventually came out, she kept Julia a secret from certain parts of her life, so Julia was more concerned that Eileen was about to make a similar reveal.

Was Eileen specifically looking for a younger woman? Yes. Aside from having always lived in cities where dating and friendship groups are not so tightly segregated by generation, Eileen says she has never felt her age: she doesn't have "rigid expectations" about how things should be, or how she should behave as a woman in her sixties. She's had numerous relationships with women who are ten or fifteen years younger, and her friendship circles have always been mixed.

But more than that, she's attracted to youth. And she's a visual person. "I'm a real whore for beauty; I like beautiful cars, beautiful art," she says. "Julia's a beautiful and a deeply erotic woman, which is just an extraordinarily powerful combination . . . If people could stop judging for a minute, they'd see that there's nothing pathological about celebrating what I am not." But her penchant for youth is not just physical. Eileen is up-front about the fact that she's drawn to Julia's youthful energy—her warmth and lack of cynicism, which she says are by-products of her having spent thirty-seven years less time being beaten down by life. As Eileen puts it, "the world hasn't soured her," yet. She's drawn to her spontaneity and energy: "There's a sort of reining in that happens when you get older and it's sad, and frustrating, but that's what it is." She refuses to see Julia as a victim; when she celebrates Julia's youth, she's celebrating her power.

Just as Eileen has a preference for youth, Julia is attracted to maturity. Around the time she and Eileen became official, she posted a video on YouTube where she talked to her subscribers about her age gap relationship. Dressed in a T-shirt that read "why be racist, sexist, homophobic, or transphobic when you could just be quiet," she says she'd prefer to look at Madonna's body at sixty-one than when she was young and she finds older women more physically attractive than young women.[18] For her, it's simply a "type," like how some people are drawn to blondes, or people who are tall. She's looked back over her childhood to find a moment that "explains" her attraction. She was an only child who spent a lot of time around adults. She grew up with a single mother with whom she has a companion-like relationship: they look after each other, and Julia often takes on a maternal role (when we discussed this, Eileen looked thoughtful before saying, "Having a close relationship with a single mom has set you up to have a very mature way of relating to older women"). Her sexual and romantic preferences mirror her friendships; she's drawn to maturity and intellectual conversation.

Aside from being physically attracted to Eileen, Julia was

taken by the depth of her political knowledge, her direct and up-front communication style, and, after they'd met IRL, how articulate and calm she is when she communicates face-to-face. She was secretly grateful that Eileen wasn't from a generation used to googling every potential date; it took Julia about a month to confess that she was a YouTuber because she thought that this older woman would find it immature and vacuous. Eileen was open about her identity, not thinking to obscure her first or last name, so Julia did some online stalking and found her Twitter and Instagram. She read through her tweets and was taken with how she seemed to be able to so eloquently convey the same political views that she held.

They had their first date on Eileen's couch. When she was getting ready, Julia recalls thinking how close she already felt to the woman who had become her 24/7 confidante. Eileen decorated her flat with fairy lights; they ate pizza (well, Julia tried to eat it, but she was so nervous she only managed a slice) and drank prosecco. They ended the night with a kiss, but there was no sex until they met for the second time.

Their relationship moved quickly, dates became regular, and soon they were spending all their time together; when they weren't by each other's side, they used their phones to keep in touch. Their schedules worked well together, which is not an insignificant hurdle when it comes to negotiating the dynamics of a new relationship. Neither is bound by a nine-to-five office job, and Eileen is happy to go about her business while Julia spends hours in front of her computer editing video footage to meet YouTube sponsor deadlines. Eileen can easily accompany Julia when she's spending a weekday afternoon filming. After a few months together Julia was on one of her daily phone calls with her mother when Eileen asked if she could translate into Portuguese if she said a few words.

They'd been an official couple for nine months when Julia

moved into Eileen's small one-bedroom flat. Julia filled the bedroom with her collection of shoes and clothes, leaving the living room shelves for Eileen's amaro and gin. Armed with a nail gun and paintbrushes, she headed a renovation project, fitting shelves so Eileen's bedroom would accommodate her belongings, and together they adopted their kitten, Britney. "You're probably thinking, wow, you have only just met and you're moving in together," Julia said to her subscribers on a YouTube video when she announced the news. "We're not just acting impulsively; we have talked things through," says a more serious Eileen, who sits by her side.[19] They'd been together just shy of a year when Julia crouched on the floor of the pair's kitchen using her iPhone to film herself, while pizza whirled around in the microwave. She whispered to avoid being overheard by Eileen and told her fans that she'd decided to ask Eileen to be her wife.[20]

It was the summer of 2019, a few weeks after their wedding, when I arrived in London to meet Julia and Eileen in the flesh. (Eileen is American, but her mother is Irish; she moved to London when she was in her thirties. Julia is Brazilian with German ancestry, so she also inherited an EU passport and came to London on her own when she was eighteen.) We'd communicated for most of the year—largely on three-way WhatsApp calls or voice memos, Eileen's preferred way to keep in touch: she loves to talk, and she hates reaching for her glasses. I got off the tube in South Kensington and weaved around sluggish tourists trying to find local museums on the short walk to their flat in Chelsea, clutching the boxes of instant Kraft mac and cheese Eileen had asked for to surprise Julia—an American "delicacy" she hadn't tried. They got married the month before I arrived and had squeezed Julia's best friend, Lara, and her aunt and mother into the living room for two weeks while they prepared for the wedding, so they were exhausted and broke. We decided to spend our first day together in their flat. Julia could fix us rice and beans, leftovers from the sixty meals she'd frozen to feed the house full of women.

I was greeted by Eileen, who was in house clothes and running shoes, and a makeup-less Julia, who seemed smaller and shy IRL (most people who meet her are taken aback by her introversion). They'd just finished writing a long email to producers from a reality TV show they'd decided not to participate in when the producers mentioned they wanted to focus on wealthy age-gap couples. Julia, who is much more media savvy than Eileen, knew that was code for something exploitative, and besides, neither of them has much money. If there's one stereotype that bothers Julia the most, it's the gold-digger trope. She's independent and a hard worker. She came to London on her own as a teenager without any English, worked for a grim winter frying churros at a market stall, was poorly paid as a babysitter, got into Goldsmiths, University of London to study classical singing, and worked her way up to nearly 300,000 YouTube subscribers—all by the age of twenty-five.

When I spent time with them, it was clear that there was a productive intergenerational exchange and a difference at the heart of their relationship that kept things exciting. It was as if they were adventurers exploring each other's worlds together. If they had official roles in the relationship, Eileen would be the communicator. She often helps Julia draft replies to emails or texts and helps her resolve conflicts with her peers. On the second day I spent with them, a long and involved "feelings talk" broke out when Julia, who has trouble being direct, didn't ask a friend to leave when I arrived. Julia gives Eileen advice on how to reply to direct messages and generally manage her social media presence, advising her that it's best not to engage because then it will become a conversation, "and you can't have

a conversation with thousands of people." Eileen wants to reply to every comment and message she receives; she's not used
to terms like "ghost" and "blank" and was socialized during
a time when there weren't as many ways to use technology to
avoid direct communication.

Eileen says she has "a package, a skin," that is a lot stronger
than that of Julia, who is so sensitive she often cries mid-sentence.
But if anyone occupies a maternal role in the relationship, it's
Julia. She'll bring Eileen tea when she's sick, does the cooking,
makes sure she doesn't binge on junk food, and keeps a watch on
her finances. Eileen is not as disciplined as Julia, who was raised
by a hardworking single mom who taught her how to stretch
her resources. But domestically, Eileen's more organized. She
marvels at how Julia manages to run her own YouTube business
when she can't even keep her bedroom clean.

Eileen is more set in her ways about certain things, like how
her food is sliced or what hotel she stays in—the sorts of routine
comforts that come with age. As Eileen puts it, when "one gets
older, there's a need for life to be controlled or manageable."
Julia is creative; Eileen jokes that she'll turn everything from
making toast to wrapping a gift into an elaborate form of self-
expression. Eileen is a realist, whereas Julia is an optimist. Eileen is not as open-minded or politically correct as Julia; she has
trouble getting her head around concepts like gender fluidity
and using the pronoun "they."

Julia is not shy about showering Eileen with affection and
praise. On camera and IRL she'll stand back staring at her, saying, repeatedly, "You're so beautiful. You are so hot."

In fact, she's committed to extreme forms of public affection.
On their first restaurant date, Eileen was taken aback when Julia
unabashedly kissed her under bright lights in a high-end sushi
bar. When Julia's childhood friend Lara was in London for their
wedding, she noticed that they couldn't go anywhere without

Julia embracing or stroking Eileen and telling her how much she loves her. "It's like, 'Oh my God, I love you, I love you,' all the time and I'm thinking, 'You love each other?' Thank you. I wouldn't realize, if you hadn't said it three times!"

At one function we attended together, an influencer event at a local night club, I came back from the bar to find Julia straddling Eileen, lips and tongues on faces as if they were alone in their honeymoon suite. I watched Julia nestle her head on Eileen's breasts and slide up on her lap, and I'll admit I was thinking, "Is that really necessary?"

One thing they share, which contributed to their initial connection, was feeling much more comfortable expressing themselves online. In fact, perhaps where they "connect" the most is through their shared love of social media and their desire to express themselves, to be seen. But while Eileen had experimented with online expression before she met Julia—for example, in the lead-up to the 2016 U.S. presidential election, she was on Twitter twenty hours a day—when they met, YouTube was an unknown world to Eileen, who thought it was mostly full of videos showing you how to do things like make bread or change a tire. Shortly after they moved in together, Julia encouraged Eileen to try making some videos of her own.

When she was a child, Eileen didn't even consider that marriage would ever be an option. She was born in 1957 and grew up in New Jersey, where she lived what she calls a Mark Twain childhood. She was a tomboy, in a boomer neighborhood where kids seemed to spill out from the two-parent houses like clowns from a car. She roamed the streets, knees bruised and scraped from hockey or football with gangs of boys and her big toe poking out of her right sneaker. There was no pressure to wear dresses, immerse herself in pink, or play with dolls. As she puts it, "The world was wide open to me. I wasn't forced to be girlie."

Her family were informed by the media that beamed out of New York City about a forty-minute drive from their home. Each day her father returned from his job delivering Wonder bread with a copy of the county paper and the *Daily News*. Media consumption was communal and came from a single source; there weren't any computers in bedrooms or movies in hands on phones. There was the drive-in, the radio was set to a New York City station, and the TV was always on, but she didn't see or hear about sexual relationships between women anywhere when she was growing up. She remembers the gay tennis player Billie Jean King but more as a sports star and a strong woman; if there were rumors about King's sexuality, they went way over Eileen's head, and she was in her twenties by the time King was outed in 1981. A major network didn't televise two women kissing until 1991 on *L.A. Law*, and when Ellen DeGeneres came out as gay in 1997, she was the first woman to do so on primetime TV.

Looking back, she can see that her very first crush was on a female babysitter; whenever her parents announced they had evening plans, she was thrilled. Her feelings toward this woman weren't sexual; it was a strong sense of affection and connection she'd never felt toward someone male. She made best friends with her neighbor, a gymnast, whose company she found "intoxicating"; again it wasn't sexual but more that she wanted to be around her constantly. She was addicted to her presence; she wanted to inhale her as if she were a drug. She had those same passionate feelings for a classmate; they were playing pool in her basement one day when Eileen spontaneously gazed into her eyes and said, "You look like a tiger." She remembers turning red and feeling embarrassed while her friend looked at her confused. She had a boyfriend in her senior year of high school, whom she lost her virginity to. When she says those words today, she says she feels creepy, "like they assigned women this idea of virginity and that a man could take it away," as if it were a lump of gold or some other sort of trophy he could put on his mantel. "The truth was that I elected to sleep with him; he wasn't taking anything from me." It wasn't the best experience, there was no conversation leading up to it, it just happened. She did get some pleasure from kissing him, but when she looks back, she can see she was just going through the motions and wasn't acknowledging the stronger feelings that she had toward women.

In her second year at college she met a female singer whom she says she fell in love with, but there was no sex; the singer was straight, which is also what Eileen was still calling herself. They had what Eileen calls a "romantic friendship." One night they went to a lecture by the motivational speaker Leo Buscaglia, who talked about love. On the way back to the dorms Eileen turned to her friend and said, "I really love you." At the time she meant it in a platonic way, to describe her intense friendship, but again, looking back, she can see she was struggling to articulate a passion she didn't know how to express.

While Eileen credits the cultural invisibility of being gay for disconnecting her from her sexual identity, she also acknowledges the impact of a chaotic home life, which took a lot of her emotional energy when she was growing up. Eileen's mother was diagnosed with rheumatoid arthritis when she was thirty, just after Eileen was born. Eileen doesn't remember a time when her mother wasn't in pain. There was a specially fitted hospital bed, a nurse, schedules for taking medicine. Eventually the joints in her hands and feet were removed and replaced with plastic. At times Eileen felt as if she were more of a caregiver for her mother than a daughter: but she loved the woman who had a thick Irish accent (she once took her mother to school for show-and-tell; she saw her as an exotic souvenir—just like the dinosaur she got on vacation in Florida). Eileen was twenty-four and living at home having left college when her dad woke her and told her to hurry. It was unedited raw footage, her mother dead in her nightie on the kitchen floor, blue, bacon frying.

Eileen says she learned about being gay through word of mouth; this was the early 1980s before the internet. There were two women who were important guides as she went on her journey. One was a friend she met in a photography class at college who revealed that she was sexually attracted to women. They spent the summer together at the beach, they'd get drunk, and occasionally kiss. She says that was the first time she had the concept of being something other than straight; being gay just wasn't in her consciousness. A year or so later a high school friend she always looked up to and wanted to emulate who'd dropped out of Dartmouth and moved to New York City told Eileen that she'd had sex with a female dancer. She presented the story in a matter-of-fact way, as if it were just another tale from her sophisticated life in New York, but like her other friend's confession it had a real impact on Eileen: "It awakened something inside me . . . another step in uncovering the edifice of my sexual identity."

She was studying psychology at college and every week religiously reading *The New York Times Book Review*, where she learned about the lesbian-feminist poet Adrienne Rich and sought out her work. She still remembers sitting in the library with a pile of books reading Rich's poems and feeling aroused. It was visceral; she felt a strong sense of identification with the kind of eroticism that Rich felt toward women: "Seeing it right there on the page was such a powerful experience." That was when she began to connect with her sexuality. "What was remarkable about it was that it was hidden, not that I was hiding it from anybody," Eileen says, "but it was hidden from myself in the sense that I didn't know this was a way one could be. You can't rush your brain to know things that it won't know unless it comes across triggers. It was just such a potent treasure to find someone who felt the same things I did."

She got in touch with her friend from New York and told her she thought she might be gay. The woman encouraged her to explore that further and gave her the address of a bar in Manhattan. Eileen was brave and independent, but embarking on this journey alone was terrifying. Still, it didn't occur to her to ask anyone to come with her; there were no similar experiences she could call upon, like "'so-and-so did that!' maybe I could see if she wants to do this with me." She says to forge connections, she had to "jump off a cliff alone."

She'll never forget the anxiety she felt that night. There was a heavy door and a long, dark walk to a bar full of beautiful women who seemed to be in established couples or at least on dates. She kept her focus on a pay phone toward the back of the room where she inserted a coin and pretended to call a friend. The phone was some sort of protective armor, the 1980s version of scrolling your iPhone to let people know you have connections somewhere else. She fought through her anxiety, ordered a drink, and when she told the barkeep that it was her first time there, the bartender told her about a club night that was more suitable for singles (this was before you could google things like "best lesbian bar for meeting people, Manhattan").

The next weekend she made the journey again. She'd never been to a nightclub, so she showed up at 9:00 p.m. sharp and stood in her best white jeans watching cleaners tidy an empty room. She was killing time eating Chinese food in her car when a homeless man pounded on her window; the shock sent garlic broccoli all over her lap. She took a deep breath and entered the club alone, the smell of soy sauce like an aura. The first woman she spoke to was a direct New Yorker who, perhaps sensing she was out of place, asked her, "Are you gay?" "No, I'm bi," Eileen replied, and the cliché made her new friend laugh.

She showed up there again the next weekend, and this time, after a woman bought her a drink, she told Eileen about another bar in the West Village. The first night she went, she met someone and went home to her place in Staten Island to have sex. "It's hard to describe the feeling of arriving at home and of knowing that it's your home. It was like, I love women; I have found my home with women," she says. She'd had sex with boys, which she described as "interesting" but not fulfilling. "Do women really find that fulfilling?" she once asked me; there's a part of her that doesn't believe heterosexuality is real. But sex with that woman was everything she'd fantasized about, and at times she didn't even really know what to fantasize about; she hadn't even seen any gay sex in porn. She'd found herself at the end of a long, analog tunnel.

Eileen came out in 1983, and to her "coming-out" culminated when she had her first girlfriend (that one-night stand turned into a three-year relationship). There was no official announcement to her family; it was "understood" that she was gay when she moved in with her girlfriend and brought her to gatherings. Back then she would have said she didn't feel the need to assert labels or define who her partner was. But today she has a different take. She was shy about her difference. She wanted to avoid an uncomfortable conversation; she didn't want to draw attention to herself or "force the moment to its crisis." Her sexual coming-of-age was not fraught; it was unguided—a journey to an identity with a route she had to figure out herself. And it wasn't until she was in her mid-twenties that she was able to express it. She never felt unaccepted: "You didn't know to ask so much of the culture back then." As she puts it, "I didn't have any barriers to my sexuality; I only lacked models."

Julia came of age almost thirty years later, late in the first decade of the twenty-first century, in São Paulo with her single mother—an industrial designer—one of very few women who worked in a building full of men drafting blueprints for cell-phone towers. While Eileen's media was mostly flowing one way from centrally produced production companies, Julia's coming of age coincided with the increased visibility of heterosexual young women—like Britney Spears, Paris Hilton, and the Olsen twins—on TV screens. A whole identity was created for their audience—the tween—with its own commercial feminist language of "girl power." She witnessed the rise of broadband internet during the nascent hyperconnected media era.

Growing up, she didn't find herself attracted to boys and, like Eileen, didn't know what that meant. As she puts it, "I didn't know I was gay because that just wasn't something that was talked about." Dress and makeup were how she showed her difference at her Catholic school. She adored pink, sparkles, and all the trappings of normative femininity; she'd throw on a fuchsia backpack and stiletto sneakers with her school uniform. She was obsessed with the concept of love and romance and longed to have a boyfriend. She wanted a constant companion, someone to take her on dates, and she was especially taken with Valentine's Day. Each year when the day passed, she'd say to her best friend, Lara, "Next year we'll have boyfriends. I don't want to spend Valentine's Day alone again." She was going with the script the culture had handed her.

Julia longed to get married, but she didn't want marriage to "mean what it did." She recalls a time when she was a child and her mom and her cousin were in deep conversation about cleaning products. When she saw Julia roll her eyes, her mother said, "When you grow up and have a husband, you and your friends will be talking about cleaning products, too." Julia couldn't identify with this woman excited to get married, stocking up on Windex. "I think especially when you marry men and in Brazil, it's a sexist place, so I associated it with that sad life," she says. Or as Eileen puts it, summarizing Julia's youthful thought process,

"I think you just described your understanding and rejection of a certain role that was going to be dumped on you."

When Julia was fourteen, she had her first crush, on her female literature teacher. She was careful to keep the taboo information to herself; Brazil is still a very traditional Catholic country. "I thought it was perverted," she said years later. Her friends were confused that she always turned down date requests from boys, so when she was seventeen, she gave in "so I could prove to myself that I could be 'normal,'" she once told me, pointing at her heart and then making scare quotes.

She was with a group of female friends when someone asked, "If you had to kiss a girl, who would it be?" People were throwing out famous names, but one looked up and said, "Julia." On a dare, they went to the restrooms, and as Julia looked at the pretty girl with dark curly hair who was just standing there, she realized that they were both women so she had no idea from romantic movies or TV who was supposed to make the first move. Afterward, she felt both guilty and liberated. The weight had become so unbearable she felt as if it would never happen. She immediately told her mom, who'd always been her best friend. Her mom accepted her sexuality from the outset, and when she heard this news, she smiled and asked if Julia liked it. Julia was too ashamed to say she did; even though her mother is open and far from homophobic, admitting to pleasure was embarrassing because of the wider cultural attitude she'd absorbed growing up. So she downplayed it and hid her feelings. She even begged her mother to keep it a secret; she'd internalized so much shame about her sexuality.

For Julia, being gay was "a bit embarrassing," and based on stereotypes and slang, it was not something she related to. She recalls the Portuguese word, *sapatão*, which roughly translates to "big shoes." "Not that there's anything wrong with being a masculine woman, but I was always super girlie; I didn't identify with that," she says. She didn't see any gay women around her, either IRL or on screens. There was the singer Ana Carolina, who was mocked for being bisexual. The gay men she saw on comedy shows played negative stereotypical roles, usually an effeminate foil to the hero's masculinity or a punch line to a joke.

But she had access to something Eileen didn't: the internet. It was 2011 and Julia was seventeen when she saw a lesbian, knowingly, for the first time. But that lesbian wasn't one she saw in real life. It was the drama series about the lives of a group of young gay women living in Los Angeles called *The L Word* that marked a turning point in Julia's self-perception. She found it online; the show was not screened on Brazilian TV, which was heavily censored. It was a revelation, the first time she had ever been given a window that showed her a future where she could be normal. These women were married, had kids, went to work; they weren't alone and miserable. They were out to everyone, to their friends, to their family, and at work. Those fictional women gave her a script for who she was, how she might be in the world. As she put it later, "Watching that show, I realized you could be gay and still have a normal life."

That representation was powerful. Lesbian women just existing, being human, out there in the world. They were fictional, yes, but she could relate to the characters, see herself in them, and she stored that at the back of her head; if only she'd seen a show like that on TV when she was thirteen. Before that she was saying she was bisexual because she was ashamed to say what she really was, how she really felt. But after watching *The L Word*, Julia finally gained the confidence to say three powerful words: "I am gay."

What was she to do with her desire? Could she have a girlfriend? How would she find one? She was underage, so clubs weren't an option, not that she knew of any gay clubs anyway; that sort of thing just wasn't spoken about in her circle. She knew that straight people used the internet for dating, so she did what most teenagers

born in the 1990s and later do and went online. She met her first
girlfriend on a "local lesbian Facebook," and when they were ar-
ranging their first date, the woman had one request for Julia: bring
your mom. She wanted her blessing, given that there was an age
gap and Julia was a stranger she'd met online.

Julia and her mom drove to the mall just outside São Paulo;
Julia was going through a Goth phase and was dressed in a cor-
set. They broke the ice over smoothies, but Julia was so nervous she couldn't talk. She's always felt bold online, but with the
pressure of immediate social presence, she's more likely to hold
back. About midway through the date Julia invited her to the
restroom, and while they were away from their chaperone, they
had their first kiss.

Unlike Eileen, Julia is deeply uncomfortable with "don't ask,
don't tell," or pretending her lovers are her friends. She would
never be interested in the sort of arrangement that Joe and Susie
or the Synergy crew have. She felt humiliated when her girlfriend occasionally did that to her. Because she'd felt so invisible growing up, she has strong feelings about the importance
of being "seen." She decided that openness matters, and that's
something she's still committed to. "If we hide things, they will
always be taboo and hard on the next generations, but if we talk
openly about who we are with, then it will normalize it," she
says. If she's in a relationship and her girlfriend keeps her secret,
she'll think, "Does she not love me enough to stand up to society
and tell the truth?" Openness is the most important thing to Julia, and she sees it as direct political action. It's not always easy,
but it matters.

Julia started vlogging a few years after she moved to London. At
first she filmed tutorials about things like decorating Easter eggs
and making Brazilian food, and on average she'd get about ten
views. But she experimented and found the response was more

enthusiastic when she posted more personal content—like confessional videos where she tells embarrassing stories or tours her bedroom. Her relationship with her subscribers became more intimate, and she realized that she hadn't talked about her sexuality, which was too important a part of her identity to keep hidden, so in 2016, when she had more than twenty thousand followers, she made a video about coming out, which got over sixty thousand views.[21]

She wanted to do for others what *The L Word* did for her. As she put it, "Being gay is a lot more normal now, but the more the merrier. I want to show younger people that they are not alone and it's okay to be who you are and be happy." But unlike those fictional characters on *The L Word* there's no director, production crew, editor, or media corporation controlling her image and she's not a scripted character. She's a human who continues to exist when the camera is turned off. She's fully in control of representing herself using her iPhone and editing tools on her computer, and the ease of accessing an online audience is something that no prior generation has known before.

There's an authenticity to her self-representation that's important. Like the members of the May December Society, those Instagram users who take control of their representation by posting photos of themselves online, or anonymous redditors, she shows people who are not like her that she exists and lets people who might not have seen their own experience reflected before know that they are not alone. As Julia puts it, "I think you can get a lot closer to people on YouTube because it's not scripted, there's no directors or major rules you have to follow like on TV, and that can be very powerful. When you watch someone often enough, they can feel like a close friend, so when I am giving coming-out advice, it's like having a close friend giving advice about something that they have been through before." Julia's online confession is personal, but it's also generational. If there's a hidden agenda to her media performance, it's that she wants to be seen on her own terms so that her sexuality becomes normal.

Julia's age-gap activism is a by-product of her quest to be visible as a gay woman. Her relationship with her subscribers is deeply personal, so when something happens to her, she shares it—from describing the awful texture of her first kiss with a man, to joking about why she keeps one finger nail shorter than the rest. But she also wants to normalize her desire, in this case by letting people know that she's sexually and romantically at-tracted to an older woman. Eileen admits that she found it a bit awkward at first, but ultimately she's in awe of Julia's openness: "That's how people learn to be comfortable with hard things. That's how things become normal."

When Eileen posted *her* first YouTube video, which was a monologue about coming out in the 1980s, she got about 120,000 views (when Julia posted her debut she got 20).[22] When I watched it, I thought of that woman discovering her identity alone in a nightclub back in the 1980s wearing soy-sauce-soaked jeans and wondered what she'd think if she could look into the future at her adult self sharing her coming of age with the world. She started making more and found that the genre suited her desire to be seen. It was cathartic. She gained more and more followers; the rush of likes and comments was addictive, like a drug.

In fact one of Eileen's biggest life regrets is that she never fulfilled her potential. She feels as if she wasted her talent doing technical and copywriting, and she's always wanted to express herself creatively, write a memoir, a play, or a novel. She says her failure in this realm is the direct result of her lack of disci-pline, or, in her more self-deprecating moments, "because I'm a bit of a mess." When I thought about how power is present in Julia and Eileen's relationship, one thing that seems clear is that when she met Julia, Eileen found a way to access that almighty beacon of power—media power—because she was introduced to a very useful way of finally, aged in her sixties, expressing herself.

Eileen's friend Farzana describes Eileen's transformation as like a butterfly emerging from a chrysalis: "She thawed out after a dark period of not expressing herself much and met someone on Tinder who changed her life." Eileen says that meeting Julia was a gift: "It's sort of like when you hear someone ask a writer, well, how did you learn to write? And they say that when they were a kid, someone got them an empty journal. I feel like that's what Julia's done for me with YouTube."

Our tendency to judge things that are unfamiliar is powerful. When Julia was making herself at home in Eileen's flat, Eileen filled her in on gossip about the neighbors. The woman who lives downstairs is a real character. Eileen was making small talk with the old English nana type about how thin the walls are. "I hope you don't hear me stomping about, because I am *not* light," quipped Eileen. But her neighbor wasn't bothered; she was planning her own apology. "I hope you don't hear me masturbating," she said. "Apparently she said it twice!" Julia told me, her eyes wide, giggling. "But you see, she doesn't look like the . . ." She paused, choosing her words. "She doesn't sound like the sort of woman who would do . . . that. She's older, very serious looking."

They were shocked not only that a woman well over middle age would still experience sexual desire but that she'd brashly discuss it with a stranger. And I was surprised by the story, too. After all, none of us have been taught by the culture that older women may still be complex sexual beings whose libido doesn't suddenly explode during menopause. There was cognitive dissonance; we couldn't hold those two ideas together at the same time. Julia and Eileen know that their response to the masturbating granny is hypocritical. But that's how powerful cultural and social norms are.

In fact, Eileen openly judges heterosexual age-gap relationships, perceiving the power dynamic to be inherently tainted. She thinks power is different between two women. "Part of it is the bare transactional nature of it, which disgusts me about heterosexuality across the board. Nowhere is it more clear than when you see an older man and a younger woman," she said to me, prompting Julia to interject: "You don't know that, Eileen! People say the same about us." When Julia exposed her hypocrisy, Eileen didn't try to defend her position; she admitted that her gut response is that these types of relationships are suspicious. Then, when she was ruminating on her judgment, she hit on something important: "It's because I don't see something familiar." That reminded me of how she once said that she doesn't understand heterosexual female desire, because being attracted to a man is so unfamiliar and there's part of her that doesn't believe heterosexuality is real. For something to become normal, it has to be made familiar, but at the same time it's worth accepting that there's something about the way we decide what's normal that has more to do with our own subjectivity, and that's something that no amount of exposure or empathy can necessarily undo.

Making an alternative script for marriage familiar was one of the reasons Julia and Eileen allowed a reality TV crew to film their wedding and planned a big rollout for when they released the footage on Julia's YouTube channel. When it appeared online a few months after I met them in London, I settled down to watch.[23] They are both wearing white and have pink hair. It was held at a hotel in central London; Eileen's sister-in-law walked her down the aisle, Julia was accompanied by her mother, and the two registrars were women. Eileen takes Julia's hands and says,

"In my long and varied sixty-one years, I've never met anyone so genuinely kind and gracious as you . . . The reward of your love is a late-in-life gift that I'm not sure I deserve . . . And, as you will almost certainly outlive me, I want you to know that I want you always to be as open to love as you were before me so that I know that after me you will be always wholly loved and appreciated for the entirety of your beautiful life." I heard so many older partners in age-gap relationships express that sentiment, and each time it made me reflect on something important that extreme age-gap relationships expose. The older partner who has lived a long life full of love and loss knows that happiness is fleeting. No relationship is forever. If you stumble upon a chance for happiness that might come without a template, a precedent, and if achieving it means you aren't hurting anyone else, grab it. Or as Eileen puts it, "Be grateful for the things you can't really hold on to; have them while they are yours to have." Why does permanence have to be the end goal?

Not long after I met Julia and Eileen, I heard back from Jane Beckman, a woman I'd contacted through the May December Society whom I'd also seen on a British documentary series about age-gap relationships. The sixty-six-year-old writer, who lives in San Jose, is married to Andrew Crockett, who is thirty-five. Given the lack of media representations that existed when they first got together in 2007 before ubiquitous internet and Instagram and YouTube and hashtags like #agegaplove, they'd felt compelled to tell their story to try to normalize their relationship and to let other people in intergenerational relationships know they are not alone, and they still feel that sense of responsibility. They'd had mixed experiences when they appeared on TV—they were on TLC's *Extreme Cougar Wives* and on the U.K. Channel 5's *Age Gap Love*—so they'd taken awhile to consider my proposal.[24] "We have always been about trying to show others what can be possible outside of the 'normal' and well-traveled path," she wrote.

We met first via Skype. Andrew, a financial analyst and former part-time gardener, was in what I would learn was his signature "look": a waxed mustache, bolo tie, and denim "utility kilt" from Portland. The tall, attractive, dark-haired man combined the style of Charlie Chaplin with the energy of a cultural studies professor. Jane, a technical writer, was in a summer dress with a loose gray ponytail. When Andrew was twenty-one and he met fifty-three-year-old Jane, he had a pretty stringent list of things he wanted to avoid; the top three were cats, tattoos, and a penchant for roses. "Roses?" I double-checked, figuring he had a problem with commercial romance or perhaps the way they smell. The trained botanist explained that they're a nightmare to prune. Not only did Jane have four tattoos and two cats, but she lived in a house called Casa Rosa in the Rose Garden district of San Jose. "Love might not look the way you think it will," he said, knowingly, when he told that story.

When Jane met Andrew at a local self-actualization course, she was overwhelmed by a feeling of familiarity; his bolo tie and calm demeanor reminded her of her older brother who was in his late seventies, but it was also a sense of recognition. "Almost like meeting some version of myself in some younger time," she says. That sense of familiarity is vital for Jane; it's just what it takes for her to connect. But the pull and intensity were unprecedented. Andrew also felt this tug of familiarity; he looked at this older woman dressed in a Japanese haori jacket and thought it was as if she'd been beamed in from a different world. "If you are an unconventional person, you learn how to identify that in others," he says.

Their strong intellectual connection quickly revealed itself. There was small talk about history, their various collections, and botany. Andrew was working part time at a plant nursery, and Jane's first degree was in historical ethnobotany. He says that Jane was the first person he'd ever met where the conversation flowed seamlessly; it was as if their "minds connected." They became friends and started to study together, but Andrew didn't even consider that she could be a romantic or sexual partner. It wasn't a possibility; he'd never seen such a relationship before. Wait, there was that woman who lived down the street growing up. She had a much younger husband and was gossiped about so much that neighborhood kids would hide when they saw her. At one point he said to Jane, "It's a shame about that age difference because you're exactly the sort of girl I'd like to date."

Jane says her attractions are "age blind"; she's always been drawn to interesting, intelligent people. She'd had a long-term relationship with someone who was fifteen years younger than her, but she'd date up or down. Given the family she came from—her father remarried a woman who was eighteen years younger—a fifteen-year age gap didn't even register. "It was just the water I swam in," she said. She's willing to try new relationship structures; she's been in polyamorous relationships, and she's been monogamous. When they were alone, Jane found herself observing Andrew's body, his arms, his long torso. "Stop thinking like that, dirty old lady," she'd chide herself. She might have been "age blind," but thirty-one-years' difference was pushing the limits of even her own sense of normal. When they eventually got together, Jane says that it felt as if they "sailed off the edge of the world and it was free fall." They were engaging in something quite transgressive.

How did people in their life react? Some were directly insulting. Andrew's housemate's girlfriend said he must be Jane's "boy slave." When they traveled to San Francisco for a weekend break and checked into a hotel, the attendant asked jokingly if she needed a key for her son. Jane managed it directly: "He's not my son; he's my lover." The judgment stung, but they appreciated that attendant openly acknowledging who they were because it was like wearing a cloaking device. People just didn't recognize them as a couple. As Andrew noted, "If someone doesn't have a concept for something, they can't see it." Andrew and Jane say that over time most people's discomfort gave way when they observed their connection firsthand. It was probably the hardest for his parents, who had a pretty conventional dream of his settling down and having kids.

During our first conversation we discussed the first time they had sex, their philosophy on monogamy (they're against it; as Jane puts it, "Asking one person to guarantee your total happiness is very unfair"), and the burden of forging a life that the world judges. They were keen to talk about their two experiences appearing on TV, where in one instance they were set up to perform, as Andrew puts it, "a cougar minstrel show." They were happy for me to spend a weekend with them so I could get to know the "real" Jane and Andrew.

I arrived at Casa Rosa, a freestanding 1930s house in downtown San Jose, on a sunny fall Saturday. After admiring the collection of ornaments and decor spilling over on the porch, I was ushered into the front room by an upbeat Andrew. Their house resembled a museum, with its shelves lined with Jane's antique cookbooks and nineteenth-century women's magazines and Andrew's collection of rare books about politics and philosophy. "Show her your oldest one," he suggested, touching Jane gently on the arm. Looking like a Northern California Princess Leia with her gray hair swept up into a bun secured with a chopstick-like *kanzashi* and wearing a long, floaty housedress, Jane carefully retrieved a tiny book from 1614 and showed me recipes for things like "puff paste" and a "qudini of quinces." It was probably that size so you could hold it in your hand while you were cooking, like an iPhone, she said.

I was struck by their similarities, that familiarity or "connection" that Jane had felt when they first met. They agree with you in unison with a slow *mhmm*. Andrew listens patiently to his wife's stories. She's clearly a writer, telling narratives laced with pithy details; then he gives verbal "footnotes," adding insight or detail that she's missed. It was a monumental display of active listening and evidence that he's absorbed the details of his wife's life as if it were his own (in fact, he once went to a lecture about the history of one of the companies she worked at before she met him). They were like twins. Jane caught me staring and smiled, explaining that their main difference is organization: she's chaotic, and he's a neat freak. When they first moved in together, he organized her kitchen cupboards, and Jane did not react well when she couldn't find her cleaning sponges. Now their code word for a petty fight is a "scrubby pad."

We sat around in their front room talking about their childhoods. Jane's dad was a revered art director who had a long career in Hollywood building sets for films like *Gypsy* and TV shows like *Cheers*. Growing up in a pre-internet world, she expanded her horizons through books and the intellectual stimulation of her father's creative peers; she jokes that she came of age on Warner Bros.' Stage 5, and Tyrus Wong, the Chinese American artist whose illustrations inspired the aesthetic of *Bambi*, was often at their house. She was precocious: by the time she was two, she could recite "The Owl and the Pussycat" and write out her name.

Socially, Jane was set apart from her peers. When she was a toddler, she developed a speech impediment after she almost drowned in a kiddie pool. There's no trace of it today, but she drew out her words with a slack drawl "like Elmer Fudd"; she winces at the memory. By the time it was fixed with speech therapy, the social damage had been done. She also wore orthopedic shoes, which earned her nicknames like Duck Foot and Frankenstein. She dealt with bullies the same way she deals with them today, head-on. "I'm Frankenstein, am I? You know what he does? He gets people!" she'd yell. She became a protector of the downtrodden. If standing up to bullies got her in trouble, she'd challenge her teachers. From a young age she was aware that adults can be, as she puts it, "unjust and arbitrary" and that age and power don't necessarily equal righteousness.

Jane's dedication to nurturing those less fortunate has continued throughout her life: She helped her neighbor raise her daughter, and she's an aunt figure to so many of her friends' kids she's lost count. She used to read to blind children, and she met her first husband in a very early Usenet group she created for people who felt "misunderstood"; it even had a spinoff group called the "Empaths Mailing List." She has many stories about defending the underdog, but my favorite is the time she pulled a sword on her neighbor's violent boyfriend when she heard him beating her in the night. After college, Jane got a job in Silicon Valley, where she's worked since the late 1970s writing technical manuals. Her intelligence and list of achievements are intimidating: she's published an academic journal article about southwestern food in "Dining with the Dons" (it's an abridged version of her eventual cookbook, Andrew informed me), she's a member of numerous historical societies, has numerous postgraduate achievements, is writing a novel, and dabbles in French and poetry and erotic fiction.

Until Andrew met Jane, he hadn't experienced much social kindness. He grew up in a loving home, but when he started preschool and bounded up to his first potential new friend and said, "I'm Andrew and I love you," it didn't go down very well. The abuse was mostly verbal, but it was isolating. He was picked on, singled out, ridiculed, and called names like "faggot." That exclusion instilled in him a feeling that remains to this day: you are not welcome in this world. Andrew's relationship with older figures of authority was different from Jane's. If there was an option to stay inside with the teacher during recess, he'd take it. For young Andrew, maturity and age were signs of shelter, whereas peers were the enemy.

We were looking through his childhood photos when he told me this, and I noticed bags under his eyes and a stressed look while he posed next to his science fair project as if he were a businessman worried about a merger. "That's the face of a kid who just pulled his first all-nighter," he said. He was hard on himself. He'd get frustrated if he didn't complete academic tasks perfectly. By the time he was sixteen he was six feet tall, which disconnected him from his peers; he couldn't look them in the eye.

During our weekend together they led the charge, taking me on a tour of their natural habitat. At their favorite Ethiopian restaurant we ate injera and discussed the history of migration to San Jose. They took me to the Rosicrucian Egyptian Museum, where we looked at a reproduction of an ancient Egyptian birthing room, while Andrew loudly discussed abortion and global marriage customs. Jane was thorough, slowly reading through each information box, seeking out interesting facts about women and everyday life. "This is the way our lives go," Andrew said proudly after making friends with the librarian at the Egyptian Museum, whose knowledge of the Thirty-First Dynasty intimidated me into silence. I struggled to keep up. At one point, I misquoted Hunter S. Thompson, which prompted a challenge from Andrew that was so dizzying I didn't even try to fake my way out of it ("That's an interesting supposition because that phrase comes out of Protestantism"). I kept my mouth shut when they named each and every seedling in the museum's Peace Garden and playfully debated the origins of okra. "We supplement each other's knowledge," Andrew said, smiling, "like when two encyclopedias meet." I liked their company, but I couldn't imagine either of them being in a relationship with anyone else.

But just like Julia and Eileen, the pair are also very physically attracted to each other. Jane says that after over a decade together they have sex five times a week (though Andrew insists once a day is more accurate). Sex with men around her age often felt like a lot of effort, but with Andrew Jane can be "young and vigorous." Many of the older men she'd been with didn't have much of a sex drive. For Andrew, who has only had one other sexual partner, the downside is that Jane has already tried anything that might be novel to him. He'll come bounding up excited and say, "Look at what I read about!" And she'll say, "Nah, I tried that back in the '70s." That's one area where the age gap doesn't work in Andrew's favor; it's not as if he were embarking on an adventure alongside her as a companion.

Given that they'd been together for more than a decade, I wanted to know how their age gap had played out over time. Had there been any issues as they'd gotten older? I was especially curious about health and Andrew's desire to have kids. What will happen when Jane retires? What if she gets sick? She's active, takes regular fitness classes, and has a healthy diet, but she's had heart problems and was recently diagnosed with rheumatoid arthritis. They've decided that they're open to alternative relationship models, which they'll adapt to if and when their age restricts them from doing things together like hiking or exploring the outdoors. They're officially polyamorous, and while they haven't dated anyone else, they'll look into that further if and when Jane's health prevents her from being a companion to Andrew. When she met Andrew, Jane didn't want to have her own children, but she now realizes it was because she never found anyone whom she cared to bring life into this world with. Andrew's commitment to new frontiers means that he's willing to look into non-normative paths to achieving that—perhaps a surrogate or a third partner?

One of the most common reactions to someone with an older partner is that they have mommy or daddy issues. According to this armchair psychological theory, the younger partner has a fraught relationship with their mother or father and is projecting those issues in their romantic and sexual life, resulting in the search for a mother or a father figure, which is uncomfortable and not "normal." Anticipating this reaction from readers, but reluctant to pathologize or imply that relationships with a large age gap need an explanation as if there were such a thing as normal development that was bent out of shape, I asked Jane and Andrew about their relationships with their parents and was surprised to learn that Jane, like Eileen, grew up taking care of a sick mother.

Jane's mom had post-polio syndrome and complications from a C-section when she delivered Jane. By the time Jane was in junior high—her coming-of-age years—she was more like her mother's partner than her daughter. They lived together in a home in the country, and she kept her illness hidden from the man she chose to be her life partner. He spent the week at work in L.A., and when he arrived home for the weekend, she'd operate as if she were on a movie set—everything was fine. Jane carried the burden of her mother's condition as if she had the emotional maturity of an adult. When Jane was twenty, her mother finally gave up her battle with life and used a gun to shoot herself in the head. Jane told me this matter-of-factly when she was unlocking the car door to drive me home.

When I learned this, I was tempted to psychoanalyze both Jane and Eileen and flip the standard "mommy issues" narrative on its head. Maybe they subconsciously rejected the caregiver role. I imagined how I'd want some youth, some lightness, and would want to avoid taking care of a sick or dying partner if that had been my childhood. Or perhaps it makes sense: they are used to being the more mature person in a loving relationship. Or, maybe it means that age and timing are different in the worlds that they come from. When I told Dr. Saltz about Jane's and Eileen's mothers, she pointed out that any parental modeling is not unique to age-gap couples: our parental relationships are a primary relationship for modeling. "In all relationships there is a certain amount of comparing, contrasting, looking for, gathering things that have to do with that family-of-origin relationship as the model for love and caretaking," Dr. Saltz said. Perhaps that's something that extreme age-gap relationships expose: all of us are working out our relationship with our parents or caregivers in our romantic and sexual lives.

Andrew hates the word "cougar" with its predatory connotations. He thinks it "infantilizes the man in the relationship." If he wasn't wearing a utility kilt when he said that, I'd have gone with my instinct, which was to challenge him as sexist. But he went on, clarifying that calling Jane a cougar "downplays that she's tremendously desirable and intellectually robust and a spiritually wide-ranging magnificent example of humanity." Jane is okay with it. She embraces its power and feels that by reclaiming the word, she's making a statement: as an older woman who has been denied sexual satisfaction by her incompetent male peers, she's opted for a youthful sex injection, displacing older men in the process. Perhaps the reason the figure of the cougar upsets older men so much is the same reason women are threatened by men dating younger women: they are challenging their sexual worthiness.

Like Julia, Andrew regards just existing as a couple as an opportunity for activism. During our weekend together they literally stopped traffic: a trio of men on motorcycles were so busy staring at the pair clutching hands they missed a green light. When we had lunch at a casual Ethiopian restaurant, everyone was looking. At one point I was suspicious when I saw a man stare at us holding his phone. A cook even popped out from the back to have a peek as if he'd heard there was a celebrity dining there. And that desire to be seen, to offer a template to guide others, was why they appeared on TV, and it was why they agreed to talk to me. As Andrew reminded me, "We are statistically abnormal, not psychologically abnormal. We are outliers, and because of that the number of folks who have encountered a couple like us is actually very small. People's lack of familiarity lets prejudice run rampant. That's one of the good things about mass media: it allows things to become known."

But it can also distort reality. Andrew describes *Extreme Cougar Wives* as an "exploitation" show. Andrew says producers were trying to find the sort of relationship that caused the most outrage and frustration to boost ratings and decided on cougars after organizing a survey which showed that age-gap relationships between older women and younger men have the least amount of social approval. The pair say producers lured them by pretending to be open-minded and committed to telling their story, but when filming started, it was clear they had a predetermined version of reality that they wanted them to fill. It started with exaggeration, and when that failed, they made things up. One producer wanted them to pretend they had plans to adopt a child and showed up with a hyperactive four-year-old who ran around the neighborhood banging on trash can lids. They filmed Andrew revealing "his adoption plans" to his sister, but she was so supportive the scene was cut. Scrambling for drama, the producers asked them to pretend to evict a roommate. Jane, who was more amused about the experience than angry, joked that they'd managed to make married sex look lascivious, "quite the achievement." But she knows how they saw her—the same way the culture does—as "a sad old woman with a nerdy boy toy and a fetish for Civil War underwear," as she put it. That's why Jane embraced the opportunity for self-representation afforded by the May December Society: like Julia and Eileen she wanted to be seen on her own terms.

I challenged Jane and Andrew on their decision to get married. Jane had sworn off it after her disastrous first marriage, and she's a staunch questioner of monogamy. Why not shun that institution, too? Andrew said there was an incentive to marriage that was alluring—especially given that he had entered a relationship that was judged and considered suspicious and certain to fail. Marriage legitimizes their union. It proves it's not fleeting; it's real. "It conveys: I am very much committed to this woman. I do not intend on leaving her side between now and when nature parts us," he said.

After my weekend with Jane and Andrew, I checked in with Jordan, that eighteen-year-old founder of the Age Gap Lesbian Love Facebook group. She quickly replied, saying she got back together with her older girlfriend and things were going well. I went to her Instagram page and saw that she'd changed her profile photo to a picture of her smiling with a woman with salt-and-pepper hair; her partner had decided to step out from the shadows and live openly as part of an age-gap couple. I scrolled through her feed, which was full of close-ups of the two together. On the beach Jordan holds the camera, and they lean in together laughing, wearing baseball hats, above the caption "Beautiful day with an even more beautiful woman by my side! I couldn't be happier . . ."

In the hyperconnected era there are more opportunities to take matters into your own hands and represent yourself if you can't find your identity or experience reflected back by mainstream media, and maybe that means a future where certain ways of being might just become more known, more normal? Or are we doomed to always judge other people's relationships based on what's personally familiar to us? Are we all biased?

# 3

# Maddy

Maddy is really funny. Deadpan, self-deprecating, laugh-out-loud funny. On her appearance: "I'm 26 but I pass as a tired 17-year-old." On her disabled baby cousin (who can't talk): "She's great company!" On her sexuality: "My mom accepts me as a lesbian, except I'm not a lesbian." And motherhood: "I might donate my eggs, I'm not going to use them so I may as well, and, you can get a lot of money, especially if you are an ethnic minority. I've even thought about what my profile would say: Aromantic; asexual; dropped out of college; prefers not to talk . . . is so introverted she doesn't perk up when she's on cocaine. If you want a kid who will not bother you, use my eggs!"

She owes her seamless delivery to the fact that she carefully edits her jokes. She'll send them to herself in Facebook Messenger, or by text, so she can polish them and never run out of material. Typical of an introvert who was socialized using email and SMS, she's not a fan of being put on the spot: she says she needs to mentally prepare to wake up in the morning.

Why is she so funny? Is it because she's spent her life on the social edges, observing the world as if she were an anthropologist in some far-flung location? Or does it come from her mom, who is comical in a hapless-old-woman kind of way. Filipinos don't have the *f* sound in their language, so Maddy's mom intentionally over-compensates: pencil becomes "fencil"; perfect is "ferfect." She also says that when you get over fifty, you lose control of your farts; she does them audibly in public—at the mall or on one of their many mother-daughter trips to Disneyland. She'll stop walking and make eye contact with Maddy while she does the deed.

Growing up, Maddy was a TV kid; she says she almost exclusively learned about romance and crushes from shows like *Boy Meets World* and *Charmed* or anything on the Disney Channel, which she jokes was her second mom. She was drawn to the unpopular guy/popular girl trope, which today she thinks was probably because she identified with the male nerd. She wanted to be noticed by the popular girl, too.

She was especially drawn to narratives revolving around "trauma-based friendships" where two people go through things together. She looked up her favorite TV shows online and discovered fan fiction; many of the stories were erotic, which is how she first learned about sex. While she was happy to read about sex when it supplemented the narrative, she got annoyed when it was the focus. Once she penned a caustic review pointing out that "M can mean other things" and complained that the writer thought they were being deep by relying on sex. That's something that still frustrates her today, having settled into her identity as aromantic and asexual.

Maddy's twenty-six years observing behavior and rituals that don't apply to her have affected the way she watches movies and television. She hates it when mismatched characters are forced into sexual or romantic relationships. She'll think, "Why isn't a person moving through life on her own, or someone whose most valuable relationships are friendships, good enough for the story?" Why are people intent on believing that a romanceless, sexless life is a sign of weakness or dysfunction? She didn't get the language for her identity until she was in her twenties, but if someone had given her the definition when she was in middle school, or if there had been anyone like her on TV, she'd have instantly recognized herself.

When it doesn't apply to her, Maddy's okay hearing about sex and romance; she's not what you might call "sex repulsed," which generally means someone who gets anxious or uncomfortable even thinking about sex. When they first met, her platonic life partner would occasionally forward her some of the more edgy texts she got from her male lovers. "I've been a recipient of dick pics; they just came via a friend," she once joked. Does she find people attractive? Of course—in fact, she moderates a subgroup on Reddit called "POC LadyBoners." When the page's main administrator asked for help curating photos of naked Sikhs in sultry bathroom selfies (complete with steam and erections) or young Dominican men in Speedos, Maddy volunteered, thinking, "I've got moderating skills and I can appreciate an aesthetic, in the same way I can appreciate something pretty, like a car."

I first met Maddy in 2018 in Algiers Point, New Orleans's second-oldest neighborhood, where we spent the weekend in the moist heat of a Louisiana summer at a coffee shop she frequents a few blocks from her home. We met after I'd approached the asexual-aromantic Facebook group that she helps moderate, looking for people who identify as both. I wanted to see the world through the eyes of an aromantic asexual woman, specifically to learn what it was like to reject the social expectation that the ultimate goal in life is marriage and children. But then she mentioned that she was living with a woman she met on Reddit and was helping her raise her two kids. As I spent time with Maddy and learned about her world, I discovered in her friendship with this woman a story as good as any romance.

Maddy's mother, a nurse from the Philippines, met her dad, a commercial chef from Sri Lanka, at work in a Kuwaiti hospital. They moved to San Diego, where they got married and had Maddy and her older sister. The matriarch paid the bills, cooked, fixed broken taps, and managed her daughters' schedules, while her husband, who never kept the same job for more than a few years, sat watching TV and sipping vodka or brandy. Growing up, her mother was strict and fearful of the outside world so she forbade her daughters to spend much time with friends or do any unsupervised activity. Maddy signed up for as many after-school activities as possible. Church kept her busy on weekends; she edited the youth group newsletter and was an altar server. But when she was eighteen, she became an atheist and quit.

Like most middle-class kids born in the 1990s—the nascent hyperconnected media era—she started socializing online when she was young. She was ten when her sister got a laptop that was connected with wires to the internet, and Maddy would bug her to use it to play the virtual animal care game *Neopets*, which was all the rage at her school. She enjoyed the routine work involved in caring for her pets. In seventh grade, her life was dominated by *MapleStory*—a role-playing game that was still in its beta edition. She liked escaping to an imaginary world and becoming a magician or an archer, but the main appeal was social connection with her peers. It was part of school social life, the cool thing to do, especially among the boys in her class. She'd plan group missions with her classmates and meet up online in the middle of the night; they were probably her first online friends.

Her mother didn't mention periods or sex—aside from her regular warnings that her daughters shouldn't "goof." Starting in fifth grade, Maddy's sex education was a conservative Christian curriculum full of euphemisms led by a no-nonsense veteran who taught them about body parts, but not what to do with them, until at one point she got flustered with the lack of clarity and exclaimed, "Look, I'm just going to say it. The penis goes in the vagina!" At the back of the room a popular boy punched the air with his fist and exclaimed, "I knew it!" which made the whole class laugh. Maddy already knew about such matters from the fan fiction she'd read online, and she recalls being baffled by her classmate's naivete. The program was more comprehensive at her public high school: the kids were taught how to use condoms, and in biology class a week was focused on sex.

As she approached adolescence, Maddy felt as if she were waiting for something life changing to happen. Like an entomologist, she watched this communal metamorphosis that seemed to come suddenly and without warning; it was as if someone had bashed her peers over the head with a sex-scented hammer. But not her. Why didn't "normal" sexual development assault her like the rest of them? That's when she first noticed her difference. She knew what was supposed to happen. She'd watched those girls on Disney shows giggle and lust after their crushes. She saw her female classmates' identities get hijacked by whatever boy they were into, but she just didn't feel that way about anyone, or anything, at all.

But this didn't mean she could opt out from the drama playing out around her. She was standing on a chair writing homework assignments on the whiteboard when a boy asked her to go to the middle school dance. She felt cold, her hands shook, and she lost sense of where she was. She assented, reluctantly, but she can't recall much about the event; she says she's actively blocked it out, a habit she has when it comes to unpleasant memories. It was clear he "liked" her, even though she showed little interest in him. In fact, they hardly even talked. She'd once complimented him on a home run in baseball class, but that "good job" was the extent of their interaction.

On a middle school field trip, her admirer slipped away and returned with a giant stuffed Minnie Mouse, clutching a red heart. When Maddy took it home, her mother wrapped it in cellophane to preserve it and let it sit on her mantel until that grim reminder of that boy's affection blended in with the wallpaper. Her mom seemed happier about it than she was; perhaps she saw it as a sign her daughter was developing in a "normal" fashion. As Maddy puts it, "I remember thinking maybe it was because she knew I didn't like people 'like that,' so it was reassuring to her."

Moments like this made her feel a certain way when she was younger, and they feel the same to this day: they produce a feeling of rising dread at a sense of rising obligation to reciprocate, a sensation she describes as the "decomposing feeling." It's as if someone were fermenting something deep in her gut, and a dark cloud nudges her shoulders with its anxious weight. Then she plays out all the possible scenarios. It's not fear or repulsion but an anxious crisis of perception where she fixates on how she must exist in someone's mind as a romantic or sexual being and feels as if she's been locked into a script and assigned a role that she does not want to play.

Her peers' sudden sexual awakening was accompanied by another so-called rite of passage that also left her cold. At a church youth retreat, the girls were separated into groups and told to put makeup on each other. Uncomfortable around these strangers from another school, Maddy, who still finds it easier to go with the flow than draw attention to herself by causing a scene (she hates conflict and will always opt to avoid a confrontation), gave in. She closed her eyes and tipped her head back as a kind peer gave her a full-on pageant look. "I look like a fool. I'll never pass. My facial features are too weird. How could an amateur free style my face?" she thought, gulping air and trying to hide her shaking hands.

Lipstick, blush, and eyeliner came to symbolize a club she couldn't join: normal teenage girlhood. She questioned why she wasn't concerned about her appearance the same way she'd question why she didn't like anyone romantically, and together it seemed like hard evidence that something was terribly wrong. For a long time when she thought of putting on makeup, or high heels, she'd get that same decomposing feeling that strikes when she thinks of someone asking her out. As she puts it, "Maybe if I had a womanly body and I wore makeup, it would increase my chances when it came to getting a job. I also think people wouldn't wonder out loud if I am a virgin or not."

While she didn't feel romantic or sexual attraction to either boys or girls, she did develop intense feelings of admiration for women. If there was a common thread, it was that they all appeared to be very independent, strong, and capable—usually older or popular—and when she fantasized about them, they weren't having sex or planning a wedding but spending time together as friends. She was familiar enough with the norms of femininity to keep quiet about these strong platonic feelings. She didn't try to get close to them, though; she didn't want to. As she puts it, "I was fine living in my head."

She felt especially intense feelings for her sophomore-year chemistry teacher, whom she describes as "the strong, silent type." One day, the teacher presented each student with their own personal whiteboard, warning, "If you can't be responsible, I'll take them all back." When her classmates scribbled all over them, Maddy watched in awe as the woman made good on her promise. But it wasn't just the strong, silent type who interested her. In seventh grade, she was fascinated by an older, popular, rebellious, potty-mouthed Catholic who was head of the school's Asian clique. "I wanted to be the seventh-grade version of her," she says. During Mass Maddy would crane her neck to study the way she stood so she could copy it later. There was another teacher that same year, a young Filipino who was a fan of rap music.

She wanted to feel sexual or romantic feelings toward someone, and she could appreciate when someone was objectively attractive, but when she tried to imagine more than that, there was a disconnect. She felt as if a crush should come before feelings of sexual desire, and that was, as she puts it, "the bigger holdup." Maybe it will happen with time, she figured, and began to fake crushes on boys so she'd fit in. By the next year, she gave that up; the act was too exhausting. Instead, she waited for that sexual mace that had gripped her peers to overwhelm her and reveal that she was normal.

By the end of high school, she realized it wasn't going to happen. She came to see relationships as a sign of weakness. She'd given up waiting for something to change, and she feels guilty admitting it now—just as she's ashamed to say that she reads relationship advice columns as entertainment because she sees the problems of couples as comedy. She'll think, "Why do you need to rely on another person to get through life? If you can't even function if you have to sleep by yourself at night, you probably have things you need to work out."

David Jay, who was born in 1982, came of age in St. Louis in a liberal household with architect parents who sent him to progressive schools. During middle school he noticed that when his friends suddenly became preoccupied with sex and crushes, he was left feeling cold. As he told me years later, "There was a real sense that this was a rite of passage. You talked about the crushes you had on people as a way of showing you were growing up and you were no longer a kid. But I wasn't feeling the things they were feeling, and that was scary and disorienting." What did it mean? the intelligent kid wondered. He went to the public library and searched through books, and visited the high school computer lab where he played around with keywords using early internet search engines in the hope of finding an explanation for what he *didn't* feel. Common sense told him to research the word "asexuality," but when he did, all he came across was scientific literature referring to self-reproducing organisms like lizards and potatoes. He tried different words and phrases like "someone who doesn't have sex" or "people who are not attracted to people," but that just led him to books about celibacy or sexual dysfunctions like impotence or low sex drive caused by depression. Where was all the information about people who could enjoy sexual stimulation but have no desire to share that with someone else? There were a handful of LGB (as the acronym was back then) coffee shops that David also scoured with no luck.

He wondered if he was just a late bloomer, but he'd gone through puberty in sixth grade and shot up to six feet one, so that theory didn't make much sense. Why wouldn't an adolescent boy be a sex-crazed, hormonal mess? He felt as if he weren't normal, he should be attracted to someone, and he wasn't sure how to talk to anyone about what he felt was a catastrophic difference. He was terrified; he was sure that there was something very wrong.

One summer, while he was in the midst of privately making sense of this alienating difference, his parents, whom he was close to, sent him to an "inclusive" summer camp. A counselor was defining unfamiliar words when she wrote the acronym "LGBA" on the blackboard. "What's with the *A*?" David wondered and shot up his arm to ask. "Well, if we are covering everything possible, there's probably some people who are asexual and they are fine with that . . . This may be hard for you to understand," she said, eyeballing him; her explanation seemed loaded with the implication that a disinterest in sex would be impossible for a horny teenage boy to grasp. Though misreading him, that counselor had been the first person to make human asexuality seem like a possibility. He left the camp with a feeling he'd never had before: there were other people like him.

It was a sign whose importance can't be understated; he'd struggled for so long in part because he felt completely abnormal. If there's nobody else out there quite like you, what other conclusion can you draw? Now he knew that human asexuality existed. There were other people like him out there, and maybe, if he just looked hard enough, he'd find them.

When it was time for college, he chose the independent liberal arts university Wesleyan in Connecticut and bounded onto campus in 2000 confident that he'd find other asexuals. "I'm on the East Coast now. Surely it's brimming with asexual infrastructure and support. This place has its queer shit together!" he thought, convinced back then it was just his location in the Midwest that had restricted his access to community. He set up an anonymous email address and drafted a note to the head of the queer alliance, asking them to point him in the direction of the campus's asexual students or organizers. "We don't know what 'asexuality' is" was the gist of the very short reply.

Momentarily nonplussed, David began to read up on people who didn't experience sexual attraction. He scoured the university library and learned about Boston marriages, those turn-of-the-century New England unions between women who wanted to avoid being financially dependent on men. He found the sexologist Alfred Kinsey's 1948 landmark survey of the sexuality of American men, which showed that about 1.5 percent of the adult male population fall into what he classified as X— meaning that they didn't experience any "socio-sexual contacts or reactions"—but David longed to talk to other people who felt the same as he did.[1] If an asexual community existed, it was very hard to find.

During his first winter break he flew out west to visit a high school friend at Stanford. They were up late in the dorms when David heard some theater and literature students raving about this life-changing new internet search engine: "Have you tried it? You've *got* to try it!" As soon as he got back to campus (this was before ubiquitous laptops), he sat down at his computer and typed the word into a slim rectangular box, then sat back and waited for the results of his first-ever Google search. One of the first hits was a story called "My Life as an Amoeba," which was published on an American digital magazine by someone named Zoe O'Reilly. "There's been a lot of press dedicated to gays, bisexuals and most other sexually-oriented groups. But there is one group continuously overlooked: The asexual," Zoe wrote.[2]

David eagerly read on about how she longed for the same visibility that other marginalized sexual orientations enjoy, with ribbons and buttons and a dedicated awareness day. She complained about the absence of asexuals from high school sex-ed literature and spelled out the benefits of her identity. He was so moved he had to stop for a moment to collect himself. He spent the next few days processing the sense of validation he felt just knowing that there was someone else out there—this time an actual person with a name—who felt the same way he did. Even if he had never seen her face, or heard her voice, her thoughts and feelings seamlessly matched his.

And there was more. After he'd absorbed the weight of his discovery, he noticed a comments section. People were also describing this experience for the very first time:

> I found someone else who is asexual! I've thought for so many years now that I was the only one; I've never found another, anywhere. Physically, I'm male, but there's nothing inside to tell me what I am, no drive.[3]

> I'm so glad to know that there is a name for people like me and others. Anyone know where I could get some Asexuality buttons or bumper stickers. I don't suppose they isolated a gene for it or anything. We get no respect.[4]

I honestly thought that my total lack of desire for
either sex was a psychological abnormality. I can't tell
you how relieved [I am] that there are other people
who feel the same way . . . I am glad to have found this
little group. I feel so much better.[5]

That sense of community was life changing. When David went
home to St. Louis for the holidays, he sat his parents down and told
them what he was: asexual and happy that way. He was planning
to "come out" in public, and he wanted them to know first.

Back on campus he set about executing his grand vision. He
was determined to create a space for asexual people to gather,
interact, and share their experiences in real time, so he built
a website. He settled on a definition for asexuality that is still
referenced today: "An asexual person does not experience sexual
attraction—they are not drawn to people sexually and do not
desire to act upon attraction to others in a sexual way. Unlike
celibacy, which is a choice to abstain from sexual activity, asexuality is an intrinsic part of who we are, just like other sexual
orientations."[6]

He'd come of age listening to his queer friends talk about
their sexuality, and he firmly believed that sexual identity was
something you, and you alone, are allowed to define. If someone
says they are asexual, they are. Nobody else has a right to label
you or deny you the right to identify that way. Asexual people
aren't broken or sick or in need of a cure, and like any sexuality
there's no need to diagnose or look for a traumatic childhood
moment when they were twisted out of shape. He called his
website the Asexual Visibility & Education Network because
ever since adolescence he'd been made to feel as if he didn't
exist.

After its initial launch in 2001, David removed the website
from the college server and bought a new domain name, which

meant the website ranked higher in Google searches, and his vision was achieved: it became the very first hit whenever anyone did as he'd done and went online to google the word "asexuality." Then he watched as people registered. A handful a month turned into a few people a week and then a person a day. It was as if these asexual comrades had all been equally persistent and after years of isolated struggle took advantage of this more sophisticated new search engine, thinking, "Maybe if I look here, I'll find out what I am." Well aware of the isolation he'd experienced, David was armed and available 24/7 in the welcome forum to greet these new members. He wanted to offer them exactly what he'd craved: a sign that they weren't alone.

David also knew from researching the history of other marginalized sexual orientations that the way they're studied by scientists, and reflected in the media, has a serious impact on how they come to be known in the world. For example, for most of the twentieth century homosexuality was considered a mental disorder, and it was only fully removed from the *DSM* in all forms by 1987. He was sensibly wary of how psychologists might feed the media when they both tried to make sense of the asexual experience, and he wanted to control the narrative.

To this day, AVEN's guidelines for dealing with the media, which were drafted by David back in the first decade of the twenty-first century, focus on presenting an image of the "normal," relatable asexual. They list general tips like "smile" and warn that reporters' questions about asexuality typically fall into two camps, arousal and emotions, so try to focus on emotions because that "highlights that we are fundamentally going through the same things as everyone else, it sets people up to empathize with us."[7] David wanted to humanize asexuality and shatter the existing stereotypes that asexual people were lizards or aliens or robots without a soul.

In 2004, just three years after AVEN's launch, he was approached by a reporter from *New Scientist* who was writing a piece about asexuality based on the advent of AVEN and a recent finding by Anthony Bogaert, a Canadian psychologist, that 1 percent of the population could be asexual (Bogaert found the data in a British lifestyle survey when he was researching a paper about the biological origins of sexual orientation).[8] David was armed and ready to be the friendly, totally normal face of this new identity.[9] And that was when the emails from reporters started flowing and asexual people started arriving on the AVEN home page. The uptick in new members seemed to coincide with the waves of media interest.

AVEN's biggest spike in new registrations since 2004 came in 2006 when David appeared on numerous TV shows including CNN's *Showbiz Tonight* and ABC's *20/20* and *The View*. "Is it a problem?" asked a confused Joy Behar. "So then, why do you need to organize?"[10] Tucker Carlson, then playing the token conservative on MSNBC, was particularly brutal. He seemed defensive, disbelieving, and offended by the very idea of asexuality when he bombarded David with questions like: "You're aware that the average man has a porno movie on a continuous loop going in his brain at all times, and you don't? What are you doing with your free time? A lot of viewers will say he's gay and that he is just repressed; do you get that a lot and is that true? Do you feel like you are missing out? Why don't you just try it once, and then you'll know for certain, and whether you like it or not?"[11] His inability to digest asexuality was typical. As David puts it, "I think we were fascinating for all the reasons we felt really isolated. People thought it was impossible."

The next year, Montel Williams devoted an episode of his talk show to people who were "asexual and they are fine with it" ("people are going to say, yeah right, you were sexually abused by the teacher, or the bus driver, or the milkman," Montel speculated, using his fingers to count the possible "causes" of David's asexuality), but again, AVEN membership soared.[12] David was attractive and socially competent, smiling through the disgust, shock, and awe of people who just could not believe that he was uninterested in sex and perfectly happy that way. While journalists and talk-show hosts might have enjoyed confirming their own supposedly normal sexuality by dissecting David Jay, his exposure meant that the template for identity was now possible; the word was out there, and the experience existed for people to go online and explore. These days AVEN's English-language forums average about one hundred new registrations from asexual people and their allies every single day.

When asexuals from around the world united, things like sex and love (or a desire for companionship) were separated. Just because you don't experience sexual desire doesn't mean you don't want to go on dates, have kids, get married, or live with a life partner. As we saw in Delaware Valley Synergy and in St. Louis, love and sex and sex and love don't have to be a package deal. Language and sub-identities were formed. The term "ace" has become an umbrella term, like "queer" or "consensually nonmonogamous," to describe the various identities on the spectrum of asexuality. Online people met in forums to share ideas and create language to articulate the full range of the asexual experience. There are those who are heteroromantic (romantically, though not necessarily sexually, attracted to a member of the opposite sex or gender), homoromantic (romantically attracted to members of the same sex or gender), biromantic (romantically attracted to both sexes or genders), demiromantic (someone who can only experience romantic attraction to someone they connect with emotionally), and aromantic (someone who experiences little to no romantic feelings).

In 2010, Maddy moved from San Diego to the University of Alabama in the sports-obsessed college town Tuscaloosa for a bachelor of science degree, but her time there was grim. First, there was the shock of coming from a liberal, largely Filipino West Coast community to the South, where it wasn't unusual for her to be the only nonwhite face in the room. By second semester, she was disengaged from her studies; she compared herself with her peers who all seemed to have spent their teens exploring their interests and were on track for careers they were passionate about. She had no stories about sex or ex-boyfriends or even a social life or circle of friends, so she avoided conversations that got too deep. Her grades slipped, and she fixated on the money she was wasting, stressing that she'd leave college with nothing to show but debt. She masked her feelings with humor ("You know how people start to like each other in the sixth grade? I'm still waiting for that to happen," she'd joke to college classmates, trying to keep things light), but the truth is her lack of interest in romance or sex made her feel damaged, inadequate, and very left behind.

Maddy first heard the classic scientific definition of asexuality in biology class, where it didn't refer to humans, so the AVEN definition ("An asexual person does not experience sexual attraction—they are not drawn to people sexually and do not desire to act upon attraction to others in a sexual way") was new to her when she first discovered it online. She'd followed a digital path that started in a Reddit thread where people were sharing controversial opinions they'd never say IRL. There was a user who thought demisexuality (someone who only experiences sexual attraction to a person they have an emotional connection with, which Ken Haslam also found online and identified with) was "a load of crap." "What's demisexuality?" wondered Maddy, who googled it. That led her to a website that offered a word for something she'd experienced often but had never had the language for: "squishes," which AVEN's aromantic forums defined as a non-romantic, asexual version of a crush. This overpowering platonic desire to connect to another person is analogous to a "friend crush"—that feeling of intense adoration and admiration you may feel when courting a new non-sexual companion. Like a crush, a squish can be all consuming. Someone with a squish might be preoccupied with thoughts about the object of their affection and overtaken by a desire to be with them, or be like them.

Maddy sat there reading about this phenomenon called a "squish" and was flooded by a feeling of relief. She had never heard the feelings she had experienced so strongly—and assumed were unique to her—described by someone else. If aromantic people have squishes instead of crushes, she knew right away that was exactly what she was. She analyzed those feelings she had about her teachers and those popular girls that seemed to defy language and felt that same comfort of community that David Jay had also felt all those years earlier. It was built on a simple yet very powerful premise: other people have experienced this too. There's a name for who I am. I am not alone.

She spent more and more time on AVEN forums, read blog posts, and talked to asexual people, and she discovered that there were lots of resources and that the online world held many tools for connection. There's an international asexuality conference and well-attended meetup groups in Los Angeles and New York. There are asexual dating sites, social networking platforms, and a dedicated team of data scientists who do online surveys for an annual asexuality census. In academia there's a burgeoning subfield of sexuality studies called asexuality studies, and in the health sciences psychologists research it.[13] There's even an asexual awareness week, a literary journal, and a number of books devoted to the subject.[14]

While asexuality resonated, Maddy didn't feel comfortable adopting that identity right away. "Am I really asexual? Or do I just have a low libido?" she wondered. So, during her asexual questioning period she tried to date. First she went out with a male colleague. They made out a few times, but the experience left her feeling as if a dentist were rooting a gloved finger around in her mouth. Her second attempt was with a guy she met on Tinder (she opted for a "nerdy average-looking person"; as she puts it, "I understand that I am probably a catch for someone normal"). They met for coffee, and awkward conversation, but she didn't feel anything more toward him than you'd feel toward a friend. He asked her out a second time, and she conceded, but she's blocked out memories of what they did; she recalls strained small talk and the end of their date, when he leaned in to kiss her. Maddy thought, "This chance won't happen often, might as well," but when he issued her a peck on the lips, it was as if he flicked an off switch. He asked her out for a third date, but she ignored the text. She was trying to "fix" that decomposing feeling she's always felt about physical intimacy, but it didn't work, and that was her last attempt.

Maddy has never looked at another person and thought, "I want to have sex with them." As she once asked me, "Is that how it even works? Is that the thought people have when they're sexually attracted to someone? That's pretty crazy to me. It sounds fake." These days, she uses genetic anecdotes to get nonbelievers to understand that she's not just in denial or repressed. "Imagine if the ability to like someone in a romantic way was something in your DNA, like a gene. That gets across the message that this is not something that is optional for me," she says.

When I started to talk to asexual people, I respected the AVEN definition that makes it clear that it's not about whether you are capable of arousal but the fact that you don't experience sexual attraction. But I was still curious: Do asexual people masturbate? Do they have sexual fantasies? David Jay said he'd purposefully try to steer reporters away from this question when he was on the talk-show circuit. Why? Asking about masturbation suggests you're looking for evidence that asexuals are really just repressed or too uptight, immature, unattractive, or scared to get laid. If they can get themselves off, why aren't they interested in sex with people? On the other hand, if someone says they don't masturbate, people may assume that means their body is broken or their hormones are somehow askew, and according to David Jay, focusing on the mechanics of an asexual's body medicalizes asexuality. So I didn't broach the subject.

But most asexual people I talked to raised the topic themselves. Stephanie, a former sorority sister who works as a publicist in L.A., told me that when she's premenstrual she gets to a point where she *has* to masturbate: "I don't picture myself doing anything. It's always imagining other nameless, faceless people." Likewise, Maddy delivered this information to me unprompted one day by email: "I could watch a movie with a sex scene or read an R-rated book or fanfiction, or even watch porn and I still get something out of it. I have the parts and they work." Sometimes she masturbates to help her sleep. Her sexual interest reveals itself in fantasies about fictional characters, but she's never personally involved. As she puts it, "I do think I have a libido, but I don't care to use it . . . I have tried to fantasize from my own point of view and I get the same dentist glove in the mouth, procedural feeling I got when I kissed that dude . . . I'm asexual in the way I'm able to view other people, and in the way sex plays a role in my life, which is little to none."

Asexuality may thrive in online forums and networks, but what hasn't changed much is its fairly limited mainstream media presence. The positive representations that do exist tend to be animation or fantasy and science fiction, with the notable exceptions of an asexual magician in the TV and web comedy *High Maintenance* and a minor character in an episode of the Netflix teenage series *Sex Education*, which aired in 2020.[15] The character in *Sex Education* is a confident drama student who has no connection to sex; when she talks to a sex therapist about her lack of desire, she gets affirmative advice: "Sex doesn't make us whole, so how can you be broken?" (After it aired, one AVEN member noted, "I just finished watching that episode and I honestly can't stop smiling."[16]) There is an asexual character in *Game of Thrones* and the adult cartoon *BoJack Horseman*. When the *Archie* comic was adapted for TV in the 2017 teen drama *Riverdale*, its asexual character, Jughead, was made sexual. This infuriated many on AVEN's forums: "We really need to see more heterosexual young men on TV, that experience just never gets heard" is how Cole Brown, AVEN's CTO, put it. In 2012 an asexual couple appeared on Fox's *House*, which was the first time a major US TV network featured self-identified asexual characters, but it pathologized asexuality (the husband had a brain condition that killed his sex drive, and his wife was pretending to be asexual to keep their marriage intact).[17] Sheldon Cooper in *The Big Bang Theory* is perhaps the most mainstream asexual. But he's a quantum-physics-obsessed computer nerd whose lack of romantic or sexual interest is ultimately treated with a girlfriend.

Asexuality and aromanticism challenge what many people assume is a basic aspect of humanity—the stuff that's supposed to charge us: an interest in sex and a desire to find a partner to love and share that with. Or as Anthony Bogaert puts it, "It's almost like humanity and sexuality have become so embedded that we assume that anyone who violates that is a worm or a car or a piece of grass or an alien."

If you'd asked Maddy if she was happy to be aromantic and asexual when she first started identifying that way, the answer would have been no. She still had to live in the off-line world, where she compared herself with everyone around her and felt as if she were years behind socially and emotionally. She uses computer imagery to explain her state of mind back then: "You know how in video games there are checkpoints? So if you reach a checkpoint and then if you die you at least go back there rather than having to start at the beginning? I used to think that being in a relationship was one checkpoint in life that you have to cross before you keep on going and growing up. I thought, maybe I'll just never grow up."

What do researchers say about asexuality? For most of history, not much, but today in the wake of the activism prompted by AVEN, there is a thriving body of work on the subject. The Canadian psychologist Lori Brotto first learned about asexuality in 2006 when a psychiatrist colleague at the British Columbia Centre for Sexual Medicine asked if she'd seen Anthony Bogaert's paper showing that about 1 percent of the population didn't experience sexual attraction. At first, she was skeptical and approached asexuality like a clinician, wondering if it was possible that these people have an extreme form of hypoactive sexual desire disorder, which is when people do not experience sexual desire and are troubled by that. But she was intrigued enough to want to learn more, and the findings of her first study (an online survey and in-depth interviews) didn't show people who were unhappy or wanted to change; they appeared to be perfectly content. An expert on women's sexual health, including desire and arousal, she was used to working with people who were distressed about their low sexual desire, so this finding was surprising. Brotto says that asexuality is most likely a unique sexual orientation, and for the most part her research doesn't show many differences between sexual and asexual people in terms of mood or anxiety—aside from the effects of other people's negative perceptions of them. She's gone on to publish numerous studies that clearly differentiate asexuality from sexual dysfunction and along with David Jay was part of a task force that had asexuality included as an exception from the definition of hypoactive sexual disorder in the *DSM-5*.[18]

Over the years, many of Brotto's colleagues who were initially skeptical have come around to seeing it as a sexual identity, but there are still nonbelievers. People will say, "This looks like an extreme form of hypoactive sexual desire disorder, and I see that in my practice all the time!" she told me, imitating a shocked professor. Their responses may reveal more about scientific approaches to understanding sexuality than they do about asexuality itself. As Brotto puts it, "Some of the methods we use in our science to make these differentiations between desire disorders and sexuality are flawed because they don't really get at the human experience." She also notes the irony that most of the discomfort and unhappiness about asexuality seems to come from sexual people: "People have a really hard time believing it's possible because there's a prevailing cultural belief that it's a central part of being human." Asexuality turns that idea upside down.

Bogaert thinks that asexuality is a sexual orientation and that it reveals a lot about human sexuality more broadly. When he's trying to explain it to skeptics, he focuses on what it can teach sexual people about themselves (his students often have a hard time believing that it's real). "Everybody has the kind of strangeness, weirdness, a little bit of complexity when it comes to sex, and asexuality allows us to see that a little more clearly," he says. "If someone is comfortable living a life without sex, why do you feel like it's necessary to pathologize them for that?"

Daria, an asexual playwright from the Washington, D.C., area had an interesting take. When we talked, she was nineteen and living in a college dorm in Manhattan, where she had a front-row seat to the ins and outs of hookup culture. "While there's a lot of stuff about it that alienates me, there's also a lot about it that makes sense, because I can very easily separate sex and love," she said. "Sex and love often overlap for people, but for others they are completely different, and I think that's one of the things about asexuality that scares people. It's similar to being vegan. People get very mad at vegans, and I think it's because they see an alternative that makes them question their own life and that's hard work, and I think a lot of people don't want to do that."

Asexuality may be hard for some sexuals to accept, but aromantic asexuality is even more challenging. I asked Cole Brown, AVEN's CTO, what fear they think aromantic asexuality taps into, and their answer gets at the preconceptions that asexual people deal with whenever their identity is discussed: "There's this perception that to be sexless and non-partnered you will be miserable . . . I think people want to be empathetic, but when they put themselves in the shoes of an aromantic asexual, they feel sad and can't get past that." Julie Sondra Decker, an aromantic asexual from Florida who published one of the first books about asexuality in 2014, agrees: "My detractors will say, 'But what's going to happen when you are old and alone?' And I think, is that why people are getting married? It doesn't sound like a good reason . . . There is no guarantee of permanence. You could easily lose your spouse; you could also end up being the one giving care rather than receiving it."

I reached out to aromantic people via online forums and communities (including the Facebook group that Maddy helped moderate) and asked those who were interested in sharing their experience to tell me exactly what being aromantic meant to them. Susan, a thirty-seven-year-old woman from Toledo, put it like this: "To me, romantic attraction is the want to be physically close to someone. I love hugging, but kissing, sitting right next to each other on the couch, spooning in bed, or holding hands are all unnecessary for me . . . I enjoy reading about romance and I may even tear up when I see people on TV have a happy romantic ending, but I don't want it myself." "But can you tolerate it?" I wondered, thinking of Maddy's decomposing feeling. Romance makes Susan uncomfortable because she doesn't know how to reciprocate; like Maddy, it feels as if she were being forced into a role she doesn't want to play. Amanda, a twenty-one-year-old student from D.C., says growing up, she was annoyed whenever romance was introduced into a book or a TV show. Then, when she got a boyfriend in high school, she found the whole experience "pointless and dumb." Whenever she talked to him, she felt as if she were reading from a script.

Lori Brotto has just worked on some of the first qualitative research about aromantic asexuality, and her findings show that aromantic asexuals are more likely to be introverts and prefer solitary activities. As she puts it, "There was more of a global picture of solitude but again, without discomfort."[19] They aren't depressed; they really just prefer to be alone.

To this day, there's no better way to end a friendship with Maddy than to tell her that you like her "like that." When people hit on her, it's usually women. She was living in Alabama and working at Chipotle when the "Crush Mist incident" took place. She was becoming friends with a female colleague, and they were trading jokes when the woman paused and told her she'd got her a gift. Oblivious, Maddy went into the back room and turned on the light to discover a purple cylinder of Crush Mist spray from Victoria's Secret nestled in a gift basket next to a box of chocolates. "What do you even do with that?" she wondered. "Do you spray it in the air to attract somebody? Is it for your body?" she asked me, years later. After that she pulled back into herself; it was as if all her previous platonic interactions were tainted. She felt guilty, as though by being friendly she'd unwittingly led this woman on. After that she showed up at work "silent," which is what she calls her natural state.

Compared with Maddy, thirty-two-year-old Felicity is a Luddite. In fact, she says she had a grudge against the internet ever since she was fourteen and it led her mother into chat rooms, an affair, and eventually a divorce. She didn't use the computer or a smartphone until she was well into adulthood, and even then she had to take a class to learn how to use Microsoft Excel. But when her older daughter, Sky, was nine months old and she was pregnant with her second daughter, Emi, she went online at work to kill some time. Typical of the hyperconnected era, a search for scary stories led her to another website, which led her to a forum on Reddit where she found an endless supply of suspenseful entertainment. She was browsing other subreddits; she'd previously been active in antiracism groups and was married to an African American man with whom she had a daughter, so when she found one called "Black Ladies," she joined. She was discussing the politics of the white pop star Miley Cyrus twerking when she met another ally.

Maddy was also drawn to Reddit's subgroups that described an endless array of hyper-specific experiences. She created a subreddit for South Asian Americans. "Why aren't we a visible community like in the U.K.?" she wondered, having thought more about her Sri Lankan identity since moving to the South. She spent her days glued to the screen on her phone or laptop, talking to fellow South Asian Americans about food, college, and politics. She was always online, clicking, scrolling, posting, and presiding over her digital empire. Being a moderator gave her a sense of purpose and power, and she was socializing in a way that suited her best—with her physical self left behind. She'd found her real niche: online friends. In chat rooms and forums she was extroverted and secure; she had time to plan what she wanted to say and was judged for her humor and intelligence rather than her physical presentation. Like Felicity, she'd joined the Black Ladies subreddit as an ally during the trial of George Zimmerman. At first she'd just pop her head in, but the more time she spent there, the more involved she got and soon became immersed in this community, too.

If Maddy first met Felicity in person, she says it's unlikely they'd be friends. Maddy, who was still settling into her aromantic asexual identity, was a virgin. Felicity was into kink, had practiced polyamory, and was pregnant and married with a kid. Maddy grew up with middle-class parents in the suburbs of San Diego. Felicity grew up very poor in New Orleans and lived without a shower or kitchen for a year when she was displaced after Hurricane Katrina. Maddy had spent her young adult life on the computer, working at Chipotle, and barely studying biology at college. Felicity was a poet who had been volunteering in an anarchist bookshop and attending Social Forum rallies, traveling to San Francisco to protest on the fifth anniversary of the Iraq war with a bandanna on top of her long red hair. "It was the type of thing that could only happen the way it did online, because I got to know her thoughts first," Maddy once said.

After striking up a rapport on Black Ladies, they began to message privately. Felicity would vent about her complicated life—she was pregnant and going through a hard time with her husband—and Maddy would encourage her to talk. Maddy became a constant, comforting presence. She was always on her laptop or her phone, and Felicity kept a window open to Reddit on her computer at work so they could talk in real time about everything from heavy topics like Felicity's relationship, their childhoods, and their parents to the lighter details of whatever had happened during their days. Felicity even messaged Maddy when she was on the way to the hospital to give birth. Maddy felt safe sharing details about her life with this woman whom she figured she'd never meet IRL, and she noted that she might not have felt as comfortable getting close to her if she wasn't older than her, pregnant, and married with a kid; she figured it was unlikely her friendliness would be misconstrued as flirting.

Felicity, who identified as queer, wasn't fazed when Maddy told her that she was an aromantic asexual. She firmly believes that sexuality is a spectrum and that sexual identity is self-defined; besides, they were friends: What did it matter to her if her new confidante was not the sort of person to fall in love or have sex? After a few months communicating, they knew so much about each other and were too invested in each other's problems not to call themselves best friends.

Maddy was at home in San Diego for mid-semester break when Felicity sent her an urgent message, saying her husband had attacked her and smashed her phone, destroying all the photos she had of her daughters. Maddy was calm and direct. "Send it to me," she said. While she waited for the package, she asked for the specific make and model and went online to look for instructions about how to retrieve the data. When she got the package of broken telephone, she locked herself in the bathroom, away from her mother's prying eyes, and immediately got to work like MacGyver, operating on the phone with screwdrivers and a miniature saw. When she finally retrieved the images, she emailed a photo to Felicity to celebrate.

When Felicity got that photo, she was thrilled. She made a rare Facebook post with the caption "Maddy is my motherfucking hero!!!! Genius, spy, phone fixer . . . I have no idea how I have survived this long without you." Maddy was there throughout the last gasps of Felicity's relationship; her presence seemed to radiate comfort and calm support from behind the computer screen. She sent Felicity a package of DVDs to distract her, and even printed out hard copies of photos of her babies and carefully arranged them in a photo album. She taught Felicity how to hack into her husband's email and the Instagram account he devoted to his life of sex with strangers. "I could change his password and lock him out, that's an option that exists," she typed to Felicity, who was touched by her virtual sidekick's support. "Let's wait for the divorce to finalize first," Felicity said.

Maddy was the only person Felicity was confiding in about the intimate details of the pain her husband was causing that was too shameful to say out loud—even to her sister or close friends. Maddy was easy to talk to, she didn't judge, and she asked lots of questions. Maddy realized there was probably nobody in the world who knew as much about Felicity as she did. From behind the veil of the computer screen the young woman from another city had just about told Maddy her entire life story.

One of the charges most commonly leveled against asexuality is that it's "made up," that it's an internet construction without any historical precedent. But unlike homosexuality, there's never been a law prohibiting it. In previous eras asexual people might have entered sexless marriages, lived as "spinsters," or said they were celibate, so how do you mine history for asexuality when there's no action or behavior to find? Maybe something coded? As Cole Brown, who assumed they were bisexual before they found the language on AVEN's website, put it, "Asexuality had to have existed before the internet; we just couldn't see it."

Cole's words rattled around in my head, and when someone I'd met through AVEN sent me a link to an online archive of a dispatch from a conference held by the New York Radical Feminists in 1972, which mentions an "asexual manifesto," I was intrigued. The dispatch, which was published in the feminist news journal *Off Our Backs*, is illustrated with a photo of a group of "lesbian activists" in front of a board that lists a range of identities to select from: "Straight, *asexual*, lesbian, bisexual, anti label, dyke separatist, ?, lesbian feminist, anti sexual or whatever."[20]

I read the article and learned that when conference goers arrived, they were handed paper buttons and encouraged to give themselves a label. The day was packed with feminist activities.

Someone read a poem called "Women Who Love Men Hate Them." Jill Johnston from *The Village Voice* declared, "Who you sleep with most is yourself."[21] And Gloria Steinem was there; she showed up late, in a babushka. There were workshops on trust between women, dealing with anger and ageism, and a curious reference to a workshop on asexuality, held by someone named Barbara Getz. There isn't much detail about the session, which the article's author attended, except a summary of remarks made by its leader: "Asexuality is an orientation that regards a partner as nonessential to sex and sex as nonessential to a satisfying relationship."[22] Then there's a reference to an asexual manifesto that could be obtained by writing to a P.O. box address for the New York Radical Feminists. What was in this manifesto? I had to find out.

I started my hunt for the manifesto, using a well-trodden path. Googling away, altering keywords, but all I could find was Tumblr postings and posts in forums where people from the asexual community had written about their own search for the document. I found an excerpt from the journalist Margot Adler's memoir; someone had called in and read the manifesto on her early morning radio show, which prompted days of phone calls from the "solitary and celibate."[23] I emailed the special collections at Duke University, where the New York Radical Feminist records are held, only to hear back from a librarian apologizing that they don't have it and saying she'd had requests before.

Those counselors at David Jay's summer camp must have heard it somewhere, I reasoned, typing "Barbara Getz," the name of the asexuality workshop organizer, into a public records database and limiting the search to women who would have been at least sixteen when that workshop was held. There were four results, including someone in her eighties who seemed to be alive and well and living alone in Manhattan. "I might have found the grandmother of contemporary asexuality," I thought to myself as I printed out letters, addressed them to all those Barbara Getzes, enclosed a photocopy of the article, and mailed them out. The letter began, "I'm desperately trying to find the Barbara Getz mentioned in the attached article. I hope that it is you."

Felicity was the first to suggest to Maddy that they meet up IRL; she was only about a four-hour drive away from Alabama in New Orleans. But Maddy didn't feel as if she needed a physical encounter to validate or enhance their relationship; her social and emotional needs were served just by communicating with Felicity, so she canceled a few times before she finally plucked up the courage. When they'd been fostering their friendship online, Maddy had downplayed her discomfort with social situations and preference for solitude. She was so edgy when she approached Felicity's house that she missed her driveway and had to drive around the block and try again.

Felicity, on the other hand, was excited to see her friend. After showing Maddy around the four-generation, all-female house she lived in with her mother, grandmother, and two daughters (that's five women—seven if you count the cat and their bird), she took her to her neighbor's house for her annual anti–Black Friday event—"slack Friday," where they play board games to boycott the sales. Maddy tried to keep her cool. It was a tame gathering, but among so many strangers she was way out of her comfort zone. She continued to feel awkward that night when she lay down to sleep in the living room across from Felicity's boyfriend, who was also spending the night on a couch because Felicity shares her bed with her daughters and the bedroom policy is strict: no men allowed. When she thinks back to that night, she has no idea how she pulled it off. Aside from seeing family, she probably hadn't socialized since that experimental Tinder date two years earlier.

The next day, the pair went together to buy a Christmas tree. Felicity likes to make an effort for the kids during the holidays, and she wanted the whole affair of decorating the Christmas tree to be an occasion. She invited her father and his wife, and her boyfriend and her mother and grandmother were also there. The adults duly gathered around upbeat, while they dressed the tree. Maddy was uncomfortable around so many strangers, earnestly oohing and aahing, so she kept a low profile, opting to take photos, instead: like a true introvert, if you give her a role at a party, she does just fine.

On her last day in New Orleans, they talked about tattoos. "Let's get one together," Felicity suggested, picking up the phone to see if her friend had space in his studio. It was Felicity's idea, but Maddy had always wanted to get one, and high from the emotions of the weekend she felt emboldened to finally do it. Maddy went first. She rolled up her trousers to reveal a patch of flesh on her ankle. Felicity opted to get hers on her rib cage, in that painful spot just under her breast. Maddy is not one for touch in general, so she tried to act comfortable when Felicity clutched her hand while the tattooist drove his needle deep into her soft white skin. They both emerged with bear paws.

When she got back to Alabama, Maddy was both exhausted from the drain of social activity and flooded with adrenaline. It was the first time she had ever had a sleepover with a friend. She'd done something normal, she thought to herself. She visited again around Christmas and then came back a few weeks later, and then again, until it became a routine. And when Felicity asked Maddy to move in with her, she didn't think about it for too long before she said yes. Felicity's a single mother who has been through hell, and she needed the help. Maddy needed somewhere to live; she'd dropped out of college, and her life working at Chipotle didn't make much sense. She'd come to see her IRL friendship with Felicity as a way to force herself to branch out and do more "social stuff." "We'd be platonic life partners—like a queerplatonic relationship," Felicity typed, and Maddy googled the term to see exactly what that meant.

The word "queer" didn't sit quite right with her: Is a platonic relationship between an asexual woman and a queer woman actually queer? "Do I have a right to claim that term?" she wondered. Should asexuality even be included under the LGBTQ umbrella? Surely there's something uncomfortable about the specter of a heteroromantic asexual couple bounding up to a Pride parade and scoffing at the free condoms (the sex advice columnist Dan Savage was initially dubious about asexuals as an oppressed class, but he has since come around).

But she poked around, trying to find a real-life template. "I guess it's like Oprah Winfrey and her friend Gayle," she figured, reading a blog post that described their relationship that way. Felicity felt closer to Maddy than any other adult in her life, so she wanted their bond to have a special title   something that would put it on a pedestal above "friend." Maddy told her mom she was moving to New Orleans to live in a friend's spare room. Later, she heard from her sister that her parents assumed she was gay. At work, Maddy had become close to a manager who had moved to Alabama to be with her closeted partner whom she had met online. The pair had lived together as "roommates" for years. Shortly after Maddy told her about her plan to live with Felicity, she sat her down and tried to give her advice. "Listen, you're just a lesbian and you're unable to accept it," she said.

But friendship wasn't Maddy's only motivation. Human relationships are rarely completely selfless. Maddy also figured a life with Felicity was probably her best hope at some version of normal. Back then, she lumped the fact that she was introverted together with being asexual and aromantic as if it were a package deal that would exclude her from doing anything vaguely "normal" with her life. She thought her being asocial was something she had to fix. "Social people just have it better," she once said to me, revealing the way she separates the world into "social" and "asocial" as well as "sexual" and "asexual," "romantic" and "aromantic." She'd internalized a pressure to be social, just as she'd internalized those messages that everybody's ultimate goal should be to get married and have kids. Like losing your virginity, they are markers of "normal" social development and, these days, applicable to everyone, regardless of your sexuality. "I was thinking, this is the closest that I will ever get to that, so I feel like I said yes for that reason," she reflects. When I heard this, I was stunned: Did she really move in with Felicity just because of the pressure of fitting in? You *must* have been lonely? Were you craving company, I pressed, projecting my own social needs onto her. "I wasn't lonely. I just really thought that I was 'in,' like I'd made it into the adult club. I have a family unit too," she said.

When she began her full-time life in New Orleans, Maddy was determined to pass as a social person. But she was nervous. Could she cope in a social city where bars and clubs stay open twenty-four hours and you can drink on the streets? Would she be able to get used to living with five others in a four-generation, all-female house? Their life together started out well. Maddy helped with the cooking, laundry, and childcare and babysat the kids while Felicity went to night classes (she'd enrolled in college and was studying to work in child justice) or stayed at her boyfriend's house. Maddy got a full-time job and reenrolled in college to get enough credits to graduate with her bachelor of science.

And for the first few months, Maddy tried hard to keep up a socially active persona. She fought her nerves, forcing herself to go to parties and bars as if it were part of a training regimen in her quest to be normal. "Do things you don't usually do. You can be the social person you always wished you were," she'd repeat like a mantra while she went through the motions. During one night out she realized she had never sat at a bar. "How do you do it?" she thought, adjusting her legs. When men approached her with flirty small talk, she was uncomfortable; those evenings, which usually ended at dawn on a stoop, were not the best for Maddy. "You're so beautiful. Where are you from?" men and women would say, sliding up alongside the woman whose appearance was considered exotic in a city where Asian people make up only about 3 percent of the population and not talking to strangers is considered a social offense.[24]

Her visits to parties and clubs marked the first time that her sexual orientation was subject to public scrutiny. When Felicity told a curious friend about Maddy's asexuality, the woman, who trumpeted that she was liberal and down with alternative sexualities, screwed up her face processing the information. The insinuation was clear, "That doesn't exist." Felicity was overwhelmed with a protective urge. "Fuck you! You'd never question a trans person, so don't fucking question her!" she yelled. The last time Maddy went out at night, it was to a dance party. When Felicity invited her, Maddy just stared at her and said, "Will there be chairs?" She managed to find a stool. "If you need me, I'll be over there," Maddy said as she took a seat and spent the night on her phone, occasionally glancing at sweaty bodies gyrating on the dance floor.

After that, Maddy gave up the act. Just as she eventually quit those fake school crushes, or going through the motions with the guy she met on Tinder, she couldn't pretend to pass forever. When Felicity went out, Maddy stayed home. She developed a close relationship with Sky and Emi. Sky is an extrovert: she tears around the house, plays loud games, and likes to ask adults heavy questions ("Why am I alive?" "What animal am I eating?"). Emi, who often goes completely silent around strangers, is an introvert, which was more Maddy's speed. They'd sit together and quietly draw. Felicity and Maddy weren't physically affectionate; they'd occasionally hug (according to Felicity, "literal standing hugs"), but Maddy often hugged the girls, who seemed to need constant cuddles. It was as if she were a power cord and their batteries needed a recharge every five seconds. Felicity observed her life partner with her children, thinking that Maddy provided something that most people can only hope for: a supportive companion whom she could trust implicitly with her kids. It was like no relationship she'd had before—not quite like her sister or a friend, stronger than that. When I asked Felicity to compare it to something, she said there simply wasn't a template.

The pressure to be social wasn't the only challenge that Maddy faced. When she brought Felicity with her to her work Christmas party, she introduced her as her "partner," but she was uncomfortable with the smarmy glances and smiles; obviously they thought Felicity was her lover. It wasn't the assumption that she was gay that bothered her; it was the idea that they thought she was romantic or having sex. But to counter that, she'd have to tell them that not only is she not interested in a romantic relationship but she's also asexual, which she thinks they'd just dismiss as repression or denial. If she presented Felicity as just a friend, it minimized their relationship. And what about Sky and Emi? Saying they were her friend's kids didn't cut it when she had to run out of work in the middle of a shift if they got sick or there was a childcare emergency.

And to Maddy, together in physical space with bodies and voices, the differences between her and Felicity had become too stark. She could laugh off or ignore Felicity's TMI references to sex when they chatted online, but in person it was harder to avoid. When Felicity invited her to a kink club, she was annoyed—not that she said anything, but she was thinking, what would possibly give her the idea that would be a setting she'd enjoy? Then there was the weight of the responsibility of being a primary caregiver for two young girls. She fixated on the fear that Felicity would die. What if she was out late and got caught up in a shooting, like those people on the steps of a bar on South Claiborne Avenue one Saturday night, when a gunman came running down the street? When Felicity's mother texted from her upstairs bedroom to see if Maddy knew if her daughter was anywhere near the scene, Maddy's nerves were shot.

Maddy also found the social energy that goes into caring for kids draining. When the girls would say, "I love you," she felt uncomfortable. She knew it wasn't deliberate, but those words have a way of making her guilty. "Do people just say that so they can hear it back?" she wondered. "Why did they need me to say it? Isn't love something you show?" She knew they were children, but it was still unwanted. She's not sure why; all she knows is that she can't handle feeling obligated to help another person with their feelings. They'd been talking about buying a place together, and each time Felicity excitedly sent her links to open houses, she got a terrible feeling in her gut.

Maddy was in over her head. "I could have been a friend. You don't have to be somebody's partner to be good for them," she once said to me, reminding me of a complaint many aromantic asexual people have that friendships aren't given the same importance as sexual or romantic relationships. At home, she'd speak only if she had to. Like at Chipotle after the Crush Mist incident, she retreated into her natural, silent state. When she got eczema all over her face, she joked that it was her true self scratching its way out. Maddy found herself in front of her laptop watching endless hours of the anime series *Naruto* about a ninja who competes for the adoration of his peers. In *Naruto*, the most significant relationships in the characters' lives are usually friends.

"How will the girls feel if I leave?" she wondered, unease sloshing in her gut. When Sky grabbed her leg and announced, "You're my second mom!" Maddy went back on Reddit to those relationship forums she'd once used for entertainment, this time seeking advice. On a subreddit for stepparents, she was overwhelmed by the number of posts from people who seemed to be in over their heads. "Felicity believes it takes a village to raise a child," Maddy reasoned. "They have lots of adults who care about them. Maybe it will be easier for them to sort out my role in their lives when I move out? My presence is probably confusing." When she couldn't find anything specific to her situation, Maddy solicited help. The replies were cold:

> You are not in a relationship with them, just leave!
> They are not your kids, get out!
> You weren't even in a sexual relationship with her,
> go . . .

"I've been in their life for years now. I can't just dip out," she said, realizing the irony of her living situation. "Of all the people in the world, why would an asexual aromantic virgin be the one chilling with a family so young?"

A few days had passed when my phone vibrated with a text message: "You found the Barbara Getz you were seeking!" The long-searched-for woman from that *Off Our Backs* article was alive and well and living in Manhattan. She'd got my letter and immediately raided her archives, where she found the document that had been collecting dust in her apartment ever since the 1970s. My first thought was "Are you asexual?" We arranged to get together at a diner in Chelsea that coming Labor Day weekend. "She has no plans on summer's last long weekend . . . maybe she is," I muttered to myself when we were planning our rendezvous. She asked me for a very detailed physical description (including height) and offered one of herself: "I'm five foot six, on the slim side, hair white with turquoise." I couldn't wait to meet her.

"I can't remember the workshop," Barbara said, rubbing hand sanitizer in her palms as if she were trying to warm up. I tried to hide my disappointment, which made me realize how much I wanted her to be an undiscovered pre-hyperconnected-era asexual. We were sitting in a windowed annex of a twenty-four-hour diner when she explained the backstory: In the 1970s she started writing the manifesto with a radical feminist—a woman named Lisa Orlando—but she either lost interest or got too busy—she can't remember—and dropped out. When Lisa finished writing, she sent Barbara a copy of the manifesto, which she'd filed away in her apartment and hadn't even read until she got my letter. I was dying to hear what it said, but she'd only brought a photocopy of the first page of the precious document. She was reluctant to show me the rest without its author's approval. She's from a different era, I reminded myself, slightly annoyed, softening my grip on the phone that was hot in my pocket ready to take photos.

Luckily, Barbara wanted to share a sample. She cleared her throat before reading its opening few sentences out loud: "In September 1972 the coordinating counsel of New York Radical Feminists formed caucuses, membership in each being based on similarity of sexual orientation. The members of each caucus were to explore their personal and political attitudes about their sexuality and communicate their views to the larger group. Barbie Getz and I..." I stopped her: "Barbie?" She often used a nickname when she wrote radical stuff back then. In fact, these days she goes by B. Junahli Hunter, which explained Barbara Getz's nonexistent online presence. I let her go on: "Barbie Getz and I realized that we would not feel comfortable in any of the proposed caucuses and formed our own."[25]

I was confused. In their usage, was asexual a resistance to the gay or straight binary? No, that wasn't right. They were trying to challenge the way that feminists were classified in sexual terms—it was a political resistance to being defined by your sexuality—as a straight or lesbian feminist. I told her the contemporary definition of asexuality, and she curled her lips. That was not what they meant. "I don't think either of us stopped having sex; at least I didn't. Our ideas were not popular," she said. Could her co-author, Lisa Orlando, have been asexual? Maybe she wrote the manifesto because she'd never experienced sexual desire? Junahli didn't think so, but how could she know for sure? She didn't, and they had drifted apart; in fact she hadn't seen her since.

I settled in for the dinner date. I was curious about the life of this woman in her eighties who had spent the last fifty years without a partner or children. Over a very carefully ordered vegan burger, Junahli told me a bit about herself. She grew up an only child with a largely stay-at-home mom and a military father. She got married but things didn't work out, and she was divorced by the early 1970s, when she was in her thirties. She decided New York was the best place to be an "older" single woman back then, so she stayed, and she's been on her own ever since. Not that she's given up: she was planning to attend a workshop on finding your soul mate. Junahli learned about feminism after reading books like Germaine Greer's *Female Eunuch* and joined the Radical Feminists. She had a "midlife crisis" in her forties, and enrolled in a doctorate program in social work; her dissertation was about attitudes toward the changing American family. She worked as a social worker at high schools throughout New York City until she retired.

Junahli seemed happy. She'd lived a full, independent life. She had a meaningful career and a PhD, she'd traveled, and she'd been active at the height of the women's movement—in New York, no less. I pictured her smoking and bashing around on her typewriter huddled together with feminist friends late at night in her apartment on Manhattan's West Side. She is still writing, has had roommates (her last one was a student from China), travels regularly (she's planning a trip to India), and keenly participates in conferences (her passion is fighting climate change). Later, as I spent more time with Junahli, I learned that she also has a writing coach and a personal assistant. "She has a whole team," I thought when she introduced me to her PA.

We were wrapping up dinner when she told me about the panic that set in during her early fifties, after she quit smoking. She woke between 3:30 and 5:30 each morning for two and a half years. Weekends were especially tough; she didn't have work to distract her, so they could be painfully long. She was so desperate for a human voice to talk to she ended up calling suicide prevention helplines; when she told them she wasn't about to kill herself but just needed human connection, they'd let her talk, anyway. She was frustrated with the quality of help she got there when she had an idea: What if she trained people to listen to her on the regular? She recruited college students, taught them the art of empathic listening, and put them on the payroll ready to take her calls. One of her listeners was a college student when she started working for Junahli fifteen years ago, and she's still on the team. "I called them empals. I coined that phrase," she said proudly. And I was impressed. She'd figured

out a virtual way to find instant human company in a time before the constant connection afforded by chat rooms, email, or
text. I thought back to what Felicity said about Maddy's listening
technique: she didn't judge, and she asked lots of questions, like
an empal.

We parted and I walked home to the Lower East Side south
along Sixth Avenue, zigzagging down side streets, watching solo
diners through the windows of restaurants, and imagining what
their lives were like. I was plotting how to track down Lisa Orlando and when I got home immediately went online to google
her name. I found references to some articles she'd written for
*The Village Voice* as well as her master's thesis, and after some
online research emailed most of the people she'd mentioned
in the acknowledgments, figuring that someone had to know
where she was. She had some heavyweight friends, I thought,
as I wrote to academics like Gayle Rubin and Judith Butler. I
looked her up on public records, too, but what if she'd changed
her name? There didn't seem to be anyone around the right age,
but I sent letters to all the Lisa Orlandos I could find, anyway.
Gayle and Judith both replied quickly saying they'd lost touch
way back in the 1980s.

Disappointed, I tried to figure out exactly why I was so determined to find a historical source that positively defined asexuality as a sexual identity. Was I influenced by younger asexuals
who were frustrated by the way the mainstream media seemed
to credit David Jay as the "founder" of contemporary asexuality? Among their complaints was the fact that his constant
presence in the media had marginalized the voices of asexual
people of color and those who are female or gender noncon-
forming. Had there been an erasure of women's involvement in
the construction of asexuality? Why didn't Zoe O'Reilly—the
author of that formative personal essay David Jay read when he

used Google for the first time—get more credit? Or was it because I'd got slightly annoyed with David Jay when he scolded
me, a self-identified single person, for using the word "single"? ("It implies that if you are not in a relationship that fits
a particular script, you are not in a relationship.") Was I being
narrow-minded, having internalized the sex positivity of my
own liberal 1990s coming-of-age that "normal" development
necessitates embracing sex? Or was it really because I was still
questioning asexuality? Did I secretly agree with those critics
who refuse to believe that asexuality exists, that people who
are repressed and scared of sex were having their identity validated on the internet? Was my determination to find an asexual pathfinder fueled by a desire to strengthen asexuality with
a clear-cut historical precedent—something to use as evidence
that it's real?

After a few days plotting different ways to find Lisa Orlando,
I suddenly realized it didn't matter. Just as I'd discovered when
I read those letters to Deborah Anapol at the Kinsey Institute,
there were much more limited ways for people who felt the
same way to mobilize, to talk to each other, to form a global hyperconnected community and ultimately a collective identity. As
Zoe O'Reilly had written in that essay David Jay read all those
years ago, "I think I'm asexual, therefore I am." It was because
of the visibility and language formed online that Maddy and
others growing up in the hyperconnected era have been given a
name for how they feel, a name that now comes with a clear, established community and a template that allows them to know
who they are.

After about two and a half years living with Felicity, Maddy
moved out. She'd been very careful with the girls, telling them
often that soon she would not be sleeping there anymore but she

wasn't going to disappear. And she hadn't; she'd been babysitting two or three times a week. One night when she was taking care of them, Felicity came home to find her sitting with Emi at her children's desk. I called Felicity a few weeks after Maddy left. It was the first time we'd talked one on one. The adjustment had been hard for her: she'd sent a few late-night whiskey-fueled texts where she'd perhaps gone too far expressing how much she adored her. Maddy hadn't replied.

Felicity missed her partner. She really hadn't wanted her to leave, but she was trying to focus on the positive to get through this type of platonic breakup, which was a new experience for her. So she'd been house hunting and concentrating on the relationships she still had: making sure her daughters felt comfortable and supported and that her dynamic with her boyfriend Andy stayed "healthy." And it was going well, which she says was in large part due to the balance she'd learned from Maddy, who'd got her into the habit of resisting her instincts to be overly emotional. It occurred to me that Felicity had probably never had a chance to talk to another person whom Maddy had confided in. "Maddy is like nothing else. It's very clear to me that she's been life changing. I can't really say this to her, because I don't want her to feel obligated," she said, referring to Maddy's tendency to take on, and feel uncomfortable about, other people's emotions, "so I'm saying it to you."

"Was it always hard to tell her how you feel?" I asked Felicity, who said that initially they talked often, though Felicity would follow Maddy's cues to make sure she was comfortable with the tone of the conversation. But as time passed, they talked less and Maddy retreated inward; Felicity described it as like settling into a monogamous relationship where you don't have to verbalize your feelings so much, but because there wasn't any physical or romantic intimacy, she constantly questioned where she stood. Likewise, there were moments when she couldn't convey how she felt about Maddy using words, and she realized that in romantic relationships sex often served that purpose. Unlike her romantic or sexual relationships, she didn't feel entitled to lash out. "It might be a little self-serving to say that's because I care so much about Maddy moving through the world that I put her needs before my own. Which is kind of how I feel about my children," she said.

Maddy taught her the power of nonsexual, aromantic relationships. "Occasionally I've been hurt by things that she says, but that's nothing compared to the damage that's been done to me in romantic relationships. She does not seek to do people harm. Our struggles never end in a battle where we are trying to prove that the other one has fucked up. Together we found a way to not damage each other, insult one another, or intentionally go out of our way to hurt each other. So little has sucked with Maddy; she's been an ideal support . . . If she walks away right now and never talks to me again, I will have a hard time having any ill will toward her; she's been amazing," she said. When she spoke, I thought back to Felicity's Facebook post when Maddy triumphantly fixed her phone from her San Diego bathroom, saving those baby photos she thought were gone forever: her genius, spy, hero.

Maddy moved into the dorms, where she planned to stay until she finished her degree in medical technology, which she'd started earlier that year. The plan was to get work quietly processing lab results alongside fellow introverts—a job suited to her personality: she can help people from behind the scenes. Then she hoped to either head back west, to her mom, whom she'll keep company in her old age, or to her sister, whom she'll help if she has a baby (she'll leave when the baby starts talking). Once Maddy had her degree, she'd be able to work as a traveling technician anywhere in the country. She had a list of modest goals: save up to get a season pass to the NBA, work on her TV show memorabilia collection, maybe push her comfort levels and try her hand at stand-up comedy. She even started doing open mic nights and went on a solo road trip to meet some of her closest South Asian friends from Reddit. For the first time ever she felt excited about the future. "I don't have any of those tick-the-box life goals anymore," she said. "There are so many life expectations that just don't apply to me. I really have the freedom in life to do whatever it is that I want."

## Postscript

Just over a year after I found Junahli and "The Asexual Manifesto," I was doing an online search for recent writing about asexuality when I came across a blog post about "The Asexual Manifesto" by an ace activist that included an interview with Lisa Orlando. "How did he find her?" I wondered, heart pounding, feeling like a weak reporter while I quickly drafted an email asking the writer, Siggy, if he could put me in touch with the long-lost radical feminist. He replied within a few hours explaining that he didn't find her; she found him. He'd written another online piece about asexuality and mentioned "The Asexual Manifesto," which had attracted the interest of Lisa Orlando, who had done a Google search for it (something she did periodically, having lost her only copy of the precious document). When she came across Siggy's article, she left a comment and Siggy got in touch.

I emailed Lisa, who was now in her seventies and living alone, riding out the COVID-19 pandemic in an Airbnb in Albuquerque. She was excited to discuss the manifesto, which she remembers well. She wrote it during a period in her life when she had decided she was sexually and romantically sick of both men and women.

Lisa was twenty-one when she discovered feminism. She'd just finished reading *The Plumed Serpent* by D. H. Lawrence when she came across an article about women's liberation in *Glamour* magazine. "I thought holy fuck," she said. "I've been paying attention to D. H. Lawrence's take on women's sexuality since I was fourteen and he's full of shit." She eventually joined a women's liberation group in Miami, but she says all the "bikini beach life" made it hard to recruit other women, so she was explicitly "looking for the revolution" when she arrived in New York City in the early 1970s. Her first home was an apartment she found via a friend, but it was full of actors who "had no politics," so she was frustrated and trying to figure out how to meet like minds when someone suggested she talk to her neighbor who turned out to be Jacqueline Ceballos, who was then the president of the New York chapter of the National Organization for Women. That well-connected feminist told her about Mother Courage on West Eleventh Street—the country's first "feminist restaurant." She went and encountered a tableful of interesting-looking women who invited her to pull up a seat. It turned out to be the coordinating council of the New York Radical Feminists. She joined and became their liaison.

After a woman she'd met at a bar and spent a weekend with tried to strangle her (she'd become obsessed and stalked her), Lisa swore off both men and women. She was already becoming disillusioned with the ideologies of lesbian separatism, saying she'd always been attracted to both men and women but "had been really naive and had this idea that all the problems in my relationships were because of men and if I didn't involve men I wouldn't have problems." She wanted to devote her life to social change, and relationships were destroying her ability to do that. When the New

York Radical Feminists formed caucuses to explore the straight/ lesbian split that had impacted other feminist groups, Lisa decided to create an asexual caucus, as she put it in that interview with Siggy, "for ex-lesbians who were turned off because they discovered that women were as fucked up as men."[26]

In her usage, asexuality was a political choice available to any feminist who was disillusioned by the exploitation present in relationships with men or women. Junahli (then Barbie) was the only other person who joined the asexual caucus, and the pair worked on the manifesto together before Junahli, who was a social worker, pulled out because she was scared it would negatively impact her professional reputation.

When she finished the manifesto, Lisa remained celibate for a short period of time, but her "asexuality went out the window very quickly" when she fell for a woman who was married with kids. Things didn't work out, and Lisa left New York with a broken heart. She cut off all her hair, bought a hunting knife and a backpack, and went hitchhiking around Canada, where she enjoyed a lot of sex. "I went from an asexual lesbian to hooking up with men," she said, explaining that casual sex while traveling was a good way to keep herself out of relationships. These days she lives alone and says her "practice" is asexual in the sense that she hasn't been attracted to someone sexually for many years and she's doubtful that she will again anytime soon. "I had so much sex in the periods I was having sex, and it drove me crazy. Relationships drove me crazy," she said.

The construction of identities like asexuality in the hyperconnected era is something to truly celebrate. Asexuality is a good example of the positive power of the current moment for knowing who you are. With all this information at our fingertips, and the ability to find new names for old or previously unknown ways of being, there is a real sense of liberation. Naming defines; identity remains important. But should we always celebrate naming something? What happens when people gather in the hyperconnected era to discuss and create identities based on desires or behaviors that are illegal or at least deeply taboo? What are the downsides of connecting with others to share language or ways of being?

# Part II

# Transgressing Normal

The stories in this section explore illegal and taboo sexual behavior. Chapter 4 contains themes and descriptions of incest and sexual assault that may be distressing or traumatizing.

# 4

# Shelly

I was on Reddit when I first came across a subgroup discussing a phenomenon that breaches one of society's most important taboos. It wasn't exactly a brand-new concept to me; in fact it was something I'd first heard about when I was a kid, in the 1990s on an episode of a daytime talk show. I'd watched biological relatives estranged by adoption discuss how they developed intense sexual feelings for each other when they reunited as adults. It's as if it had sat there at the back of my head for nearly thirty years, and when I was researching ideas for "What It's Like," I was curious if it was happening more in the hyperconnected era given that so many biological family members were reuniting with the help of social media, so I'd gone online to find out.

I searched around and sure enough found communities of people who said they had experienced intense sexual and romantic feelings toward immediate biological family members they'd reunited with after having been separated since birth or childhood. Some people were there to make sense of their feelings and get support, others were secretly living in what they called "consensual" sexual relationships with their relatives, and there were also those who said that they were "recovered" and warned against ever acting on these feelings; they spoke about the phenomenon as if it were an addiction or a disease.

I was completely unable to identify with any of the feelings they described, but I kept reading. Their narratives used a common language to describe the intensity of the attraction, and the familiarity of their partner they said filled a void that had left them feeling empty for their whole life. They described it as like having the perfect match designed in a science lab, or looking into a mirror and falling in love with your own reflection. Like magnets, they had to be together; it was as if the pull were too strong to resist. Many said that when they were in these relationships, they finally felt complete. They described the attraction as being so fierce it was almost as if there were something in their shared DNA pushing them together.

I was surprised when I began to feel empathy for their situation. They seemed confused, distressed, and overwhelmed by emotions that didn't make sense to them and were not the sort of thing they could comfortably talk about to people who they knew in real life. But at the same time, I was thinking, is it a good thing that people are gathering to talk about this? Does sharing their experience so candidly lead to an atmosphere where acting on these feelings is normalized? And more broadly, what is the downside of a completely virtual and anonymous community?

In one forum a woman wrote about how she felt toward her half brother when they were reunited after he found her on Facebook: "I sensed this overwhelmingly powerful attraction and by the second night of my visit of four days we had an intense connection in every way. More intense than any experience of my whole life. We literally felt like we had been taken over by a 'force.'"[1] Some wrote poetry or long diary-like posts about the all-consuming completion they felt when they met an estranged family member for the first time. One man wrote as if he were speaking directly to his sister, treating the forum like a confessional: "It was as if we were one mind and soul which had been ripped apart . . . You fulfilled a need I did not know was missing. You were a part of me and me you. I didn't just want to be with you, I desperately needed for us to be together, somehow, someway. The supercharged urges for us to bond in some physical way were overwhelming."[2]

In those forums and communities many described experiencing something they called "genetic sexual attraction," or GSA. The term emerged in the 1980s when a woman named Barbara Gonyo went public with the feelings she experienced following her reunion with the son she was forced to relinquish for adoption when she was just sixteen years old. They reunited when Barbara was forty-two and he was twenty-six. In her self-published memoir, *I'm His Mother but He's Not My Son*, Gonyo saw similarities between the bonding of a mother and child and feelings of sexual intimacy. As she put it, "Bonding and Genetic Sexual Attraction may be one in the same. If it would have happened at the usual times in life, it may have been an easy process. Adoption separation has added the burden of abnormal timing."[3]

Gonyo is commonly credited with "inventing" this term that didn't exist in the medical literature and was first spoken about in post-adoption networks or whispers in therapy rooms. But, as she pointed out when I first contacted her, she didn't invent it. She first heard someone use the phrase at an American Adoption Congress conference in the early 1980s. In 2006 it found its way into the *Oxford Dictionary of Psychology*, where it is defined as "erotic feelings between close relatives, often between siblings or between parents and children, who are separated early in life and reunited in adolescence or adulthood."[4]

The online GSA community is made up of "secret" groups on social networks like Facebook, subgroups on Reddit, and a handful of other private forums like Kindred Spirits, which launched in 2012,[5] and the GSA Forum, which grew out of a website that Barbara Gonyo created and today charges a small fee for a yearly membership. On the GSA Forum, moderators and senior community members advise against acting on GSA feelings; the purpose is to support people who are struggling with sexual or romantic feelings toward family members they've recently reunited with. The general tone is that it's a lifelong affliction and those who have experienced it must learn to live with the longing. They talk about "GSA recovery" and describe the feelings as being like a drug. For example, a man who joined the forum after experiencing sexual feelings toward his younger sister wrote, "I'm finding it's a monster I can't battle myself." After lurking in the forum for a while, another man confessed the feelings he has toward his half sister, which he'd kept secret for decades: "This is the first time in my life I have admitted this ongoing issue that I have struggled with for some 20 years."[6] Members offer him comfort and support. "It's like an addiction," says a woman who became attracted to her brother.[7] On the GSA Forum people come together to support each other in abstaining from acting on their overwhelming desire. As a moderator put it when we talked on the phone, "We are all victims but we will do more harm by acting on it, so we shouldn't succumb to the emotions."

But on other forums, like Kindred Spirits (which is free), moderators and more established community members are explicit in their aim to normalize GSA relationships; they even advocate for consensual incest as a sexual orientation. The most vocal are a handful of figureheads whom I'd call anonymous GSA normalizers—that is, people who moderate the groups, respond to media requests, and act as advocates. They are active and responsive community members, but they all write using pseudonyms and refuse to step out from behind the screen and reveal who they are. Two of the most active normalizers are a woman who goes by the name of "Jane Doe" who runs the Kindred Spirits Forum and "Keith Pullman," who runs a blog called *Full Marriage Equality* that advocates for the rights of GSA relationships. Pullman became interested in blogging about what he calls "consensual" incest back in 2010 when he witnessed a close female friend of his develop a GSA relationship. She wouldn't risk speaking out about it, even anonymously, so he began to blog about it on her behalf. According to Pullman, if he reveals his identity, he'd compromise the trust he has with his online confidants who depend on his support. When I asked Jane Doe why she remains hidden, she said she was protecting herself and reporters (in the past she had what she calls a consensual sexual relationship with her father). "You cannot be subpoenaed in court to provide information on us that you do not possess. It covers you, and it covers me," she wrote by email.

Both Pullman's *Full Marriage Equality* blog and the Kindred Spirits Forum seem to be official. A cursory glance could lead you to think they have a physical storefront with a busy office and team of dedicated workers. They have bibliographies and links to resources and are regularly updated. Their founders call themselves advocates and use the word "consanguinamory" to name what they argue is a sexual orientation.

They're very up-front about their goal. They want to normalize what they call "consensual" incest and even speak as if their plight were the same as that of other groups who have historically been marginalized for their sexual identity. One day they'll have a float at Pride, or at least they deserve one.

They write as if they were sexual minorities who need law and culture changes to protect their marginalized desire, and in forums members adapt language from LGBTQ activism: think "consang-positive," "love is love," and "equal rights for all." In fact, Pullman's blog features a map of marriage laws that includes same-sex and polyamorous marriage. It even uses a rainbow flag in its logo.[8]

As Pullman writes on his blog, "Not everybody wants the same life, and the disgust of one person, or even many people, should not prevent consenting adults from having the sex and love lives to which they mutually agree."[9]

The Kindred Spirits Forum also has a logo: a pair of green leaves intertwined with a purple and red lily in a botanic cuddle in front of a black circle. According to Cristina Shy, the pseudonym of a GSA "activist" who designed the logo, gay people are "friends of Dorothy" and consang-people are "friends of Lily"—a reference to Lily Beckett from Diane Rinella's romance novel *Love's Forbidden Flower*, who has a sexual relationship with her brother.[10] The red represents the bonds of blood, which bind friends of Lily in "this rare opportunity of double love." Green symbolizes endurance and safety, because "our relationships must endure so much discrimination and hate from those people that cannot or will not understand." Purple signifies the rarity of their relationships: "We are the rare few in this world who were presented with this opportunity of 'double love.'" And black is for the mystery that surrounds their relationships due to the oppressive laws they must "live and love under."[11]

These websites downplay the genetic risks of having children with a close blood relative (which has been called the "mutant baby myth").[12] They have manifestos, talk about discrimination, and want to achieve what they call full marriage equality, where brothers and sisters and fathers and daughters can marry each other and enjoy the same legal rights as other couples and live without discrimination, in peace. It's an apocalyptic vision.

Joe Soll, an adoptee who is not an online "consensual incest" advocate, became a psychotherapist who specialized in adoption in 1990. When he began seeing clients, he was surprised by the large number of his recently reunited patients who were struggling with what they believed were unusual feelings toward their estranged relatives. A fifty-year-old woman particularly stands out in his memory. She sat in his support group and declared, "I have this intense desire to lean over and suckle my mother." As Soll says, "Her body wanted to go back and have Mommy. It wasn't sexual. She didn't want to have sex; she wanted affection. But their bodies respond sexually to the closeness because they are adults." The hardest part was convincing the couples that the relationships could be very "dangerous"; their desire is all consuming. What exactly did he mean by dangerous? "The incest taboo is huge. Huge," he replied. "When you break it, you can get into a horrendous psychological mess with guilt . . . It's often impossible to get the adoptees to stop. The parents always want to stop because the guilt is just too much, but the adoptees just want their mommy or their daddy. The bond between a parent and her child is the most sacred relationship in the world, and when it gets disrupted, things like this happen."

I needed to know more. Who were these anonymous people who spent hours online discussing this taboo experience? What did it take for someone to act on this desire? I had to find someone who would talk to me directly—on the phone with voices—about both what this experience was like and how online community had normalized their desires. I posted requests in forums, and Pullman put out a call to the members of his private community, but he was doubtful. The fear of speaking about it is immense for obvious reasons, but within hours of Pullman's memo I heard from Shelly, who at the time was eighteen years old and living in the Great Lakes region in a secret sexual relationship with her father.

I almost didn't pursue the story. When I was deciding if I should talk to Shelly, I was conflicted. She was young, and she'd spent her early childhood with her father before they were estranged, but she was willing to talk, which felt important (I'd been in touch with a handful of other people, but they would communicate only by email, and they had been clear that a phone conversation could never take place). After my time reading firsthand testimonies from people who had experienced GSA, I felt empathy for them, but I was very uncomfortable with the anonymous nature of this support system and the way that some members of the community borrowed activist language from the LGBTQ movement and argued that acting on this desire was acceptable. And like most people I had serious questions about consent and morality when confronted with these relationships, which don't (and can't) operate outside power relations. People in these relationships must navigate the implications of transgressing a prohibition that is both ancient and universal (if anything can be said to be universal). But I wanted to know the impact of acting on GSA feelings and what it meant to live in a world where something like this could be normal, so I decided to make the call.

I first spoke to Shelly from my tiny living room in New York's East Village, and we'd been chatting for about twenty minutes, breaking the ice, when she declared that she'd lost her virginity to her biological father. "I've never been in a more passionate, loving, fulfilling situation with anyone, ever," she said. She planned to marry him (she'd even started planning outfits and wedding decor), have kids, and move to New Jersey, where incest between consenting adults was decriminalized in the late 1970s. That physical space, combined with the support and activism she found online, gave her fuel to think that what she was doing with her father could be normal. Over the course of six years of phone calls, emails, and visits, I came to see the world according to Shelly.

Shelly has sad eyes—deep anime wells of blue that she usually dresses with wings of eyeliner. She doesn't have much money to spend on her "look," but she's skilled at making the most of what she's got. She streaks her hair with bursts of color and glams it up with a plastic flower or a wilted bow culled from the thrift mega-marts littered throughout her town's many strip malls. Her fiancé, Jimmy, takes her on regular shopping trips so she can stock up on cutoffs, makeup, and faded H&M tanks. She's an expert thrifter, willing to dig deep to retrieve button-downs, cartoon T-shirts, and silly sunglasses for him, too. When they reach the cash register, she might beg him for a treat like beat-up lollipops or bags of broken Easter eggs.

When I first met Shelly, she had her high school diploma and was halfway toward completing a cosmetology course. When licensed, she planned to marry Jimmy, have kids, and settle down in the suburbs. Jimmy would see if the maintenance company he worked for could organize a transfer, and Shelly could work taking care of the elderly in a nursing home, fixing their hair and painting nails.

Shelly's concept of family has always been different. Just after she was born, her mother had a nervous breakdown and sent her daughter to live with her own grandparents, where Shelly's great-nana, whom she considers her mother, cared for her. Shelly conjectures that early separation from her biological mother had a lasting impact on their relationship: "I think that's part of the reason why we've never been close. We didn't bond when I was a baby."[13]

When Shelly was two, she returned to her mother's care. By that time, her mother had split with Shelly's father, but they shared custody until Shelly was about four; then he slipped out of her life, seemingly for good. Shelly looked after her two younger siblings while her mother sometimes lay in bed or sat depressed on the sofa. "I also think of them as my babies because I helped raise them," Shelly said.[14]

Shelly's world is small. She may have access to a range of global media and information online, but she hasn't been on a plane, dipped her toes in the ocean, or slept in a house alone. Still, she's seen a lot. Diagnosed with bipolar disorder as a child and bullied about her weight, she spent parts of her adolescence in and out of various mental health institutions. She cut herself. She attempted suicide. "The more scars they had, the tighter they'd hug," she said of her institutionalized peers. She was first put on prescription drugs when she was four. Then came a scary cast of doctors. She sat in silence as white-coated medical professionals used their pens like evil wands to etch the names of pills she couldn't pronounce on their prescription pads.

Although she was hardly four when her dad left, she still has slivers of memory spliced together like a worn-out View-Master slide—that last summer day she spent with him at his house, when he surprised her with a trip to the zoo. She remembers the gift store; her dad bought her a plush bear.

Soon after that, he vanished.

She snuggled the bear as a cuddly security blanket until she was sixteen and, on a whim, decided to give him a wash. The poor animal tumbled in the warm machine, and his polyester body melted. That bear, and a miniature tea set, were the only totems she had of her dad, but she thought about him constantly. Where was he? Did he miss her? What did he look like? What became of the crate full of Barbies he had for when she visited? Why did he reject her? Where was the tall man who taught her how to blow bubbles?

Barbara Gonyo also grew up quickly. Rather than a bruising and unstable childhood, though, she'd enjoyed a comparably normal one for the times of housewives and brand-new bulbous TV sets—until she was forced into adulthood at the age of fifteen when her father threatened to have her arrested for being pregnant. Unmarried teenage girls didn't have sex in 1950s Chicago. But Barbara was in love with her boyfriend, and she lost her virginity to him while her parents were at work delivering sandwiches and MoonPies to factory workers. When Barbara stopped taking Kotex from the box that they shared, her mother confronted the scared girl, who figured she was just jump-starting the inevitable. Barbara had never been told she could be much more than a wife and mother, so she figured she'd get married, work in a dime store, and raise the kids. But, as she told me years later, "you aren't logical when you're a teenager; you just think what you feel."

As an adult, she bared it all in a memoir. The sensitive girl, who as a child often gazed at birds freezing on icy trees outside her bedroom window,[15] anxious about their safety, was beaten with a belt when her father learned of her transgression.[16] She thought he was going to kill her. He didn't, and off she was marched to a battery of doctors. There were hushed conversations; a blue-eyed doctor who jabbed her with a needle to try to induce a miscarriage;[17] the hot baths administered by her mom to make her bleed (desperate not to lose her baby, Barbara secretly added cold water);[18] the doctor who warned her mother off an illegal abortion, saying it would leave her daughter unable to have kids.[19]

In the 1950s, adoption was largely confidential, and all official agency records were closed. Women who had given up their babies were shielded from the shame and stigma of an "illegitimate" or underage pregnancy, and the recipient women were protected from judgments that they needed adoption to form a family. Some girls who failed to follow the normal script (marriage, *then* pregnancy) were sent to maternity homes and other religiously affiliated locations where they'd hide until their water broke. Babies were assiduously matched with parents who had similar coloring and appearance. The process was anonymous and, by the 1960s, brokered by a third party (birth mothers and their recipients didn't exchange names). When a baby was relinquished, a new birth certificate was issued, and the original was sealed and filed away. The purpose of this elaborate ritual was ostensibly to protect the reputation of the woman and/or her family. Many have since spoken out, saying they genuinely thought they were helping, that the secrecy would protect these young women, because the social mores of the era dictated that an unmarried woman's reputation would be ruined forever if the world knew she was having sex. New Jersey only ruled adoptees could access their original birth certificates in 2014; there were activists who had been pushing for the reform for more than thirty years, arguing that those who were denied access to their records had been stripped of the most basic of all human rights: to know who you are.[20]

Barbara went to a hideout for unmarried mothers in a predominantly African American neighborhood on Chicago's West Side (the thinking was that surely nobody who knew her would run into her there). On her first night, which was also her first night away from home, a matron filled her in on the home's strict privacy policy. Don't open the door to anyone if you are showing; send a girl with a flat belly. Do not mention your last name to anyone, no matter how much you trust them.[21] Girls had to travel in pairs during outings and wear modest dress and wedding rings.[22] After giving birth (which they attended alone, in a cab), they had to return to the home for twenty-one days to lose weight so they could re-assimilate with their reputations intact.[23]

Barbara's four-month stay was lonely. Her roommate was a bit older and kept to herself. Barbara wished she was in the dorms with the other girls. Her boyfriend, "John" (in her memoir she gave some people pseudonyms), was banned from visiting; his mother even bought him a car if he swore he'd never see Barbara again. The young man was rewarded with mobility and freedom while Barbara was left grounded, snacking on popcorn and deli pickles while her baby squirmed in her womb.[24] She prayed that when she gave birth, her parents would change their minds.

Her girlfriends came in a group and spent an afternoon perched on her bed taking turns placing their hands on her belly. Barbara recalls sensing how excited they were to get a glimpse into this taboo and grown-up world. Her dad drove her mom to visit, but despite their once-close bond he refused to get out of the car, so her mom went alone with Barbara's five-year-old sister, who had made her a bouquet of weeds she'd collected from the yard.[25] Barbara could feel her dad's disappointment emanating from the parking lot. "Whether a child or a woman, to go through this alone was the greatest horror," she later wrote in her memoir.[26] She dreamed about that place for the rest of her life—as in, it haunted her while she slept. A grand staircase; hidden tunnels with secret doors; a narrow walkway and pregnant zombies slowly moving their heavy bodies.[27]

The night she went into labor, a handyman gave her ice cream and she spent the night in the kitchen timing her contractions. She traveled in a cab—alone—to the hospital. Her parents weren't told she was going into labor; why worry them before it was all over? She didn't even yell out in pain when she felt the force of the labor, thinking that perhaps if she acted grown up, and stoic, she'd be allowed to keep her baby.[28] As soon as the cord was cut, the nurses whisked away her baby boy. When she was disturbed by a doctor scolding her because she wasn't breastfeeding she spoke in a low voice, concerned about what the other new mothers in her ward would think, "I'm not keeping my baby."[29] While she lay there, she decided to name him even if the child would never be known by it; she felt it was important. She settled on John, after his dad.

Aside from a glimpse when he was born, Barbara saw John once, when he was three days old, just before he left to start his new life. She begged her adoption agency social worker to let her see him, but she was too scared to ask if she could hold him.[30] So as the nurse held him, she stared at her baby in the arms of another woman. She eventually got into another taxi to go back into hiding, where she signed a form relinquishing all parental rights. She had felt alone before; she had felt alone for months. But now, the warm little companion she'd carried in her body was gone. As she put it in her memoir, she wept, mourning her "empty body with milk-filled breasts with no baby to suckle" them.[31]

Shelly's favorite class at cosmetology school was a free service for cancer patients undergoing radiation or chemotherapy. She'd treat these frail women to a full spa session, paint their toes and fingernails, and rub warm stones on their swollen legs. She loved their stories and identified with their isolation: "Even when they have family, they feel so alone because they don't want to burden them with their pain." This interaction made her feel less alone at college, where, like most social situations, she was plagued by paranoid thoughts: "My auto process is to think that people are talking about me, whispering about me. I've never been able to get over it." The other girls formed cliques. "It's high school all over again," says Shelly, wondering if she'll ever escape the pressure of fitting in. Generally, she prefers the company of animals to humans. When she was little, she'd regularly smuggle stray dogs and cats from sidewalks or parks back to her house and beg to keep them. One of her stepdads once bought her a three-foot-long iguana. The reptile roamed around the house going to the toilet in a kitty litter tray.

Shelly was born in the mid 1990s, and like many of her generation a lot of her information comes from one important source: Wikipedia. Back when she was still a teenager, she'd regularly blurt out dubious factoids with the authority of a child playing an old woman in a school play:

The longest time ever recorded between the birth of twins carried by the same mother is eighty-four days.

A cat's penis has worms attached to it. Those worms prompt ovulation.

You'll get hepatitis if you drink from a glass without using a straw.

There's no risk attached to having a child with a close relative. It's okay to have a child with your dad. Look at the Tudors!

When Shelly was seventeen, Facebook notified her of a new friend request. As she stared at the thumbnail, a shock of recognition jolted her. Jimmy looked just like her. She eventually accepted the request and sent him a simple message: "I thought you were dead."

He was very much alive. Unmarried. And other than her, childless. He lived only half an hour's drive away. At first, Shelly was guarded. Where the fuck have you been? Jimmy insisted he'd attempted to contact her but each time he added her on Facebook, she declined the request. (Shelly had only recently regained control of her social networking passwords from her mother.) Of course her mother had blocked her from her father, she reasoned; she always had. She began to believe that she and her dad were victims of her mother's desire to keep them apart. She formed a story fueled by the negative things Jimmy said about her mom. When they shared custody, it was her mom who refused to drive halfway to meet him. What about that time he sent her mom an email asking if he could see her? Shelly remembers crying and saying she missed Jimmy but has forgotten why he never came.

Jimmy came over, about a week after their online reunion, when her mom was home; she had insisted on supervising the visit that after all this time she still hadn't wanted to happen.

She kept her distance, though, staying inside while Shelly and her father sat in the yard, stretched out on the lawn drawing pictures, chatting about their shared interests. They are both devoted to animals, and they love to paint and draw. She kept noting how youthful Jimmy was; he seemed to be on her level, a potential friend who wasn't a stranger. She was confused: "I was seeing my dad for the first time in forever, but it was also like, he's so good-looking! And I was like, What the hell are you thinking? What's wrong with you? I saw him as my dad but then also part of me was like, I'm meeting this guy who I have been talking to over the internet and really connecting with and I find him attractive."[32] When it was time to say goodbye, Shelly begged him to come back as soon as he could because those few hours just weren't enough. After a fight, her mom agreed to let her spend a week with him at his home.

He kept his promise. One week later he came to get her. "I'm spending the week with my dad," she repeated to herself over and over while he drove her to the house he lived in with his girlfriend and her kids. On the first night, Shelly was anxious when she settled down on the floor; she always is when she sleeps in new places. Because her little sister wasn't there, she asked Jimmy to sit with her until she calmed down. They whispered through the dark, as she'd always imagined friends would at a sleepover. It was the first time she'd truly felt comfortable in the company of a stranger.

When she woke, Jimmy was asleep on the couch beside her. On night two Jimmy fell asleep next to her again, and on the third night they lay together on the floor and she drifted off with her head on his chest. When she blinked herself awake, she spent a few seconds resting on his torso, enjoying the steady beat of his heart and the safe loop of his long arms. On the fourth night they ended up on the floor together, cuddling.

That day Jimmy drove her to buy some new clothes. He'd

noticed she'd been tugging at her shorts that were a few sizes too small. She modeled for him, coming in and out of the changing room like a contestant on a makeover show. She didn't care what he thought of her body because their connection felt deeper. They headed back to the house, and she clutched the plastic bag containing her brand-new clothes close to her, nursing the first gift she had received from her father since that teddy bear.

Back at home that night they horsed around, play wrestling, tickling, and performing feeble body slams. Swept up in the game, Shelly sunk her teeth into her father's flesh and bit him. When she pulled away, she noticed goose bumps pop up from his ankles to his shoulders. He was silent when she placed his hand on her leg and moved it up to her inner thigh, where his fingers rested for a moment before he pinched her; then they kissed, and then they had sex.

When Shelly first told me this story, there was no part of me that believed her when she said she wanted it. I asked—repeatedly—did she feel pressured? She must have; he was her father. He'd abandoned her, and she'd longed for him her whole life. I didn't think she was capable of consenting to sex with her father. And as for Jimmy . . . Well, he's an abusive, lecherous predator. What sort of man has sex with his daughter? It doesn't matter what age they are; he's the one with the power.

In 1997, Kathryn Harrison published *The Kiss,* which describes her reunion with her estranged father when she was a freshman in college. She told a story of pressure, confusion, manipulation, and betrayal where she was forced to give in to her father's unwanted sexual advances.[33] When I emailed Harrison asking if she'd talk to me about the concept of "consensual incest," she replied saying that she does not believe that exists.

Shelly insisted she wasn't coerced or guilt-ridden: while biologically Jimmy is her father, she told me, she didn't grow up with him. She reminded me of this often, most succinctly when she remarked, "He's not your father. And, I'm not you." She insisted to me that her feelings hadn't changed: "I didn't regret it at all. I was happy for once in my life. We fell deeply in love . . . It didn't even feel taboo. I felt like I'd made love with a man I'd been with for years."

Online, I contacted other women who experienced GSA when they reunited with their fathers, and while they wanted to talk, nobody would risk meeting me in person or even speaking on the phone. One wrote about her reunion, which was similar to Shelly and Jimmy's. First, there was the connection online, the ice-breaking messages, the curiosity, the decision to meet in person, then that mutual shock of instant sexual attraction when they stood face-to-face: "I wanted him to see me as an attractive woman, and I flirted with him pretty hardcore that whole time to try and get him to bring it up naturally. In the end I had to raise it point blank myself, and I felt amazing when he felt the same way about me," she wrote.

Another woman repeated again and again that her desire to talk about what was going on with her father trumped the terror she felt exchanging emails with me. Like Shelly, she last saw him when she was about four. They reunited when she was an adult, and when he left after each meeting, she physically hurt, she found she was constantly looking for reasons to be with him. When she told him, he said he felt the exact same way and things got "sexual." They've continued a relationship as "dad and daughter," but occasionally things become "a lot more." "I'm glad he's back in my life . . . I'm still scared in writing this to you, but I also feel better now," she wrote.

I spent a few months emailing with a fifty-four-year-old woman named "Minnie" whom I met via the Kindred Spirits Forum. When we started talking, she'd been in a sexual relationship with her seventy-seven-year-old father for the last year and a half; she'd even left her husband to be with him. Like Shelly, she was raised by her mother and her grandmother, whom she says gave her the bulk of love and nurturing she experienced as a child. Her parents separated before she was born, and when she was growing up, the only information she was given about her father was his name; there were no photos, no biography. She was constantly told that she had his lips, the same shape.

Her mother kept letters from him, which Minnie discovered after she was married. She plowed through the correspondence, eager to learn everything about his past. She says that while they had an instant "connection" when they talked on the phone, during their first physical encounter she only felt neutral. She did sense a strong sexual energy radiating from him, though. She spoke as if GSA were an illness that took them at different times. His feelings were there when they first met, but hers took longer to incubate and mutate. She says "the GSA" "hit her" when her father showed her pictures of himself as a young man. She stared at his lips; feeling like a "giddy teenage girl," she longed to kiss them. When they finally did, there was so much "pent up sexual energy" that they remained kissing for at least half an hour. It was as if their bodies merged; they swayed back and forth as though they were the only two who could hear "some magical tune that was playing in our minds."

Her feelings were overwhelming and unprecedented. "I've never, ever felt such strong, intense, life changing emotions for another human being," she wrote. After they met, she reflected in her diary, "My heart aches and feels like it will break in two. I can't bear the separation from him." It was her father who gave her the language for what she was feeling, something called GSA, he said as if it were a diagnosis, suggesting she go online and do some research, too. "Thank God there is a word, a description, a category, for these intense, passionate feelings we have for each other. There are thousands of others who have experienced this," she wrote. "We are not weird. We are not perverts. We are not crazy or insane. We are typical adults who were denied the loving father/daughter relationship we needed to have when I was a baby." Within two months she'd left her husband of thirty-three years, packed a U-Haul, and moved to a new state to live with her father, who had also announced he was in the process of divorcing his wife.

With her father in her life, she says it was as if she saw in color again. The initial rush of GSA was like a fever and over a year later that fever was replaced with a "gentler love," but she said it was still as strong as ever, as if she were "perpetually wrapped in the warm blanket of her lover's arms," whom she is drawn to via a "magnetic" pull that she's "powerless" to change.

After she learned the term "GSA," she went online to do some research. When she found a local government publication from the U.K. that described GSA, she felt especially comforted; it was an official publication that to her sanctioned what she was going through, "like I wasn't some perverted freak."[34] But it was in forums and chat rooms that she found a sense of "community." In conversation with others, she decided that there are roughly two paths, given that most people were afraid to talk to a therapist or other professional. You can either cut off contact to prevent the emotions from growing and eliminate the chance of acting on it or "jump on in and go with it." After reading about so many people mourning the loss, she chose the latter. On GSA Forum she found that people who openly discussed acting on their feelings were ostracized, but she found that other members who were mourning the loss of their relationships worked as cautionary tales, and it was largely based on what she read there that she decided to pursue a romantic and sexual relationship with her father. "I didn't want to be one of those alienated from the one I love," she wrote, "always pining and missing him." Like those GSA normalizers she used language of identity politics. "We are truly in a sexual minority, and I look forward to the day when adults in a GSA relationship are just as normal as those in LGBTQ relationships," she wrote.

Then one day Minnie contacted me to say that she'd ended things with her father. She couldn't reconcile her actions with her conscience; shattering the incest taboo was hard enough, but she was also committing adultery. His wife was unwell and dying, and she didn't like the way he was so quick to abandon her. She made the decision to leave with the help of a therapist, and when she did, it was like coming out of a trance, like she'd been under a "spell," having strayed so far away from her values. In retrospect, she's taken by the way she rationalized her behavior. If she could go back in time and talk to herself before she decided to act on her feelings, what would she say? "Don't follow your emotions, follow your values and use your head . . . However, GSA is so powerful . . . I'm not sure that I could have heard it even from myself . . . It's a tough road, and if I was to encounter anyone else deciding whether or not to enter into a GSA relationship, I would strongly urge them not to," she wrote.

In 1891 the Finnish sociologist Edvard Westermarck proposed that the level of disgust we feel about incest reflects the amount of intimate time we have spent with the family member in question: it's not so much a genetic fact as it is one of proximity. Those who grow up as family in the same household very rarely develop sexual attraction to one another even if they aren't related by blood.[35] So what happens to people who miss out on this socially sanctioned intimacy that naturally limits sexual attraction? What happens when genetic family members meet as adults? Is there an innate desire to experience these exchanges anyway? The basic explanation for GSA is that it's a disruption in normal timing and development.

In 1994, Betty Jean Lifton, a counseling psychologist and

adoption reform advocate, wrote about patients of hers who experienced sexual attraction when they were reunited with family they were estranged from by adoption. They behaved, she
described, as if "under a sorcerer's spell or lost, like Titania and
Bottom in *A Midsummer Night's Dream*."[36] Their desire was
uncontrollable; some even reported feeling aroused before they
had met, including when they talked on the phone. "I think of
it like a form of masturbation . . . like touching a part of yourself for the first time. Not literally, but symbolically—being in
touch with yourself," said one of her respondents after reuniting
with his birth mother.[37]

To date the most organized study of GSA was conducted by
British researchers in the early 1990s. They asked a small sample
of adoptees who had sought post-adoption counseling to complete interviews, and all eight adoptees and one biological parent
surveyed reported feeling "erotic sentiments." Three acted on
these feelings and had sex (one father-daughter couple and two
sisters). Common to each participant was a "romantic falling in
love intense and explosive, sudden and almost irresistible" sentiment, coupled with a "particular" desire for "closeness." Like
those of Lifton's patients, these feelings often began well before
a physical encounter; one woman wrote her estranged son a five-
page erotic letter after their first phone call. When they did meet,
they reported a strong feeling of familiarity; as one female adoptee said of her biological father, "He was me in a male body."[38]
The common thread is the recognition, the familiarity, and that
overwhelming "connection."

It was Jimmy who first told Shelly about this thing called
"genetic sexual attraction." She was confused and ashamed about
what they'd done, and when she went online to look it up, she
says she found the only explanation that made any sense. She was
immediately linked to the Wikipedia page. She searched more
and came across forums and a private Facebook support group—

emblazoned with that Friends of Lily GSA logo that claimed to offer a safe space for people like her to talk. The voices of these anonymous people discussing experiences so similar to what she had just been through were comforting. As she put it, "I thought it was weird and unacceptable, until I went online and read about that." She searched GSA well into the night, mostly sending herself in a loop back to the same woman, Barbara Gonyo.

When my interview with Shelly was published, it went viral.[39] The story was picked up by Fox News, which was one of the top referrers for traffic to the story on *New York* magazine's *Science of Us* blog, and within two weeks it had reached 1.17 million readers. It was covered by online outlets like *Cosmopolitan*, *Jezebel*, and *Bustle*.[40] There were stories about it in tabloids, and national and local news.[41] I was also bombarded with questions from readers and interview requests from reality TV and documentary production companies who, probably excited by the sensational headline, wanted to interview Shelly themselves. I got emails from reporters pleading to be put in touch with her. But others expressed concern for Shelly's welfare and anger at me for exploiting a young woman who was already being exploited by her father. They pointed out that Shelly's experience had all the markers of sexual abuse: an abuse of power by an adult whose position as her father meant that despite her age she wasn't capable of giving consent (as *The Daily Beast* put it, "Consensual incest is rape"[42]). People noted angrily their feeling that by interviewing Shelly and presenting her situation without passing judgment, we'd effectively normalized GSA. Because she'd talked about her desire to flee to New Jersey, where she could legally live with her father as a couple, it attracted the attention of lawmakers who spoke about revising the state's law that allowed incest between consenting adults.[43]

I even heard from the legal team of a man who had embarked

on a sexual relationship with a girl who was believed to be his fifteen-year-old biological daughter. He was nineteen when she was born, and they'd reunited on social media when she was a teenager. They left Alabama together and traveled through Mississippi and Pennsylvania—they were at the Port Authority in New York, perhaps even heading for New Jersey, when they got caught. During interviews with the accused man his line didn't waver: they were very much in love. The legal team had not been allowed to interview the daughter, so they did not know if she was also claiming an emotional connection, but when I heard that, I felt sick. Had my interview with Shelly emboldened them to pursue a relationship? Of course, if they were in fact heading toward New Jersey, they could have got that information about the legality of incest there from any of the online GSA advocacy spaces, or even just an internet search, but the timing made me uncomfortable. Had this man used my interview with Shelly to justify what he was doing with his daughter? Given that our interview had been recycled on just about every online tabloid and was a staple of morning radio and TV for weeks, I knew it had reached a wider audience than people who were online googling their feelings. He'd pleaded guilty to traveling across state lines for the purpose of engaging in illicit sexual conduct, and his legal team wanted help with the tone of the sentencing submission. "It's incredibly hard to put this phenomenon into words, striking the right balance of empathy for the client and showing that he accepts responsibility," their intern wrote to me by email. They didn't end up mentioning GSA in their sentencing argument; when they flagged it to the prosecutor and sent her all the literature they could find about it (including my interview with Shelly), her response was one of disbelief, as if this man were mining the internet for an excuse so his lawyers thought the judge would have a similar reaction.

Shelly was understandably frightened by the interest her

story had generated; she never imagined her experience would become what historian Brian Connolly in the *Los Angeles Review of Books* called an "international sensation."[44] What if someone read it and recognized her and she got caught? I was worried about her: I wasn't convinced that just because she couldn't see it, or couldn't voice it, her situation wasn't abusive. I also knew that the secrecy added to her difficulty; it further isolated her. Yes, she had that online support network, but as we have seen, in the hyperconnected era online support doesn't replace real-world support. Talking out loud to other humans matters, too. As Shelly later told me, "Back then there was nobody in real life I could talk to about it but you."

Had her sexual abuse been normalized online as GSA? Did I have a duty of care to report what was going on? Was it worth trying to persuade Shelly to end it? Should I tell her mother, or the police? She's an adult, and I'm documenting her life, not involving myself in it, I reminded myself. But still, I wrestled with all of this. I admired her for talking about what she was experiencing, for offering a detailed account of this experience that so few are prepared to speak about to a reporter, and I knew this wasn't an isolated case. Just because we rarely hear about something doesn't mean it doesn't exist, and if something is happening, we can't ignore it. But by responding neutrally and without judgment, were those critics right, had I normalized it for her, too?

After Fox News and the *Daily Mail* linked to the story, the comments became especially critical, and many referred to details of Shelly's life as evidence that I'd made the story up. "This article has a distinct whiff of bullshit about it. Methinks the author is trial-ballooning an awkward young adult novel qua perks of being a daughter-wife. I am confident this interview occurred in the author's fantasy-fanned salon. The responses to the interview are ridiculous," wrote one.[45] "I was wondering when this one would be published in a screenplay. Ridiculous . . . Normal pheromones would prevent this crap from happening," typed another.[46] I recently found an email where I'd written to my editors asking if I could reply and defend us both. I felt bonded to Shelly as a victim of online hate.

I needed to finally meet Shelly IRL. Maybe in person I could persuade her to end it? I also felt it was important to meet face-to-face. I was uncomfortable with the virtual nature of our relationship, and I wanted to see Jimmy for myself, naively hopeful that a physical encounter might let me properly assess the amount of danger she was in. And it's very difficult to admit, but there was a very small part of me that thought maybe it could be okay. I didn't trust Jimmy or his motives, but because Shelly insisted he made her happy, and because I didn't want to treat her like a vulnerable child who didn't know what she wanted, and because I understood the power of those GSA feelings because I had spent so much time talking to people who were experiencing GSA—reading discussions in forums and emailing with people I'd met there—I'd reluctantly gone along with her version of his presence in her life.

I decided to drive west to spend the weekend with her and Jimmy. She trusted me enough to meet me IRL. Why? In a way we had become friends. We weathered a media storm together, and she'd become part of my life. She'd mentioned hoping to one day visit me; she longed to go shopping on Broadway and be in Times Square when the ball dropped on New Year's Eve. Perhaps the thought of talking to someone who listened without judgment was too appealing. Minnie, the woman I had met on Kindred Spirits, once told me that even though she had the help of a therapist, a psychologist, and the anonymous contacts she'd made in online forums, what she really craved was a friend to confide in; all that support was not the same as having "someone you trust to talk to about it like friends do." Since we'd never met, Shelly wisely suggested we get lunch somewhere neutral. She directed me to meet her at a Mexican restaurant nestled between a Best Buy and an Applebee's in the medium-size city in which she lives.

I was anxious about meeting Shelly and Jimmy alone, so I asked an old friend, Devin, to come with me for moral support. We drove west from New York in his parents' Volvo, and along the way I felt a wave of nausea that I had been nursing in the buildup to the trip; I wound down the window and vomited, violently. We drove past cornfields, gas stations, and sepia antiabortion billboards, and I wondered what sort of reasonable man says to himself, "You know what? I'm going to go ahead and have sex with my daughter."

It was hard to tell that Shelly was eighteen years younger than Jimmy. The pair matched: they were both dressed in plaid and decorated with piercings and tattoos, with the same mournful stare. Devin and I sat across from them in a booth, and we all nervously ordered food and made small talk about the weather, what soda Shelly should order, and our journey to meet them. I was expecting Jimmy to be wary or standoffish, but he seemed to accept my presence without question; if anything, he seemed slightly embarrassed. It was Shelly who turned the conversation to the matter at hand, their relationship. Jimmy looked sheepish when he said, "You know we didn't choose this. We didn't decide this would happen." Then, when Shelly went to the restroom, he mumbled, "I know it must seem really crazy to you." I shook my head to signal that it didn't, but I didn't say no.

The next night, I offered to buy them dinner if they took me to their favorite spot. They both agreed on a diner, near the college campus. Their neighborhood is peppered with discount marts, check-cashing kiosks, and factories that leave a briny aroma in the air, like tequila. I sat in the back with Shelly while we drove downtown. She offered a running commentary on the scenery, hanging her head out the window like a kid at an amusement park. There was neon everywhere, chalkboard signs and blinking lights advertising beer and shot specials, bar crawls, and Irish-themed day-drinking events. Drunk people stumbled out of doors, and woozy drivers wobbled across lanes, ignoring red lights and blaring Rihanna. Shelly, who had always wanted to go to college and live in dorms, was mesmerized. "I can't wait till I can go out on my own," she declared, before laughing about how comical it is that she can legally drink with her boyfriend because he's also her dad.

When we got to the restaurant, we found a table on the porch and decided what to eat. Jimmy scanned the menu searching for something to fit his specific dietary requirements, and after filling us in on the history of the area, he talked about his health. They were living off about five hundred dollars a week, so they usually ended up eating fast food. He recently started collecting free boxes of fresh produce from a local charity. "Last time I got a bag of oranges, nine melons, and a whole flight of mangoes," he said, boastfully. He went on to blame Shelly's mother for too many medical interventions that he says messed up his daughter's thyroid, claiming that it was one of the things they fought about when they shared custody. He wasn't raised that way, he insisted, despite his bad behavior (he could never sit still or focus in class, so not surprisingly he didn't do well at school): "When I was growing up I had all these diagnoses, and my mom refused to medicate me for anything apart from asthma. She told the doctors to just let me be normal. I think parents medicate because they don't know how to raise their kids."

I was very uncomfortable hearing him criticize Shelly's mother or anyone else's parenting, so I snapped at him: "There's also the fact that medicine wasn't administered so liberally back in the

'70s, when you were a boy." Before he could answer, Shelly took the opportunity to lay into her mom. "Well, me and my siblings were zombie children and still are," she said, explaining that her siblings are medicated, too. "They figure she's fucked up, so are they. I guess I do have mood swings. To be honest, I probably am bipolar; I've just learned how to deal with it naturally."

By "naturally" she meant Jimmy. He knows how to calm her down. He did it that first night she stayed with him. Forced to sleep in a strange room in her estranged father's strange girl-friend's strange house, he sat with her while she attempted to drift off. He's learned to spot when she's slipping into one of her "moods"; sometimes he holds her, rubbing her back until the yelling stops. "It's drastic," Shelly explained. "I can go from to-tally happy to completely outraged, ready to knock the head off someone. Like a flick-of-the-switch, drop-the-hat kind of thing."

During the weekend I spent with Shelly, Jimmy didn't let her out of his sight. He paid for everything; in fact, Shelly didn't seem to have her own money. He was responsible for driving her to meet us; it was his car, and when we were planning the weekend, Shelly seemed at the mercy of his schedule. When I thought about it, he was often there in the background when we talked on the phone. In retrospect, it seems bizarre that I was looking for extra evidence that he was controlling or abusive: he was living in a sexual relationship with his daughter.

The official story was that Shelly had moved to live with her father to get to know him and to get away from her mother, whom she was constantly fighting with. It was the truth—just not the whole truth. And if you asked her back then, she'd have insisted that her life had improved. In this new, calm environ-ment, she buckled down and finished the last few credits she needed to graduate from high school. Jimmy persuaded her to stop taking a cocktail of meds and watched as she flushed the contents of those brown containers down the toilet. Shelly made Jimmy quit his two-pack-a-day habit. They established a routine, something Shelly had never experienced. They ate dinner together and were in bed by 10:00 p.m. And Jimmy had even driven Shelly to visit her mother and the kids.

For the last few years Shelly had fiercely guarded their secret. The stakes were too high. Their relationship was illegal. Technically, they were both breaking the law, but when it comes to "consensual" incest, it's usually only the parent who is prosecuted—the courts siding with the party perceived to have less power. If Jimmy went to jail, where would Shelly go? Who would love her? The thought of losing her fiancé and her father in one hit was too much. She'd always sworn she would only come clean when they were safely in New Jersey. She had a dream: when her brother and sister were over eighteen, they could join her, and they could live out in the open; they could have a normal life.

It was around noon one day after our interview went live, and just before I drove to visit her, that her phone buzzed with a message from her mother. "Are you engaged to Jimmy?" the SMS read. The day of reckoning had arrived: the word was out. According to Shelly, her mother, who was suspicious, had gone online and found her interview with me. She's not sure what led her to it, maybe when it appeared on *USA Today* under the headline "18-Year-Old Plans to Marry Her Long-Lost Father."[47] But when she was finally confronted, Shelly couldn't lie. "I had to face the battle. I would have told her from the beginning if I could. So I just texted her back and said, 'Fine, you caught me.'" She sent her a link to the Wikipedia page for GSA. When her mother called, she answered and listened to her objections (he should have been more responsible; he's brainwashed you). And then she dropped the bomb Shelly knew was coming. "You can't see your siblings, and don't come over anymore."

Shelly was puttering around the house when she noticed a squad car parked outside. She anxiously monitored it for the next few hours, telling herself it was just another neighborhood drug bust. It wasn't. When Jimmy returned from work, the police cuffed him on the doorstep before leading the pair to the station for questioning. Shelly was certain they'd both be locked up, and she cried while they rode in the back of the car, but she stopped herself from reaching for Jimmy's hand. When they were separated, it became clear that everyone was confused. They'd received a call from a woman saying that her daughter was being brainwashed into having sex with her own dad. Alone in an interview room with Shelly, a nervous young female officer reached up to rub her eyes. Shelly noticed a large ring on her engagement finger. Unease sloshed in her gut: Could she ever have a normal life like this woman's? The officer seemed uncomfortable, explaining that Shelly's mother was worried about her mental state. According to Shelly, her mother had begged them to arrest the asshole who took advantage of her daughter and was calling the station asking for updates. Shelly reminded the officer that her mother couldn't tell her what to do: she was over eighteen. She pointed to her glistening ring and asked her, "Did you have any control over who you fell in love with?"

The woman didn't answer right away, didn't answer at all—maybe she didn't have time—because Shelly continued speaking, explaining exactly what genetic sexual attraction is, and once the crash course in the phenomenon was over, the officer walked out of the holding room with a scrap of paper on which she had written the term. The police were at a loss: a conviction depended on either a confession or evidence that they'd had sex, which Shelly refused to give. When they reunited, they were spooked, exhausted, and not thinking clearly. They decided to flee to the Garden State, which had become their symbolic asylum.

The next day Shelly rose early and began to pack. They

barely had any cash, but they were determined to make it work. They filled up the car with bags of clothes, plastic crates of CDs, and their dogs and said goodbye to their roommate; then they drove east toward New Jersey, taking a long route to avoid tolls. Shelly used her smartphone to summon help from the network of online friends who shared her secret and were in similar relationships.

A man in Philadelphia told them they couldn't stay with him for the night and that their exodus was an admission of guilt. If they made it to New Jersey, they could be extradited and charged with a felony. Was he giving sound advice, or was he apprehensive about harboring these fugitives he'd never met in person? Another woman from one of their secret Facebook groups, who was herself married to her half brother, ignored Shelly's request when she asked if they could come and stay (later, the woman admitted to me, "I shouldn't judge anyone, but the parent/child stuff creeps me the fuck out"). Overtired and frightened, they turned around to make the journey back home minutes before they reached the New Jersey state line. It was clear that if there was such a thing as a GSA community, when it came to her movement through the IRL world, Shelly was alone.

It was a Friday morning when I arrived in Mount Prospect to visit Barbara Gonyo, the woman who was made to relinquish her baby all those years ago and who was now in her late seventies. I walked from the train station, aware of the silent sealed houses that projected their wholesomeness via manicured front lawns, porcelain swans, American flags, and seasonally decorative plastic pumpkins. Six years earlier, *BusinessWeek* had named the pristine suburb about an hour's train ride from central Chicago the best place in America to raise your kids.[48] The Barbara Gonyo I had imagined was a construct of stories in tabloid news reports and TV shows, her name inevitably brought up whenever GSA is, her voice when asked to comment on shows like *Dr. Drew* (including my interview with Shelly).[49] But who was this woman who had shocked the world saying she was sexually attracted to her son? Was she thinking about her family's privacy when she went on a mission to publicize this phenomenon? Or was she a victim of a different, 1950s form of child abuse: shunned from polite society and institutionalized alone for months, forced to give away her baby and left haunted by his absence?

Barbara's a little lady with a loud, dry voice. She opened the door a crack to contain her miniature poodle, Chloe, who leaped around like a cotton ball. "In my next life I'm only having dogs, no kids," she said, leading me in. She'd just got off the phone with her youngest daughter, whom she called her "problem child." She was dressed in a neat denim shirt, baby-blue slacks, and pearl earrings, her dark gray hair cropped in a short haircut. She ushered me in, chatting away and explaining that her husband, Bob, was grocery shopping, and, before I'd taken my coat off, grabbed a framed family portrait and verbally annotated it, introducing me to her three other children. "That's all my kids but John," the son she gave up for adoption. He died of brain cancer about seven years ago, she said, opening a drawer to find a paper funeral brochure.

Barbara got married soon after she returned from the maternity home. Desperate to fill the hole left by her absent baby and boyfriend, she latched onto the first person who showed her any affection. They had three children together, but then the marriage ended; according to Barbara they just weren't compatible. In her memoir she describes him as a casualty of her loss: "I married him to replace my baby. He never had a chance."[50] She moved in with Bob, a childless fireman, almost immediately after her divorce.

Barbara never really stopped thinking about the baby she was forced to relinquish. October was always a dark month. As

John's date of birth approached and the days got shorter and colder, she'd relive the powerlessness she'd experienced as a teenager. In the early afternoon one day in 1979, she was watching TV when a woman who had tracked down her birth mother caught her attention. She'd never heard a birth child talk about what it felt like to reunite with their mother. Barbara scrambled to find a pen to write down the name of the group that had led the search: Truth Seekers in Adoption.

It took Barbara three months to make the call. The friendly woman at the end of the line, who had also adopted out a child, invited Barbara to a meeting that was being held that night. She didn't want excuses. "I'll pick you up myself," she said. Barbara became a regular and eventually took over running the entire Illinois operation. It was this network of people skilled at searching records and archives who were able to trace down the baby she last saw being held by another woman twenty-six years earlier.

Once his identity had been confirmed and she had his phone number, she wrote a script.[51] It took her another six hours to work up the courage to pick up the phone and call Mitch, which was what his adopted parents had named him. During their first conversation they agreed to meet. He came to her house for dinner; all her children were adults and had left home, so it was just her and Bob. The details are blurry: she vaguely remembers Bob getting emotional watching the pair together, but she very clearly remembers how she felt. Physically, he reminded her so much of his father. They had the same voice and they walked the same way, but his personality was all Barbara. He had her sharp, sarcastic sense of humor. He was chatty, warm, and socially generous. She was shocked when Mitch told her he was an artist; he even brought some of his work to show her. "Is my talent genetic?" she wondered. "What a phenomenal feeling," Barbara wrote in her memoir. "I get to relive my youth with this young replica of his father and better yet he's part of me and has most of the qualities of me that I like. Talk about an ego trip!" When it was time to say goodbye, she was too scared to say she loved him and too shy to hug. She wrote that when he left that night, she experienced "the same feeling as after you've given birth and your big body which was so full of life and action and the wonderment of that little person living inside of you, depending on you to continue his life, is now empty, unmoving, still and lonely."[52]

The more they got to know each other, saying goodbye became more and more painful. She felt as if every time she watched her son walk away, she would never see him again. They didn't hug until their second meeting. When he wrapped his arms around her small body, she felt as if she were watching herself in a movie. "I knew instantly that holding him beat any feeling I've had in my whole life. Any sexual experience seemed petty in comparison," she wrote.[53] That hug was the very first time they had ever really touched, and when she felt the charge of that physical connection, she knew just how much she craved him.

The feelings she had for Mitch, all grown up, were unusual. It wasn't a crush; it was both more and less. It felt like sexual attraction, but he was her son, so how could that be? She recalls fretting over how to dress when she met up with him as if she were going on a date. She'd visit him in his apartment, admiring his decor and searching his bookshelves for signs of his personality like when first invited to a lover's home. She gushed about his artistic talent while downplaying her own. When he brought girlfriends to meet her, she'd lure him into a world of personal jokes. She didn't want to share, so she invited him over when nobody was around. She was frustrated. Friendship wasn't enough. She felt like a needy girlfriend—always calling, checking in, anticipating their next meeting, reflecting on it later. What the hell was she going through? She really didn't know.

Barbara didn't waste time before she said exactly how she felt. Her life had been shaped by secrets, lies, and keeping up appearances. Isn't it important to let the toxins out? She reasoned: if you sit on trouble, it will only fester. So at a Truth Seekers meeting she bravely told a crowded room that she was experiencing sexual feelings toward her son. She didn't mince her words, telling the group that she wanted to "touch him" and run her "fingers through his hair." "I want to smell him the way I smelled my other babies so many years before," she said.[54] She explained that when he was near, she "felt very aroused," and when he wasn't, her "thoughts belonged to him."[55]

She'd hoped her honesty would break down a wall; maybe someone else would admit to the same feelings and she wouldn't be alone. A woman told her she was sick. The rest sat in silence. It was probably just her, she figured—disgusting, oversexed Barbara. As a teenager she had been made to feel as if her sexuality were criminal. Maybe her parents and the nuns were right: her sexual desire was what always got her into trouble. What sort of a deviant was she?

Not long after her confession she got a phone call from the wife of a member of Truth Seekers who had heard what she'd said. She told Barbara she thought her husband was struggling with sexual feelings toward his biological mother. Hearing directly that this was happening to someone else was an immense comfort: it had happened to someone else, maybe she wasn't crazy. But she was listening to a woman talk about her reunion with her brother at an American Adoption Congress conference when she first heard someone give those same feelings a name. Barbara will never forget how the woman described it: when this woman's brother parked his motorcycle in her driveway, took off his helmet, and shook out his hair, she felt "a pull so innate, so deep down inside, that it felt like it must be some sort of *genetic sexual attraction.*"

This wasn't a pathology unique to her. Barbara told Bob, she told her friends, and she even decided to write a statement about it for an American Adoption Congress newsletter—what good was it to keep it to herself? She wanted to be a cautionary tale, to fight back against the institutions that put her in that position in the first place. She'd encourage openness so that others would not have to go through what she had, and in the process maybe she could claim back the power she lost when she was young.

During Truth Seekers meetings in hospital rooms, parks, event spaces at the Salvation Army, and even in her house she fielded their questions about the messy range of emotions, often sexual, some family members were experiencing when they reunited. Once, at a large national conference, the organizers canceled her GSA seminar to balance their overbooked schedule. Determined not to let anyone down, Barbara announced that interested parties could meet with her in a break room. The floor was packed; some had to stand outside and peer in the door. People might have been reluctant to share their stories, but they wanted to hear hers. She spoke to reporters, self-published a memoir, and never said no when she was contacted by TV networks: she wanted to reach as wide an audience as she could. Later, she even founded a website that eventually became the GSA Forum that is still operating today. And middle-class, articulate Barbara was an especially sympathetic spokeswoman because unlike Jimmy or Shelly she hadn't acted on her feelings.

Barbara didn't have the confidence to tell Mitch face-to-face, so she gave him the article she wrote for the newsletter and watched him as he read it, observing his shock and confusion firsthand. He didn't feel the same. She asked him to go to therapy with her, but he refused to talk about it. He didn't silence her, though. She asked for his permission each time she spoke about her feelings in public, and he always agreed, as long as she didn't use his real name. Reflecting on the experience today, she's clear about the charge of her feelings. When I first visited her, she said, "He didn't know the power he had over me, because if he had said I don't want you to do it, I wouldn't have. But if Bob told me not to, I would have ignored him." She felt as if she had to be there, telling her story, that if she was brave enough to get up and talk about it, then other people would, too. The truth that's hardest to tell should be told the loudest, after all.

"Barbara is a hero," declared Joe Soll, the psychotherapist, over the phone a few months after I visited her. They met on the convention circuit in the 1980s, and while he's one of her biggest fans, he doesn't quite agree with the label she used to describe her confusing desire. "I believe it's genetic attraction," he corrected me, deliberately removing the word "sexual." Not that this was something he'd experienced; by the time he found his own mother she was in a grave in the Bronx. "When a baby is adopted, the natural process of bonding with its mother stops. That bonding that began in the womb, and then it is interrupted, and when they meet later, feelings like sexual feelings emerge, and nobody can make sense of them." I told him I found the punishment, isolation, and ultimate theft she was subjected to when she was just a child the most disturbing aspect of Barbara's narrative. "That would destroy me now and I'm in my thirties," I said and he agreed: "She was brainwashed into giving up her child because of society's fucked-up rules. She's a groundbreaker. To discuss the attraction she had? Talk about brave." Barb wanted to be a cautionary tale, but we can't always control how our narratives are received, or where they end up as they are unhinged from context and circulate across time and space in the hyperconnected era.

As for the feelings themselves, Soll says he understands and doesn't judge, "but what makes me angry is when an adult male takes advantage of his daughter." That's where he draws the line. Barbara had told me she has the most sympathy for women who have relationships with their biological fathers. "You don't know if the dad is really taking advantage of them, or if he's feeling the same thing. And when it ends, the women feel used, really badly used," but she didn't want to ignore the birth parent's emotions. She knows adoptee women who had sexual relationships with their dads and fell so in love with them they couldn't see straight, and then "when it goes pear-shaped they hate them because they feel like they have been used. Even though they probably haven't, the father might be feeling the same way they felt. They lose everything in one hit; it's just tragic." She knew a father-daughter couple who decided they couldn't see each other anymore because the taboo was too much for them to shatter in public. She was heartbroken. "She told me, 'Every time I see pictures of him I break down and cry.' They were crazy about each other, but the guilt was too much. They had to cut each other off and it killed her."

It had been about three years since I met Shelly in person when I saw an Instagram photo of her skipping down a street somewhere with a caption declaring that she'd just got married. I froze. They actually did it. "Why hadn't I told her not to?" I said out loud as if it were my fault. I'd carried a complicated weight of guilt ever since I'd decided to interview Shelly. I was one of the only people from outside the GSA community who knew the true nature of her relationship with Jimmy. Because I'd listened to her without judging—or reporting her to authorities—I felt as if I'd sanctioned her decision to act on her feelings. I also felt as if our interview had put her, albeit anonymously, in the middle of a tornado of media attention she wasn't prepared for and that she'd been exposed in a way that she wasn't equipped to manage. That feeling reached a climax shortly after her mother discovered the column and Shelly emailed me asking if there was any way I could get it removed.

But after zooming in on the pictures, I realized that her

husband wasn't Jimmy. Was it a joke? They were still together when I'd last heard from them a few months earlier. I fired off email, Facebook, and Instagram messages to find out what was going on. Shelly replied quickly with the news that they'd broken up. "It was toxic," she wrote. "I realized what a relationship is supposed to be like."

When I read that message, I was relieved. I even had a fantasy that this was the ultimate story of female triumph, imagining that she'd kicked him to the curb and taken ownership of their relationship by insisting he be her father and nothing else. I was hopeful that she'd found happiness with someone else. But I knew this wasn't the sort of story that could be wrapped up in a happy ending. I also knew that there was only so much I could tell from a distance. I had to see her.

She was open to a visit, but she'd relocated to a remote part of the country, kept moving, and was hard to pin down. Sometimes she'd reply to my emails or messages on social media, but never more than a few lines to say she was doing well. I'd check her Instagram account, glad to know she was still out there somewhere when I saw her occasionally post a selfie, usually modeling a new hairstyle or eyeliner, smiling at the camera.

Then we fell out of touch. Occasionally she'd reply to my emails; once she said that she keeps changing her phone number. When she contacted me out of the blue, by text, in summer a year later saying she had a new boyfriend whom she'd love me to meet, I was confused (what happened to her husband?) but excited to see her, whomever she was with. After a few months of negotiating, we both arranged to travel to her hometown, where we met on a fall Saturday night.

I emerged from the elevator to meet Shelly, who was with an older, well-dressed man in glasses and a button-down. She'd lost about a hundred pounds and cut her hair into a mature pixie cut. She wasn't wearing any makeup and was dressed casually in jeans, worn-down shearling slippers, and a tank top. "I know, I look like I've turned basic," she joked. "The other day I was wearing a cardigan and holding a Starbucks, and I caught a glimpse of myself and thought I'd turned into Britney Spears." She introduced me to Sam, whom she'd started dating earlier that year. "I'm so awkward," she said when we got to her hotel room, dumping her bags on the floor, while Sam slipped off his shoes and calmly positioned himself on the bed in his socks and started scrolling through his phone. After a few minutes negotiating what we should do, she reminded me of her social anxiety. "I'm a homebody," she said, so I settled down and tentatively asked about Jimmy.

"I've burned that chapter in my book. I never want to read it again. Nothing you knew then, I am now," she started, and I listened quietly, as usual, resisting giving my opinion while she told me all their problems. The secrecy and double life were draining. The tension with her mom was unmanageable; while she had agreed to turn a blind eye, she was tolerating their relationship, not accepting it. But it was when Shelly got close to another man that it all snapped into focus. Things turned sexual, and she realized a key difference between the way she felt about him and the way she felt about Jimmy. She now knew that her feelings had been confused. "I loved him as a lover, and Jimmy as my dad."

She was now very clear about the way that Jimmy had abused his power. "It's sad and scary how in denial I was . . . Deep down, I think I knew it was wrong the whole time, but he convinced me it was okay. He told me to consent," she said, referring to the four years they spent living together in a sexual relationship. "He manipulated and groomed me until he got what he wanted . . . I've had to tell myself over and over again that I have no blame in it. I still have a hard time saying I have no blame because I consented, but I literally didn't have any power. All my paychecks went into a bank account that he was in charge of."

She'd made a list of everything he'd taken from her, or would have taken from her if she'd continued that life with him she once hoped could be normal: "He wanted to take away my right to have kids. My right to get married. My ability to drive"— she'd wanted to learn, but he refused to teach her. "He took away my mother. He took my siblings—my kids."

What about those advocates who gather on websites and in forums trying to normalize consenting sexual relationships between close family members? She's sickened by them. That community dangerously normalized the abuse that Jimmy subjected her to. "The activism is bullshit," she said. "This is not the same as being gay, or whatever it is they try to say. I understand why they don't get given any rights! It's like, hang on now, we have to have morals. We can't all be fucking our families! We have to have morals."

She's customized a cliché to describe her prior outlook on life, where her optimism and denial were a shield. "I used to look at the world through kaleidoscope glasses, and those glasses made bad things seem okay," she said. When she got clarity about her feelings toward Jimmy, she took the glasses off and replaced them with a set of "realist glasses." "They see black and white and gray," she joked, reminding me of her sense of humor and underutilized intelligence. When her vision returned to normal, she did something she always swore she wouldn't: she called her mother and said, "You were right."

I asked her the question that had weighed on me since our interview was published: "Do you think talking to me normalized it for you, or that I somehow made you feel like it was okay?" She said that back then, when we "connected," she was desperate to talk out loud about what was happening. She wanted to express herself to someone who wouldn't be turned off by the visceral nature of her situation, someone who understood her emotional state but was objective, someone who wouldn't simply judge and turn away. I felt emboldened to finally tell Shelly how I felt. I explained I had always thought that even though she didn't grow up with Jimmy, he was her biological father and he'd grossly abused his power when he acted on his desire. Because I knew how difficult her life was, maybe there was a small part of me that wanted to believe things with Jimmy could be all right. Perhaps I was wearing those kaleidoscope glasses when I was learning about her experience; maybe I'd spent so much time in those forums and chat rooms and hearing from people like Barbara who were going through or had experienced GSA that it had been normalized for me, too.

It was when she saw how the world, and her mom, responded that she felt those kaleidoscope glasses falling off. It was as if she needed to observe her experience through someone else's eyes to be able to admit to herself that it was wrong. Likewise, when our interview went viral and I saw the extent of other people's horror, the gravity of the situation she was in became real to me. I was writing down everything she said. Shelly turned to Sam and said, "She fuels my ego," then to me, "But really, sometimes you'd message me just wanting to know if I was okay and asking how I was, and there was literally nobody else in the world who ever asked me that."

The next day we went to get lunch. On the way we walked down the same street we drove down with Jimmy all those years ago. Sam and I waited while Shelly stopped at each of her favorite haunts—petting cats in the pet shop, filling a bag with sour gummies at a candy store—before we ended up at a table outside at the same diner we went to together when we first met, which had been gentrified with a cocktail list and subway benches. We ordered mimosas in sippy cups, and I snickered when I saw Shelly steal the communal bottle of Cholula and tuck it in her bag.

We talked about the future. She still hasn't swum in the ocean or traveled on a plane; Sam promised that a flight to the seaside was on the list for 2020. However, she has finally slept in a house alone. Sam's been encouraging her to spend more time with her mother, and she has plans to become a correctional officer. "I want to help people," she said. She still dreams of a normal life. She loves children and wants to fill a house with them, saying she'll soon start trying to get pregnant, shaking her head at the memory of those anonymous voices in those forums and blogs that said having a baby with her father would be only slightly risky. They spent the summer traveling around the Midwest, camping, and she loved Michigan. Maybe they'll settle down in a cabin by the lake? Somewhere tranquil away from Jimmy and the pressures of the city and people and anyone who knows about her past.

"You look just like Madonna, so beautiful!" said Bob as he pulled Barbara into a tight hug. The TV screen was lit up with a 1990s-glam version of his wife wearing polyester and metallic makeup. She'd dug out the meticulously labeled VHS archive of her various appearances on television, and we'd been taking a tour of her talk-show fame: *Oprah*, 1987; *60 Minutes*, 1991; *Jerry Springer*, 1992; *Maury Povich* and *Montel Williams*, 1993. Bob used a brick-size remote to zoom through the faded commercials for home-security systems and TV dinners. On *The Jerry Springer Show*, Barbara participated in a sober discussion of the pitfalls of closed adoption. She has a flair for storytelling, as if she's been professionally coached. Once she'd gained the host and audience's sympathy, her narrative took a turn. "The minute he walked into the room I was a sixteen-year-old vamp. I thought I was dating his father again . . . It's a real egotistical, narcissistic type of thing like where you look at a male mirror of yourself." Then, on TV in front of a live studio audience, she calmly shattered one of the world's most established taboos.

Bob continued fast forwarding through the tape. On another

show a concerned psychiatrist offered her take on Barbara's strange attraction. She shook her head and twisted her lips, explaining that this is a unique pathology that's not well understood, ignoring Barbara's key message: this is the result of a botched social experiment that tried to ensure normality. Bob shuffled in his seat, irritated, reliving the frustration he experienced when the world didn't understand his wife's unusual situation. "Barb just wanted to educate people that this happens. Doctors don't know the reason she felt this way; it wasn't in the books," he yelled to the room. "How could she understand?" Barbara exclaimed. "I wouldn't understand either. People hear my story and they imagine their children, or their mother, but it's not the same." Bob snapped off the TV and told us it was time for lunch; he'd made chicken soup and salad with tomatoes from the yard. "I can't watch this anymore," he said, padding in his slippers into the kitchen.

Over lunch the pair traded stories about her TV days. One crew took her out to a fancy restaurant, another interviewed her in a downtown penthouse hotel suite, a lovely woman traveled all the way from England, her team set up camp at the house for a day in deep winter; Barbara beamed when she recalled the event. Bob was grumpy because they trudged in and out all day carrying lights and cables, letting the heat escape. Still, he was honored that they had flown across the Atlantic to hear his wife's story, and he snuck out to buy authentic Chicago beef sandwiches to say thank you.

Jerry Springer was the best, they both agreed, pointing out that this was before his show turned into a freak show with "everyone throwing furniture at each other." "Oh! He was so smart. He asked thoughtful questions; he wasn't disgusted by it. He took the time to understand; boy, was he sensitive," reflected Bob. What was Oprah like? I asked. "I think she was shocked— most of them were either disgusted or shocked," said Barbara, explaining that a lot of them were only interested in a prurient story and urged her to describe her sexual thoughts in salacious detail. "What did they expect me to say? I wanna throw him on the floor, take off all his clothes, and put a diaper on him?"

When it was time to go, Barbara insisted on driving me to the train station. She was still wading through memories about her time in the spotlight. "You know I think those were the best days of my life," she said, pumped up, having spent the day reliving the past. Like Shelly, telling her story gave her power. She'd recently reread her self-published memoir for the first time in decades. She was developing a close relationship with a new pastor at her church, a young forward-thinking African American woman. In a moment of heightened boldness, Barbara gave her one of the only two copies she had of her memoir, then rushed home to read it anew through this woman's eyes.

Barbara decided to share her story with the pastor after hearing her give a sermon about the meaning of life; she'd been so moved by the words of this powerful woman who'd shattered so many boundaries to get where she was. The pastor spoke about living in a world with seemingly infinite choices and options: travel, the high speed of everything, careers, the globe-spanning Library of Alexandria that is the internet, the granting of basic human and civil rights that people had been fighting to gain for years. The pastor said it can be overwhelming, but everyone exists for a reason, and if you are lucky, very lucky, you will discover your purpose. She cast her gaze around the church and assured each and every person in the pews that they had one. Barbara looked forward, the headlights illuminating the road ahead, repeating the same words she'd used on Jerry Springer's show. "I thought I was crazy. I thought I was the only one who this had ever happened to. I thought I was totally nuts," she said. "But when that woman spoke, I realized that I've served my purpose in life, because I was born to tell this story."

I thought about what Barbara's bravery had achieved. On the one hand, taking charge of her narrative and fearlessly telling the world what happened to her was a way for her to reclaim the power that had been taken from her in her youth. Her openness surely had a positive effect by raising awareness about what can happen when biological relatives reunite, giving language to the feelings she thought were unique to her and emboldening some people struggling with those same feelings to seek help. Additionally, she was privy to a lot of human support IRL. But at the same time, by talking about it so openly and making it relatable, she'd normalized it, especially when her experience was taken out of context as it became a distant whisper of a sound bite in some online forums and chat rooms in the hyperconnected era. Her message might have been diluted when she appeared on sensational talk shows, but it was fleshed out enough for viewers to know that she did not act on her feelings and those feelings were the result of an almost pathological urge to uphold social norms.

# 5

# Paul

When Fran met Paul, she'd never used a computer before. Back then he was just a stranger who'd met her roommate on the "internet," which as far as she was concerned was a strange network on a mysterious machine that connected people somehow. It was January 1996, and Paul had a brief layover in the South before his flight home to Canada. Direct and sensible Fran was drawn to Paul's politeness, manners, and the fact that he didn't see a woman and immediately want sex. Paul, who had never had a girlfriend, thought Fran was polite and hospitable, and he found the effort she put into making a stranger feel comfortable very attractive. Over dinner they had a heated debate about veganism. Fran accused Paul of pushing his agenda, and Paul noted that this woman who had only a high school education was incredibly intelligent. She asked measured questions, drew connections, and listened thoughtfully to his opinions. He was there for a few days, but he didn't make a move until he was just about to leave, when he leaned in to kiss his new friend on her head. Today he reflects on meeting Fran, who'd had a difficult childhood: "I sensed that she was vulnerable, and I tend to be drawn to those who need help." On the flight back home he was so buzzed he turned to his seatmate and said, "I think I just met my future wife."

He paid for Fran to come visit him in Canada, and at the end of the week they were engaged. An early tech adopter, Paul was used to chatting on his chunky cell phone, so the plan was to stay in touch like that while Fran packed up her life, but when he got a three-hundred-dollar phone bill, he bought a computer and shipped it off to his long-distance lover. As soon as she received the package, she had to make a few more expensive international calls so she could ask him how the hell to turn it on.

Paul had told her he'd be sending her something to help them keep in touch, and she figured she'd use the computer like her mom's cast-iron typewriter: to write notes and send them through the mail. "I didn't realize we'd be sending *internet* letters," she says. They spent weeks sending those "internet letters" back and forth, usually three times a day. Both love data and facts, and after four months communicating that way, they calculated the virtual time they'd spent together: the grand total was 120 hours—nearly two weeks' worth of 9-hour working days. Their wedding was small and cost about as much as that first phone bill. Paul baked treats for the reception. Fran's mom took the photos, and the guest list was restricted to family and a few very close friends.

Marriage license in hand, belongings in a U-Haul, the couple crossed the Canadian border on New Year's Day in 1997. Later, during Fran's citizenship interview, government officials questioned the pair about some of the more unorthodox touches to their wedding: "Where's all your family? Why aren't you wearing white?" Fran's not one for organized religion (after heated debate, the pair agree she's an "agnostic pagan"), but her Catholic mother is, so Fran wore green because she'd been married once before. When Paul's father found out he was marrying a woman, all he felt was excitement. As Paul says, "I suspect he always thought I was gay."

Fran had spent most of her youth in a small southern town, so leaving the United States was a big step, and they spent their first few months north of the border moving around, trying to find a place to live where they both felt comfortable. After a few years living in the suburbs they settled in a small rural community where the industry is largely manufacturing and the households mostly two-parent families. Both feel most at peace away from the noise and human traffic of the city. They enjoy sunsets, grilling in the yard, and snuggling by a fire.

They agreed from the outset that their marriage would be open, with a disclosure and veto policy. If either party wants to engage in extramarital sexual activity, it must be reported and approved. When it came to kids, they were on the same page: neither had any interest in bringing new life into the world. They took out a mortgage, bought a house with a yard, and filled it with dogs and cats and chickens instead.

A few months after arriving in Canada, Fran decided to take some college classes. She toyed with the idea of art but ended up getting a bachelor's degree in electronics, engineering, and math. Paul patiently mentored her through those less than pleasant times. "I don't do well when I don't understand things . . . I get angry," she says. On more than one occasion she would yell at him, and he would just quietly walk away. When she graduated, she got a well-paid job, but she became sick of spending her lunch hour waiting outside the "titty bar" while her "drunk ass bastard co-workers stuffed money in women's twats," so she left. Paul's managerial job pays enough to cover the mortgage and ensure that they have a comfortable life.

At work, and among most of his IRL friends, Paul keeps his sexuality secret. He can't talk openly about most of his desires or tell anyone his true sexual identity. But he has two dreams. One is that when he retires, he can afford a house in the country on a plot with lots of acres. The other is to start a nonprofit group advocating for the voiceless—especially teens and kids. It will disseminate health, safety, and legal advice and offer support and community, resources and education. While it will be based in Canada, its online storefront will serve people across the world who are coming to terms with what he describes as their ridiculed, ignored, and misunderstood sexual desire.

In the fall of 2014, I was lurking on Reddit, researching ideas for "What It's Like," trying to find someone who identified as a zoosexual. That's right, someone whose sexual identity is based upon their sexual and romantic attraction to animals. Why was I doing that? It might be hard to believe, but at first it was sheer curiosity and an intellectual challenge. It was still the early days of the series, but I had been on a roll learning about very unfamiliar experiences. Interspecies sex is something so foreign, something that provokes such a visceral disgust that most of us don't want to even let our minds go there, and I wondered if there really were functioning members of society who have acted on such a seemingly deviant form of desire, and if there were, what was it like to be that way? Had the internet helped them find themselves and each other, allowed them to connect and know who they are? When I pitched the idea, I didn't expect it to be approved, but it was, so I set off on a hunt to see what I could find.

My initial online search for "bestiality" revealed a very inaccessible world mostly focused on sex acts and definitions. It was only when I got to Reddit's zoosexuality sub that the sorts of desires that were largely known to me in the abstract became humanized. I was surprised to find sexual relationships with animals being discussed by real people with a serious urgency.

A few years later I revisited an archive of that subreddit to remind myself of the themes that had first captured my interest. People wrote emotional posts about their love for, and dependency on, their animal partners. For example, one man mused about his canine companion: "I'm emotionally dependent on her and I don't know if I'll handle her dying . . . I feel completely hollow whenever I'm not with her . . . I feel uncomfortable around my parents because they're devout Catholics and they keep asking about when I'll have children or find a wife and are always disappointed when I tell them that I'm not looking for one."[1] There were pleas for connections with those who shared not only the same sexuality but also the same demographics or political interests, like female zoosexuals or zoosexuals living in certain geographic locations. There was even someone seeking fellow "feminist social justice" zoos.[2]

Redditors talked about language and labels. For example, in one thread there was a discussion about the use of the term "zoophile" versus "zoosexual" to describe the orientation. As an anonymous poster put it, "To me, zoosexual doesn't quite address the affectionate/romantic aspect of zoophilia, so it feels a little more lusty and closer to just straight bestiality."[3] There were debates about the enduring unacceptance of zoophilia as a sexuality. "Should we fight, or should we hide?" asked a redditor in a thread where zoos shared their reasons for staying hidden. "I feel it just isn't time for us yet. We don't have enough scientific research to back us up . . . Maybe it won't even be in our lifetime . . . we'll fight . . . for now, it's better to hide."[4]

In fact many posters discussed the benefits of hiding versus trying to live in the open. In one thread a young man coming to terms with his desires sought the advice of older community members who had many years' experience negotiating life in the shadows: "It's hard knowing that who you are as a person and who you truly are inside is something that will never be accepted, and that you will have to hide for the rest of your life.

Having to live that false life and hiding your true self from everyone that you know, it takes an emotional toll . . . how do you get through it? What keeps you positive? What do you do that helps you truly accept who you are?"[5] In response, someone advised him to consider his zoosexuality as just another thing that buffets against society's view of the ideal person, and he finds that "society's view of the ideal person is actually quite offensive."[6] Another went into more depth: "I'm a very extroverted person, so having society tell me that I am a fucked up monster is very disheartening. But when I am with my mate, and I know what I am doing, and when others can see the close bond between us, then that makes me feel good and keep my head up."[7] I read stories about the repercussions of telling family, partners, close friends, and therapists: "No one needs to know what I do in private. But, I do let nearly anyone know that I am a zoo if they question my ZETA tattoo that is on my arm or if they want to insert themselves into my social circle. I made a promise to myself a long time ago that I would never call anyone my friend who couldn't accept every part of me."[8] The tone was thoughtful, supportive, and engaged.

My head was swirling. "What is the legality of it, anyway?" I wondered, running some more comprehensive internet searches. I discovered that for years in this country bestiality fell under the problematic umbrella of "crimes against nature" laws, which included consensual sexual acts between adults once labeled illegal (like sodomy), but when these laws were repealed in most states, bestiality was decriminalized, too. These days animal cruelty laws are used to punish those who transgress. I learned that while there's no federal law banning it, sex with animals is technically illegal in most parts of the country, with the exception of some states—including New Mexico, Wyoming, and West Virginia—and the District of Columbia. The social stigma and ethics and morality of the act are other barriers to acceptance.[9]

The main critique of bestiality is that it's impossible for animals to give consent, so the act is inherently abusive. But also, why would you want to have sex with an animal that can't talk to you? Isn't there a power dynamic that's impossible to overthrow?

I went back to that subreddit and searched for conversations about consent. The subject came up often and sparked impassioned debate. For a start, zoos discussed the nuances of nonverbal consent—indicated by "enthusiastic participation"—physical cues that animals use to let humans know if they are comfortable or not, if they are willing participants. How does an animal consent? I kept an open mind and read the view of zoos in detail: by indicating interest; being forward in their body language—inquisitive, investigative, exploring—submitting willingly without restraint; giving physical signs of pleasure. Later a zoophile used canine body language to illustrate his point: "the difference between do you want the ball and do you want a bath." I read about "fence hopping," the practice of initiating sexual contact with someone else's animal. This is frowned upon by most zoos because it shows a lack of respect for the owner, and people who don't have enough respect for the owner won't have much respect for the animal. Furthermore, if you don't know an animal intimately, you are less likely to know how to ask that animal for permission.

In conversations about consent, zoos often pointed out the hypocrisy of the non-zoo insistence that animals can't consent and that the inability of animals to consent is the main thing that makes zoosexuality amoral. In one conversation on that archived subreddit a zoo parodies a critic: " 'Consent is the most important thing.' \*next breath\* 'Look at this new trick I taught my dog! How're you enjoying your steak? Oh, and remind me to take my cat to get fixed tomorrow.' "[10] When someone asked, "I wonder why society thinks it is okay for people to pet animals and to keep animals as pets without the explicit consent of the animals but the act of a human having sex with an animal is considered not okay?"[11] the replies came hard and fast: "pure hypocrisy";[12] "pure bigotry";[13] "because keeping animals as pets enforces our superior status over them in a cultural sense, but having sex with them at least in part acknowledges them as equals, which is uncomfortable. Also, sexual activities which people don't understand are automatically labelled as deviant, and therefore terrible";[14] "because society is morally bankrupt and ethically inconsistent."[15]

Admittedly, at the outset, I assumed I'd quickly become sufficiently disgusted by an online community populated by people who love and have sex with animals and that I'd let it go. But instead I was compelled by the themes that framed these redditors' narratives, having to do with identity, community, acceptance, and shame. Many were completely terrified of being caught. Conversations about their desires were coded and laced with paranoia, the hallmark of a demonized sexuality. And after a week or so immersed in the online zoosexual universe, I was questioning everything.

How far is too far? If nobody or nothing is being hurt, why do we care who or *what* someone has sex with? When should we police another person's sexual desire? If animals are part of our everyday culture now, where do we draw the line? It also struck me that for many of the zoosexuals who gathered on Reddit, the internet was fundamental to expressing and eventually enacting their sexuality; it was where they found community, language, and terms for who they are and connected with others, whom they formed friendships with and even met IRL. As with genetic sexual attraction, I was skeptical of the usefulness of normalizing this taboo desire.

At the outset zoophilia bothered me more than GSA, and I think that's because I was clear in my position about GSA: I have empathy for those experiencing it, but I don't think it should be treated as a unique sexual orientation, and I don't think it should ever be normalized. My feelings about zoophilia were much more complicated. I know that consent is hard to establish with an animal because they can't communicate verbally, but it wasn't exactly consent that troubled me, because like those redditors I find our attitude toward animal consent to be very contradictory—meaning that I agree with those who point out that we don't ask animals to give us verbal consent for anything we do to them. What made me the most uncomfortable about zoophilia was how conflicted it made me feel once I learned that there were people who had embraced this way of being, living in secret with shame and fear defining their sexuality, and that was largely projected from a society that had probably never really considered what it was like to be them.

I messaged a few posters directly, saying I was a columnist for *New York* magazine's *Science of Us* looking for people to talk to me openly and honestly about zoophilia, and I quickly heard back from a regular and enthusiastic redditor named Paul—a Canadian man in his forties who was a zoosexual in a loving relationship with a horse. He worked full time in a professional field, had been happily married to an American woman for about twenty years, and also had a "mare friend." Unlike many people I contacted, who were reluctant to step out from behind the veil of the screen, he was interested in talking on the phone, as he put it: "I feel that you need to know you are talking to a real, normal person."

When I first asked Paul if he has any theories about his desire, he made me feel like a hypocrite for claiming to be accepting of sexual difference, as if I were unfairly and preemptively moralizing or pathologizing him. "What I'm attracted to is about as normal as anyone else, and I've never needed a theory to explain why I'm normal. Say things about your spouse and/or boyfriend, and I'd agree that you can say most if not all of those things about an equine companion," he said. He insisted that he was happy with his identity; he just wishes it wasn't universally regarded as disgusting.

He stressed that if anyone found out who he was, there would be dire consequences. There was the social stigma, which would surely ruin his life, but he also had something tangible to lose: a twelve-year-old mare named Ms. C. who, he explained, could be taken from him and killed under animal cruelty laws if the truth about their relationship ever came out. The more I got to know Paul, the more I learned just how serious that fear of being caught is: Ms. C. is one of the main reasons he has for not giving up on life.

I knew that this was an especially taboo identity to explore, and I knew that it was not something people were prepared to indulge with any sort of empathy, but I got to know Paul and was shocked to find my preconceptions thoroughly challenged. I went on to communicate more with Paul, and eventually meet him, his wife, and Ms. C. IRL, and I found myself getting a taste of the isolation that zoophiles live with. It was as if I were guilty by association. Ultimately, the story of how he carved out his identity online and found peace while living in this unorthodox way made me thoroughly question the limits of what I was willing to accept as normal.

In the mid-1990s a young female psychotherapist named Hani Miletski saw a patient who couldn't stop having sex with dogs. The churchgoing man believed that sex should only happen between married heterosexual humans, so he was utterly shocked by his own behavior that breached the bounds of what he knew was moral. Miletski was at a loss; she couldn't locate the acts or feelings he was describing in the literature.[16] When she asked a librarian to dig deeper, her only finding was a tragic creative-nonfiction memoir published in 1994 by a man called Mark Matthews about his lifelong emotional and sexual connection with horses. Matthews distinguished between sex acts and identity—between those who have sex with animals as an outlet when they lack more "normal" choices and those who form deep, emotional connections with their animal partners.[17]

She decided to devote her PhD dissertation to the topic. It's one of only a few comprehensive accounts of sex with animals as an *identity*, and in it she writes about how the subject of her research collided with the beliefs of her colleagues and friends. Her boyfriend was so disgusted he didn't want to talk about it. Each time a research participant returned a questionnaire, she was full of excitement, but she couldn't share it with him, because he was so repulsed.[18] Her medical practitioner colleagues weren't any more open-minded. They attacked her choice, concerned it would damage her career and put off future clients. When I talked to her on the phone, she said that when she put a call for participants on a notice board at a conference for the Society for the Scientific Study of Sexuality, one of the organizers tore it down. She persisted, despite the stigma, and ended up with a sample group of eighty-two men and eleven women who answered long questionnaires that, with the exception of a time she met a group of zoophiles in a chat room on someone else's computer, were all distributed by mail.[19] If someone wanted to participate, they had to call and talk to her on the phone and give her their mailing address. After she'd gained their trust, she even met with about fifty zoophiles at a gathering in an unnamed rural location. She says she had no fears about meeting the men and women whom she'd learned so much about from their in-depth questionnaire responses, and in fact *she* was flattered that *they* trusted her enough to want her there.

Today Miletski is well known in the zoosexual "community"; she validated their identity as something worthy of academic inquiry. She clearly laid out the difference between a bestialist and a zoosexual: bestiality refers to the act, while zoophilia is the identity. The concerns expressed by the zoosexuals she spoke with more than twenty years ago could have been cut and pasted from Reddit. "They were terrified of being outed or caught, but elated about the advancement of the Internet which allowed them to form a supportive community and realize they were not alone. They discussed the issue of animal consent . . . They related their experiences at the hands of psychotherapists, and described the worst thing about being zoos—having to out-live their sex partners," she wrote in her dissertation, which became the basis of a book that can now be downloaded online.[20]

In her modern history of sex between animals and humans, the University of London professor Joanna Bourke notes that Mark Matthews's book and appearances in the media drew academic attention to zoophilia. Unlike previous researchers who based their studies on people incarcerated in prisons or psychiatric institutions, this new group of academics got to know zoophiles whom they were able to find using the internet, and "to their own surprise many of these researchers found themselves in sympathy with the people they met."[21] The zoophiles in this wave of research, which consisted of a handful of studies, used the language of sexual rights activism to argue that their sexuality is not a deviancy but an orientation.[22] And as Bourke points out, while the personal characteristics of zoosexuals varied within this research (ranging in age from nineteen to seventy-eight with half having graduated from college), they all showed a cohort with high levels of "desolation, guilt, anxiety and depression."[23]

In 2014, a young zoosexual conducted research similar to Miletski's.[24] When he was in his early teens and coming to terms with his feelings, he found that hard data, which legitimated his identity, helped him accept himself more than personal narratives like Mark Matthews's did. He looked around for some but, with the exception of Kinsey's estimations that 8 percent of men and 3.6 percent of women have had sex with an animal (among rural men the rate was much higher, though, at 40–50 percent), didn't find much.[25] He decided to use the anonymous connective power of the internet to generate his own statistics and designed a survey that he linked to on his blog. Of the 414 respondents, more than half describe their zoophilia as a sexual orientation, and when asked their preferred way of identifying themselves, about 80 percent selected zoophile or zoosexual (bestialist and pansexual were among the others), and nearly 80 percent said they are not zoo exclusive.[26]

The survey delves into all aspects of zoosexual self-identification, asking respondents if they are romantically attracted to animals (60 percent say yes), their preferred sex of the animal for romantic and sexual attraction (when it comes to romance, it's a fifty-fifty male-female split), preferred label (53 percent say zoophile, and 25 percent opt for zoosexual), and their position on zoophile rights (79 percent say they want, and support, zoophile rights). The majority of respondents report discovering their attraction to animals in adolescence, live in the United States, are male, and are aged between eighteen and twenty-five. A bar graph shows the array of species that respondents desire, and when it comes to romance, dogs and horses top the list, but the objects of zoophiles' affections are a virtual Noah's ark, ranging from crocodiles to bears. Most had only ever acted out their desires with members from the cat, horse, or dog family.[27]

When I first started talking to Paul, my perception of people who do "that" with animals was mostly informed by shocking news stories about those who are either criminal or very hard to relate to. I imagined him as a sort of ominous figure in a long dark coat who was emailing me from a laptop he'd set up in a trailer or a barn. When zoophiles make the news, they're usually criminal. The tech entrepreneur Douglas Spink was sent to prison on a probation violation after his farm was raided by police who found animals they alleged had been tortured and abused.[28] The open zoosexual Malcolm Brenner, who claims to have a telepathic connection with animals, self-published a book about a dolphin he says initiated sex with him in Sarasota in the 1970s.[29] Then there's Kenneth Pinyan, also known as "Mr. Hands," a Boeing engineer who died in 2005 after he was injured by a stallion during a sex act that was videotaped and later went viral online. In an episode of Comedy Central's *Broad City*, Ilana Wexler is fired after she accidentally uploads the disturbing footage to her work's social media page.[30] When Mark Matthews and his horse-wife, Pixel, appeared on Jerry Springer's show in 1998, some US stations decided that it was more than viewers could handle, and played a rerun of a different episode instead.[31] In the censored episode, Springer doesn't mince his words when he says that it makes him want to vomit.

Paul told me that he doesn't relate to those people covered by the media. He thinks that the idea of interspecies marriage is silly and that those who believe they can talk with animals are delusional. He's not a fan of imposing a human model onto zoosexual relationships: "I'm never going to be in a situation where I'm locked out of the hospital room because my partner's dying and I'm not recognized as an immediate family member. There's no reason for animal-human marriage. I'm against it." And he doesn't claim to be able to read animals' minds: "I think people lie to themselves a lot. Which is why I never say my horse companion loves me. The truth is, I don't know what she thinks."

He carefully vetted me before committing to talking on the phone. I sent him some of my work so he could get a sense of the shape our interview would take. He read my stories, and I investigated his online activity, digging deep into his history on

Reddit, where I saw that he often gave advice to young people who had gone online to make sense of feelings or acts they would never talk about out loud. I saw he comforted a young woman who'd turned to Reddit for help with the confusion she felt after having sex with her dog. Should she tell her boyfriend? What did it mean she was? I read Paul's advice, and somehow the shocking act slipped into the background. He identified himself as a zoosexual who has been married for two decades and urged her to talk to her partner. "Either they accept it and move on, or they don't and you split up," he wrote. He begged her not to fall victim to guilt, an emotion, he says, "so pervasive yet so insidious when you live in this North American society . . . that it will kill you, slowly." Her desires are taboo, yes, he agreed, and even therapists and psychiatrists won't understand. He warned her to avoid shoddy mental health practitioners who "often do not have the training to separate their morals from your problems," and urged her to fight, rather than take flight: "Do not follow the path of least resistance here, fight for what you need and accept that it makes you different." He assured this stranger that she's still lovable and has the support of a community of proud zoos, even if their arms must remain virtual: "If you were here I would give you a great big platonic hug and tell you *welcome to a wonderful life*."[32]

Paul decided the risk of outing himself was worth it. Before he scheduled our first phone call, he had one condition: I had to give him a recording of our conversation as a sort of insurance that I would accurately represent what we talked about. He felt as though something had to be said to correct what he perceived to be the unfair demonization of his very taboo sexual identity. When we were negotiating the terms of engagement, he stressed the isolation he experienced growing up. His desire to communicate directly to "zoo-questioning" teens has remained throughout the many years I've known him. As he said during our first conversation, "It's something that makes people feel confused and alone, and they have no idea what to think about what they are, and they can't talk to anybody . . . I've heard stories of people getting shock or aversion therapy . . . I really don't understand the hatred . . . I don't understand what it is that makes people so angry. Rather than actually engage with us, people would prefer to ignore us."[33] And as he put it in the very first email he wrote to me, "I'm not the monster they assume . . . I'm just a normal person."

Paul was seven years old the first time he saw a horse in real life. The city kid was living in the suburbs when a carnival set up across the street from his house. He was fascinated when he peered out his bedroom window watching men harness the little animals to a mechanical walker before they began their sluggish waltz. He spent a few days fixated on those leggy creatures, their sleek side-parted manes hanging over their deep wet eyes, with oversize baby hooves. He'd watch them each day, heads bowed, weighed down by delighted Canadian kids. Paul launched a successful campaign to get his parents to let him go for a ride, but once he was in the saddle, he started to sob and continued weeping while the pony led him on a circular tearstained journey. As an adult, Paul wonders if he sensed the pain of those defeated work ponies. "I think I was bothered by how awful the situation was for them. All they did was go 'round and 'round. I could sense something about that in their attitude," he says.[34]

One year his parents gave him an illustrated encyclopedia of horses as a birthday present. He eagerly pawed through the pages, where he read about different breeds, their history and care, but he found himself particularly mesmerized by the photos. Until then, Paul insists his sexual development had been typical of any Catholic boy growing up in the late 1970s/early 1980s in North America. When he was about six, he played the usual "show-me-yours-and-I'll-show-you-mine kinda game" with a neighborhood friend. He had his first "sex talk" at school, but it was mostly about puberty. In junior high an uncomfortable male vice-principal addressed the room of preteen boys, encouraging them to ask questions. Paul remained silent throughout the talk, which focused on reproduction, the Catholic leader dancing around any mention of the penis or vagina.

When he went through puberty, Paul started to see those leggy creatures in a "different" way. While his classmates were busy smuggling their fathers' *Playboy* magazines into their bedrooms, Paul was much more interested in that book of horses. He knew that touching yourself "down there" was something you did in private, so at night he would explore. The pages became puffy from use, but Paul didn't consider that there was anything particularly "wrong" with his fantasies. "I didn't think to hide; I didn't think I was different or unusual. I felt like my sexual development was the same as everyone else's; I just had a different affection," he says. And that affection was strong. The first time I asked Paul exactly what it was that he liked about horses then, and what he's drawn to now, he laughed at what he thought was a naive assumption that he could dissect his object of desire into body parts, like "Yo! I'm an ass man, Alexa!" There's no one "thing" he has to have in a horse, he said, before riffing on their awesome beauty, "from the hock and the hoof to the nostrils and the thighs and the neck and the way the neck curves and the muscles along the flank."[35]

Paul excelled at school. In junior high he was made teachers' aide, so when the principal invested in about thirty cash-register-looking Apple IIs, he thought of the intellectually bored twelve-year-old and asked if he could help make the school's first computer lab. Paul had been using computers at home since he was about eight. His house didn't have a dedicated study, so his father ripped off the doors of the hallway closet and threw in a desk and chair. After a few years, Paul's technical skills got so good that if he had the hardware, he could build a computer from scratch.

Paul wasn't just sitting alone using those chunky keys to play *Ultima III* or type out school projects. He was using the machine to explore his sexual interest in horses. His online interactions are a microhistory of social networking. He got into bulletin boards, the precursor to chat rooms with file sharing, and then moved on to Usenet, where he found thousands of forums including many devoted to having sex with animals. People were even sharing pictures and videos: the first sexual image he ever saw was a sixteen-color GIF, probably ten frames a second, of a farm girl touching a male horse.

That material made him feel "abnormal," but not because of what he saw; instead, he says it was the judgment of others that told him who he was. Accompanying many of these pictures were comments, often in all caps, expressing shock, disgust, and horror. He read through the grumblings of those early trolls and began to realize that perhaps his desires weren't acceptable even in the private world of pixels and screens. At school, Paul ignored his anxiety as he participated in the yearbook committee. He pushed down his pain as he climbed ladders to rig the stage with microphones and set up the spotlight for the romantic leads in adolescent productions of *Oklahoma!* It wasn't that he was anxious about fitting in with his peers, more that he felt if anyone got too close, they might learn the truth about his "disgusting" desires. He restricted school-time socializing to surface level, watching the other boys who failed to play sports get spat at with words like "fag" and "queer" and learning through observation that if you're different, being open about yourself isn't always the best idea. If you were one of his classmates, you might have described him as "emotionally unavailable"; he was pleasant, but he didn't let anyone get too close. He was so open over email and on bulletin boards that he was never able to reconcile being secretive elsewhere.

He longed to gain access to the horse world and came up with the idea of having riding lessons. He'd get to be around horses, so that was guaranteed joy, but maybe he'd also get to meet other kids who were ignited with the same energy he was when he was thinking and talking about horses. During his first session he looked around at the ten or so girls, who'd been in the class much longer than he had, and realized he was the only boy there. He was shy, insecure about his physicality, and uncomfortable trying new things. The awkwardness of the situation was crowned when the teacher handed him a slim girl's helmet. Before mounting his pony, he quietly pressed the feminine headgear onto his head, grinning through the tight fit. In retrospect he thinks it was probably because he was a boy, but at the time he was convinced the instructor was picking on him each time she asked him to demonstrate steps: he didn't know any, he grew up in the city, and it was only his first lesson. He'd fought so hard to gain entry to the "horse world," and there in that uncomfortable female helmet he realized acceptance wasn't guaranteed. "Failing at that world, not with horses, but with that artificial world that horses are put into, was hard for me," he says.

The more Paul retreated into his online zoosexual universe, the more intense his online relationships became, and the more he pulled back from those around him, which strengthened his very carefully constructed firewall. The isolation was real. There wasn't a single person he could have been open with. That internalized social disgust combined with his failure around horses warped his view of the future. The path to adult freedom and happiness that was once so vivid got so fogged up he couldn't see the end.

And it wasn't as if the zoo community were an oasis of people who all held hands and sang the same welcoming song about their sexual identity. Gatekeeping and factions were rife. There were heated internet arguments. Who was really a zoo, and who wasn't? Were you an authentic zoosexual? Were you zoo exclusive? What were your intentions when it came to animals? Were you a "good" person who would treat them with respect and care for them, or were you a brute who wanted to take advantage of a voiceless lover? Were you someone who valued consent and forging an intimate connection with your animal companion?

In the nascent hyperconnected media era, where communication was less interactive, his lack of interest in pornography alienated him from some members of the community. On the one hand, owning porn was a sign of authenticity; when all you had was someone's word they were who they said they were, sharing porn let you break your way into the club. It proved your desire *and* boosted your social standing; the more you had, the more connected you were. But Paul was never comfortable with that. He hated looking at images where animals seemed sexually objectified, uncomfortable, drugged, or raped. The thought of harming an animal for his pleasure was repulsive to him and something he thinks zoosexuals need to be especially aware of because their lovers can't talk to tell them if they are uncomfortable or in pain.

Alongside his position on pornography, Paul's virginity compromised his authenticity among his faceless online friends. How could you *possibly* know what you were attracted to when you hadn't actually tried it? In some circles losing your virginity is important to becoming a "real" zoophile; if you haven't "done it," people are suspicious. The desire to authenticate is heightened because, with a handful of exceptions, sex with animals is illegal in most parts of the world. What if you're a cop trying to force an online confession? There are also logistical concerns: a zoosexual relationship is a commitment, Paul once explained to me, reminding me of the headline for my first interview with him, how *do* you "Date a Horse"? Owning an animal is equivalent or close to marriage, so you can't have a one-night stand unless you find someone who is willing to share their animals, and then there's the ethics around that. Having your own animal means that you can get to know it, learn what it likes, and familiarize yourself with the way it expresses pleasure. As Paul puts it, "It can be very difficult to make that initial leap."

He disassociated, sitting through class at high school as if he were watching himself on TV, thinking how much he'd be hated if anyone ever found out "the truth." After dark he'd bundle up, erect his Newtonian telescope, and spend hours gazing at faraway planets, galaxies, star clusters, the moons of Jupiter weaving back and forth, and the occasional nebula, those floaty jellyfish-like blobs of dust, hydrogen, and helium bobbing against an expansive black canvas. The vastness of the universe dwarfed him, sucking him further outside himself until he was left with one single emotion: awe. Paul felt part of the universe and as if the universe were part of him, but it was also a cold place that didn't care if his atoms returned to the ground or continued fighting entropy for a few more years. As he puts it today, "I was excited about the possibilities, but always through it all I understood I was different and that what I wanted equaled a lifelong sentence of existing outside the world humans build for themselves."

Paul left high school a virgin; the closest he'd come to physical connection was with a female classmate he took to the prom. He was so awkward he couldn't even ask her to dance. He lived at home and traveled to his local college by bus, as was the norm.

He'd been making more meaningful online connections and had even arranged meetings with people from local bulletin boards. The first was with a guy he'd been chatting with over email for a few months when they hatched a plan to meet at a sushi restaurant on the other side of town.

In the days leading up to that meeting, Paul was at once excited and anxious. He didn't consider that this person could be dangerous—this was well before the panic about internet strangers—instead his anxiety was focused on a single question: "What if this man is a 'freak'; what would that make me?" He shaved, parted his hair neatly on the side, and slipped into jeans and running shoes, hoping it went well. This was his first face-to-face meeting with anyone who actually knew what he was. He arrived early and slid into a booth where rice paper screens offered shade from the eyes of his fellow diners and prepared himself to meet the first zoosexual he'd encountered in real life. He was gripped by the same fear he has to this very day when he negotiates a real-life encounter: "I am never sure. You can never really be sure."

His balding companion reminded him of an eccentric professor from a British TV show. He was a bit older, in his early thirties, and worked in computer science. At first, they used small talk to dance around the subject they were both too scared to speak of out loud. Paul looked at the man in his nice suit and tie and thought that he seemed to have a bit of cash. As they chatted about the weather, Paul did his best to look past his companion's failings: "He was, you know, the epitome of an autistic computer programmer." Paul ignored his limited social skills. "When you're a zoo," he says, "there's so few people who you are able to meet, so sometimes you have to work with a personality you might not like that much."

The man launched into a story about a dog he'd found on

the street. He was almost boasting about his conquest. He told Paul that he'd taken that orphan home, cleaned him, and had sex with him before returning him to the sidewalk. Paul was shocked. "Why'd you take him home if you didn't want to keep him?" he asked this man, who excused his behavior with the claim that his luxury apartment didn't allow pets. Listening to this man describe sex in such a transactional way was disturbing. What sort of person could put their own sexual needs before the welfare of an animal? Paul saw no excuse for such behavior: "I thought: 'Why not get an apartment that allows dogs? Or, why take him home in the first place if you knew you couldn't keep him?' I often don't understand the choices they make, and I do think that sometimes it's because they are scared of what they could be."

Overall, though, that meeting was a relief. Their failure to "connect" boiled down to a problem with how this man treated his lovers; otherwise he was, as Paul puts it, "relatively normal," meaning that he wasn't "a complete freak, you know, smelled or seemed scary or anything like that." Paul could go on, maybe even meet someone "like him" whom he actually wanted to be around. And he didn't get arrested, he noted, while he waited for his computer to boot up after that long journey back home. Fear and shame infused his sexuality from the word go: "I hadn't even done anything illegal at that point, yet I had that thought at the back of my head that I'm so despised, I'll definitely be locked up."

Paul persisted. He was determined to meet other zoos; he still hadn't lost his virginity. Unless you wanted to break into a stable and interfere with an unwilling horse, what zoos call fence hopping, it wasn't something he could do alone. He continued to meet up with people he'd connected with online. He'd catch the bus to restaurants in far-flung neighborhoods like a string of platonic Tinder dates. There was a militant vegan from Australia, "pretty annoying to be honest." Like any sexuality, you don't necessarily have things in common with someone just because you have similar sexual desires.

Zack was different. The pair met on *FurryMUCK*—a text-based virtual world constructed by the imagination of people from all over the globe. Things were much more interactive there than they had been on bulletin boards; participants created avatars and built spaces to relax and catch up with their friends. Everything that happened there happened in text. When you entered a room, you'd find paragraphs of description setting the scene, say, an emerald forest with a path leading to a waterfall with pools spread out across multiple levels. As you get closer, you notice some towels and a hot tub. Hidden in a corner is a teleportation pad, which takes you to a spaceship with windy steel corridors leading to hydroponic rooms full of lush vegetation. Any universe that you wanted, you could find, and if not you could just hit a series of keys to create a new one.

For his debut, Paul presented himself as a brown stallion. Zack was an intelligent centaur-like alien. Paul and Zack put as much of themselves into their avatars as possible. They met in forests where they'd simulate physical connections like shaking hands or petting manes. When they met face-to-face, there was no shock of the real. Their connection in those virtual woods had been authentic. As they got to know each other off-line, Paul found that their views about zoophilia were in sync: "I didn't worry about him being weird about animals; it was comfortable." They became close and transferred those virtual meetups to a standing IRL Friday dinner date. Zack told him about his friend Russell, who, despite being a bit of a Luddite, was a well-connected elder statesman in the zoosexual community. And the retired psychology professor just so happened to live on a working farm a few hours from Paul's home.

In February 1992 a nervous Paul set off for Russell's farm. He recalls shaking when he parked his car—stress activating his "fight or flight" response as his central nervous system responded to the pending climax of more than a decade's worth of pressure. He hadn't met his mare partner, a Shetland-cross pony named Juno, and he was only beginning to get to know Russell, which added weight to the already unfamiliar situation. Russell stayed well away from the barn; Paul speculates that because the pair had only just met, he wanted to distance himself in case Paul turned out to be a narc. Zack planned to stay throughout the encounter to authenticate the act and make sure that Paul didn't do anything to hurt Juno. Well, that's what he said, but Paul often wonders if he just wanted to watch.

After introducing himself and spending time getting to know Juno, they took their positions. Paul, who was shaking again, climbed onto a stool. He looked around the barn wishing that Zack wasn't there; his presence frustrated him just as much as the fact that it was too cold to remove much clothing. He continued to shake when he took off his trousers; that's when Zack turned away, to minimize his presence. When Paul pulled on his clothes, he knew that was exactly what he'd wanted; sexually everything went just right. But he has his regrets, the main one being that Juno was a stranger. "I wish that it had been a horse I'd known a long time, that we had grown together," he said. "That moment should have been even more special than it was. I still don't know what she thought about it, of course."

Paul wasn't chatting with *just* Zack on *FurryMUCK*. Joining him in the forest was an ape that was the avatar of a man named Sam. Sam and Paul became close almost immediately. By day, on email or *FurryMUCK*, they'd talk about sexual identity and gay rights. At night, they retreated into a private space for simulated intimacy. Sam had a serious primary partner, but their relationship was open. Over the course of about six months Paul fell in love with the male software engineer who worked for a start-up across the border in California.

The night before my interview with Paul was scheduled to go live, I was approached by an editor who had concerns about the story. What would readers make of it? How did I know Paul was telling the truth? We'd spent the week editing the Q&A, and it was ready to go. It was long and included questions like "How do you find a sex partner?" "How do you have sex with a mare? Is there foreplay?" "How can you tell when a mare is having an orgasm?" which Paul answered in depth, often providing lots of technical detail (including the logistics of having oral sex with a mare).[36] He also mused about his love for his horse partner and went into detail about his sexual coming-of-age and fears about her passing away.

I met with two senior editors and the online editorial chief, who cracked his knuckles and said, "It reads like a parody. What if he's making it all up?" "Why would he do that?" I snapped, startling myself. I wasn't aware how protective of Paul's story I'd become. I walked them through all the steps I'd taken to authenticate him and showed them samples of his long history talking about his identity online. "We have to run this," I said forcefully. "We have to let him be heard."

The interview went live early on a November weekday morning, and by the end of the day it was the top-performing article on nymag.com. I was bombarded with emails. At first they were playful: "Is this true?" "OMG, where the hell did you find this man?" Then it went viral. The comments section on the article was full of outrage. Roughly half of the hundreds of commenters responding to the interview were repulsed. They said things like "This is absolutely sick,"[37] or that it's "the worst thing I've ever read in my entire life ... he tries to draw out *so* much sympathy because he 'treats her so right' but honestly it's just vile. No animal can truly consent."[38] People tweeted that I was an enabler or normalizer of dangerous desires and that the interview would feed the anti-LGBTQ right's slippery slope argument. As one poster put it, "thanks, Obama,"[39] or another: "You realize of course this just feeds fuel to the fire to the anti-gay crowd—they are going to say 'well this is what we were waiting for' in some attempt to normalize it. Disappointed you even gave it a voice. Hell, this crap was even banned from Jerry Springer."[40] Equine websites and newsletters shared it in full. Christian fundamentalists devoted entire blog posts to the interview, saying I was responsible for assisting this country's moral decline.

In Canada, Paul was having his own reaction. When he read the interview at work, he had his first-ever panic attack. He'd written about his experience for years online, but this time he was representing himself to an open, global, and mainstream audience. As he put it, "It was my life story all in one place, and I had never seen that before."[41] Paul tried to respond to each negative comment, but it got too much. By the afternoon he'd gone off-line and asked a friend to monitor the comments and step in and defend their sexuality or his style of horsemanship if anyone went too far. His biggest concern was any suggestion that he'd mistreated Ms. C.

After he'd calmed down, he followed up to let me know how well his interview was received by the zoophile community. "There are those who think I should have kept my mouth closed, but mostly the reaction has been very positive."[42] Exposing himself like that was scary, but it was also validating because he felt as if he'd given back. A few months after the interview went live, I arrived at work and was greeted by an elaborate gift basket. I unpacked the horse-themed contents—a mug emblazoned with a horse's head, honey, a candle, and a stuffed toy pony—and a note that simply said, "Thank you for objectively reporting a zoosexual relationship." The next year, an excerpt was included in the print version of the magazine. The cover, which was designed to look like the Google search page, includes the line "what it's like to date a horse."[43] In response the *New York Post* said that Paul's description of his love for horses was "poetry of the stomach-churning variety," echoing the sentiment of Jerry Springer, who just over fifteen years earlier said similar material made him want to throw up.[44]

Adventurous, industrious, and logical, Paul assessed his options for visiting the United States to meet Sam. The cheapest was an Amtrak pass that would take him to San Francisco, then New York, and all the way back. He figured he'd take a month and meet as many online friends as possible. He sent emails and put out feelers on bulletin boards saying something along the lines of, "I'm traveling across the country, would anyone like a visit!?" The anxiety leading up to his departure was unbearable. He couldn't form the words to tell his parents, so he wrote them a letter (the communicative last resort in the days before text and email). As his departure drew closer, he worked up the courage to hand his parents the note, which read, "I'm going to the states to stay with a friend. My train leaves on Monday." He was over eighteen, so they couldn't stop him, but they let him know their fears about what might happen to him alone in this foreign land where he'd surely be robbed or molested or worse. When I learned this, I was impressed by how intrepid he was; this was well before the hyperconnected era, when online friendships commonly lead to IRL meetings, often in distant places.

He stayed with Sam in San Francisco, and when they met face-to-face, it was as if they were still online: the connection was seamless. Sam was about ten years older than Paul, and he had the stable energy of a father figure. He was hospitable and warm, constantly asking Paul about his feelings. Paul was especially touched that Sam downplayed the terrible chest cold he was suffering from. Sam put his needs to the side because he was determined that they have a good time. They drove to the coast, where they bundled up in scarves and sweaters and walked together on a deserted beach.

At night, Paul and Sam cuddled on the sofa. When they kissed, it was Paul's first. They snuggled together watching movies, but there was no sex. Sam was just too sick, struggling to breathe as he said goodbye. Paul set off for the rest of his journey glowing because he knew the love he'd felt for Sam in that virtual forest was real.

His next stop was Colorado, where he stayed with another online friend. Paul was young, sex positive, and open to new experience, and while he did have sex with his male host, he refrained from sexual activity with any horses for the duration of his time in the United States. He was concerned about getting caught and thrown into a U.S. prison, yes, but more than that he didn't want to repeat that first sexual encounter, where there was no emotional connection.

When I reflect on the time I got to know Paul, I'm struck by how thin my line became between what's "normal" and what's not. I wasn't a stranger to the visceral repulsion that Paul's sexuality generated. I'd read the online furor when my interview with him was published, but as it's so easy to do when we are behind the screen, I was able to distance myself from the humans who were expressing this outrage. Unlike Paul, I didn't focus on their disgust or read negative comments in much depth. That was where I enjoyed privilege as a reporter; it wasn't my life that had been laid bare for the world to judge. Instead, I opted to focus on reactions from people who were surprised to find that after they'd learned about Paul's very unusual sex life, despite finding his preferences beyond the realm of anything they could ever imagine themselves possibly wanting, they were left feeling as if they couldn't judge.

In the comments, one poster wrote about how the interview made them feel both "thoroughly disturbed" and unable to "full-heartedly" judge, "I know what it's like being judged—and I know he'd be ostracized if anyone ever found out about his sexual preferences, such as I would."[45] Another, who identified themselves as a Christian Libertarian Conservative, addressed his comment to Paul directly: "It takes bravery to share something that most simply knee-jerk an ugly opinion about."[46]

About three years after I first spoke to Paul, I started to test how people reacted when I told them I was including his story in this book. First, I told my hairstylist—a man who grew up in a small town in Texas, who was in his early twenties. I studied his reflection in the mirror; his face wilted into a sick frown. He begged me, "Please, I don't even want to think about it." He was repulsed, and I felt judged, and deviant, by association. At work, one of my editors (a woman in her early thirties) was baffled when I told her that what I find the most interesting about Paul is that he hasn't actually had sex with his mare companion for years. "Their relationship is clearly about more than just sex," I explained, carried away, while she looked at me blankly as if to say that I was in too deep. She told me she was struggling to digest the fact that he'd done it once, or ever, at all.

Another friend, an attorney who is married and straight, asked me how my "horse fetish" reporting was going. My first thought was "STFU, you normative bitch!" I was genuinely annoyed that she'd described his entire sexual identity as a kink. "It's a sexuality, not a fetish!" I earnestly texted back to her in all caps. After a while, like Paul, I just stopped talking about it. When people asked about the book, I'd gloss over the project with rehearsed sound bites like "I'm writing about people who lead complicated lives," which was both vague and dull enough that I usually didn't get any follow-ups.

I felt as though I couldn't include Paul's story in a book that also had chapters about marginalized sexualities; in fact I scrapped two completed chapters and edited the proposed contents repeatedly based on a concern about presenting Paul's experience alongside others. When I'd made my initial decisions about whom to write about in *Finding Normal,* I was concerned about, but not deterred by, the optics of publishing certain stories alongside others. To me it was obvious that I wasn't comparing experiences or suggesting they exist on a spectrum, and I'd been so focused on the overall premise of the book—about how people find themselves as normal in new ways in the hyperconnected era.

But of course the idea that social change will end in a free-for-all with animals enjoying the same rights as humans is a hurtful conservative argument that's been used throughout history, in discussions first about interracial marriage and more recently about same-sex marriage, like in 2014, when a Mississippi Baptist pastor protested a federal judge's temporarily blocked ban on same-sex marriage by occupying the steps of the federal courthouse with a horse dressed in a wedding gown. Or in 2003, when Rick Santorum compared gay marriage to "man on dog or whatever the case may be."[47] The philosopher John Corvino has called it the "PIB argument"—the idea that, as he puts it, "approving homosexuality" will lead to a sexual free-for-all where anything goes, hence the PIB, which stands for "polygamy, incest, bestiality."[48] While I thought it was important to clearly cordon off the last two chapters to make it clear that I wasn't comparing zoosexuality to non-monogamy, age-gap relationships, or asexuality, I was worried about suggesting that zoophilia is the same as incest. I began to feel as if I couldn't write about zoosexuality at all because there was nothing I could put it near.

When I was deciding whether to include Paul's story in this book, I contacted other people who have written or spoken about zoophilia. First, I attempted to discuss it with Jerry Springer or one of his producers: I wanted to know what he thought about filming that infamous episode. However, his publicist politely informed me that it's still on their "do not discuss" list. Next, I asked Hani Miletski about how her work was received. She told me that when she first told people what she planned to write about for her dissertation, she was warned that it would ruin her career because it would put off future clients, and over twenty years later she avoids telling people what she wrote her dissertation about because she doesn't want to "disgust" them. Justin Lehmiller, a social psychologist and research fellow at the Kinsey Institute, didn't include a chapter about sex with animals in the print version of his survey of American sexual fantasies, which was published in 2018, because he was worried it would impact the way readers approached the rest of the book (one in five of his participants said they'd fantasized at least once about sex with an animal). He wanted to normalize sexual desires and worried if he dwelled on more unusual fantasies like zoophilia, it might turn off people who would otherwise benefit from his findings. However, he did think that the information was important, so he made it available online as a bonus chapter.[49] He says he didn't get an especially negative response—perhaps because he was writing about other people's fantasies—and when he did a Reddit AMA, most questions were thoughtful and intelligent.

In November 2020, during the global COVID-19 pandemic, Joanna Bourke launched her history of bestiality and zoophilia

(*Loving Animals: On Bestiality, Zoophilia, and Post-human Love*) via an online lecture in London. The video was uploaded on YouTube, and for three days her social media accounts were inundated with hateful comments. The trolling was unrelenting. On Twitter she was told she should seek therapy (or be committed), that she needed Jesus and should commit suicide.

Peter Singer, who is often referred to as the father of the animal rights movement, discussed bestiality in a 2001 book review for the online sexualities magazine *Nerve*, which was commissioned by Emily Nussbaum, who is now a staff writer at *The New Yorker*. In the provocative piece he argues that if the taboo against sex with animals originated from a broader rejection of non-procreative sex, the fact that it remains firmly intact as the culture has become more accepting of other sex once considered "unnatural" like the use of condoms, masturbation, or sodomy speaks to something else, another "powerful force": the desire we humans have to see ourselves separate from animals. We are so disgusted, so horrified, by the thought of sex with them because it is an "offence to our dignity as humans."[50] He didn't condemn sex with animals; he said that if an animal is not being abused, there's nothing wrong with it.

The backlash was swift. Animal rights organizations issued statements condemning Singer. Priscilla Feral, the president of the nonprofit animal advocacy organization Friends of Animals, called Singer's position "shocking and disgusting" and likened bestiality to pedophilia: "Bestiality is wrong in part because an animal cannot meaningfully consent to sex with a human . . . Singer's essay isn't an intellectual issue and his thinking isn't logical. It's a moral issue. Singer and his apologists just need to stop repeating every annoying idea they've developed for shock value."[51] Singer was scheduled to speak at a conference that had to be moved off campus when people complained to the dean that he was a bestiality supporter. "I wasn't supporting or encouraging it. I was just saying that as far as the criminal law was concerned, it didn't seem to be harming anyone or any animal either. If it was a criminal offense, it seemed it should be on animal welfare grounds that an animal was being harmed," he said when we talked on the phone. Those thoughts gave ammunition to people who were already attacking him for his "controversial" views that abortion and euthanasia are morally justifiable.

Ingrid E. Newkirk, the president of PETA, stepped in to defend Singer, saying that his piece was daring, honest, and nuanced, and any implication that he condoned violent acts involving animals was the result of a misread.[52] "If a girl gets sexual pleasure from riding a horse, does the horse suffer? If not, who cares? If you French kiss your dog and he or she thinks it's great, is it wrong? We believe all exploitation and abuse is wrong . . . if it isn't exploitation and abuse, it may not be wrong."[53] When asked about consent, she said that compared with humans, animal consent is very different.[54] A few years later, when an article on a conservative Christian website about the case of "Mr. Hands" described those words as a defense of bestiality, she wrote a letter to the editor saying: "There is almost nothing as shocking as a man forcing himself sexually upon an animal . . . it is almost as shocking to read my comments about non-assaultive sexual contact as some endorsement by me or PETA of sexual assault on animals . . . PETA and I are totally opposed to any exploitation and all bestiality. Philosophical musings on whether there is cruelty when a girl experiences sexual pleasure from riding a horse who is oblivious to that fact or when someone allows a dog to hump their leg are a far cry from an endorsement of bestiality."[55] Since 2016 PETA has had an official statement on its website: "Consensual sex is between two human beings who enter into it willingly, and that is never the case when an animal is dominated by a human. Having sex with an animal is raping that animal."[56]

Is Singer haunted by sharing his thoughts? Haunted is too

strong, but he has regretted it at times because it's distracted people from the causes that matter to him, like ending the billions of deaths caused each year by factory farming.

Why did Nussbaum commission the piece? When we talked on the phone, she recalled that when the Dutch book landed on her desk, it seemed like a natural fit for the publication, and because Singer had written about animal rights she thought he'd have an interesting take, so she sent it to him instead of to her regular book reviewer. In retrospect she thinks it was naive not to have predicted it would provoke such a reaction. To her, getting Singer to review it was just a smart assignment; then, when it went live, it crashed the website. She was troubled by the response, and she felt very protective of Singer, who endured threats and abuse when the story went viral. She also regrets the assignment: "I have enormous respect for Professor Singer for having done it, and I genuinely don't think I understood that it would put him in a vulnerable position to the degree that it did."

In upstate New York, Paul stayed on a farm with some friends of people he'd met online. They drove to the "Big Apple" and packed all the touristy things in one day: the Statue of Liberty, the Empire State Building, even a jaunt around Times Square; one of his friends was pickpocketed on the subway. They drove to one of the boroughs to hang out with some zoos overnight, then returned back to the country. About a week into his New York stay, Paul was tending to a nine-month-old filly in the paddock. He was happy, thinking about Sam and enjoying the fresh air and equine company. He was whistling when he came back to the house, but given the number of guests there the silence was jarring. He was wondering what was going on, when his host handed him a telephone receiver.

Sam's partner told Paul the terrible news: That cold hadn't been a cold at all. While they sat together watching movies,

Sam was dying of complications from AIDS. He was dead. Paul pushed past a tangle of concerned arms and bodies and ran out of the house to the pasture, where he screamed into a valley. Paul says it was raw trauma; his eyes still sting with hot tears when he thinks back to that day.

He carried on his trip. The southern line took him west, where he roamed around Oklahoma in shock. Most of the zoos there were around the same age, so it felt like a real community. Everyone was so open. Despite being mostly numb from grief, Paul recalls feeling free. In Texas a friend drove him to a town just outside Dallas to meet with another friend; they stayed up late talking about horses, religion, and politics. Then there was twenty-four hours in Arkansas, where his contact took him to college hangouts. Being a "normal" young man felt good, but that numbness that anesthetized him to the pain of his loss was starting to fade; it had been only a week since he got the news. He extended his trip so he could spend extra time in San Francisco to support Sam's partner. They collected Sam's ashes and honored his passing at a memorial service in the mountains overlooking a valley. About thirty of Sam's work colleagues and friends gathered to write wishes on scraps of paper, which they burned in Sam's honor. When he got back to Canada, Paul greeted his parents and went straight to his room. His grades slipped and he was kicked out of his honors physics program, ruining his dream of becoming a national physicist.

Flesh-and-blood meetings with a stranger from a strange place are normal for Paul. It was how he met his first sex partners: human, and animal. But revealing his identity to me was risky. What if I was faking it and was really one of those animal rights activists who thinks all bestiality is abusive? What if I was planning to report him to the police, or showed up and ambushed him with a camera and a reality TV crew? What if I planned to post his name and location online? What if I was sloppy and ran around telling locals why I was there? What if I let a friend, or worse a nosy colleague, know where I'd be? What if I posted pictures on Instagram, or updated my Facebook status without turning off my location preferences and accidentally revealed where I was? Paul has done this for years, so he primed me on his method of privacy: obscure but don't lie, because lies always snowball.

He let me know the best airport to fly into and did some research to make sure it was accessible by train when I told him I can't drive. Then, a few weeks before the visit, he revealed the name of a town close to where he lives. He blocked off a weekend, and I nervously booked a hotel using a pseudonym. I felt as if he were trying to put me off visiting when he wrote in an email a few weeks before I left New York: "I am a little scared on your behalf, I've seen a lot of people investigate this topic over the years and almost universally they end up disappearing or ending their work suddenly." His warning didn't scare me. I trusted him; he'd already shared so much. Later, Paul claimed that his main concern leading up to our first meeting was managing his wife Fran's emotions.

In Canada, I took Paul's privacy seriously. I felt like a scrappy secret agent with a burner phone. I'd left my computer and iPhone at home. I spent a few days in the city, where I paid in cash and avoided small talk. "Friday might not be an option," Paul texted me the day before my train ride from the city to his town. "It's date night," he said, referring to the ritual he and Fran started a few years ago. I had to stop myself from replying, "Really, Paul? *Date night*? Don't be such a liar and don't be such a fucking norm." "I really hope she wants to see me, too!" I wrote instead.

The train took me past alabaster lawns, naked trees, frostbitten paddocks, and stables, so many stables. I was apprehensive about meeting Paul: What if we didn't get on IRL? He'd put so much trust in me, but what if he didn't like me? I also had the same thought that Paul had when he was getting ready to meet a zoophile for the first time all those years ago: "What if he's a total freak?" I was nearly at my destination when Paul texted, "My wife wants to meet you."

Paul and I had arranged to have dinner at a local chain restaurant with diner booths and a salad buffet. I arrived early, found a seat away from the full tables, and texted Paul to tell him where I was sitting and what I was wearing. They arrived about twenty minutes late, bundled up in puffer coats and hats, eyes darting around. As soon as I saw them, I stood up and greeted them both with a hug.

If Fran had a "look," it would be "Amish hippie" or a life-size figure from a Vermeer. She appeared to be a woman in control with her fanny pack complete with a knife case. Paul looked much younger than his forty-six years with his soft baby face and wide eyes, like Buddha with a neatly trimmed beard. Conflict averse and patient, he lets Fran lead the conversation. When he does talk, his tone is calm and measured; he's so patient and listens so carefully I often worried I was boring him because he stays completely quiet when I talk, pausing for seconds to make sure I've finished before he weighs in. It's not that he lacks social skills; it's that most of his conversations about his sexuality have played out in text. To my relief Fran had no time for small talk. She immediately began to tell me about a visit to a relative of a friend of theirs who had recently died. As she chatted away at me, her face was pulled tight as if it might split—the same shape mine takes when I'm nervous. After that heavy intro she ordered a Diet Coke and excused herself, announcing, "I'm gonna go raid the salad bar!" Paul nodded and followed like a butler in her wake.

Communication is key to Paul and Fran's relationship; they are like two hosts on *The View*, fact-checking and deconstructing the minutiae of everyday life. A fifteen-minute conversation with them can cover a dizzying array of topics: the alarming levels of mercury in the Great Lakes; the history of swearing in the military; regional Canadian food customs; the chances that Oprah could ever be elected president of the United States (hell no! says Fran; "there's way too much racism and sexism going on"); how to build a sound card; the politics of public versus private education. Fran is pro public schools, by the way, because if you are around a range of people, then you're more likely to open your mind and reject your parents' conservative or religious worldview.

She'd reluctantly agreed to dinner to be polite but also because she wanted to sniff me out—make sure I had good intentions. She listed all the things I had going against me: "You're female; you live in New York; you're single; we don't really know you; what you know could damage Paul's life." Later, when I went to the restroom, I overheard Fran fretting about getting germs from me if they took my leftovers home. My lifestyle—alone in a big city—is her worst nightmare, and she probably wondered what sort of person would want to live that way. She'd given in but confessed that her anxiety had made them late. Just before Paul picked her up, she texted him and said, "I have a doubt." Right until the moment they got on the highway, she was making the decision: fight or flight.

When Russell offered Paul a spot on his farm, it seemed like a solution to many problems. He could learn about horses, spend time in their company, and get enough credits from the local college to complete his degree. He took every sociology class on offer, including two seminars on deviance and marriage. Russell mentored him in both horsemanship and zoosexual identity. Along with several doctors and veterinarians, he gave him the language to investigate zoonosis—diseases that can be transferred from animal to human. During the day, Paul cared for Juno and her herd. He learned how to take vital stats, look out for the signs of deadly colic, scrape dirt out of their hooves, and shine their coats. At night he stayed up late with Russell talking about psychology, sociology, and gay rights. Russell would tell stories about the zoo community from the 1950s and 1960s when he built his network by responding to advertisements in the back of muscle magazines using a P.O. box address. Paul was struck by how much communication there was before the internet. Russell had a lover who'd died a few years earlier, and when the old man showed Paul pictures of the stallion, he usually wept.

As Paul got to know Russell, he learned the backstory of a life full of adventure and experience. Russell had come of age in Montreal, where he had a career photographing bodybuilders. He went on to excel in psychology and worked his way up to professor. Paul, who'd longed to be a physicist, looked up to him for his academically rigorous career. And Russell had a full life. He liked art, he'd traveled, he had friends, community, and a lifestyle that let him be around the object of his affection. Russell was a tangible reference for a possible future—a walking example of how to be a happy zoosexual. Paul mined the college library, eager to read everything he could find on the topic, though there wasn't much. There were those statistics from Kinsey that 8 percent of men on average have had sex with an animal, but in most of the research papers he found on the topic, the words used to describe his feelings echoed the disgust he'd seen online: "sick," "deviant," and "wrong." He waded through the medical and scientific literature, which described his sexuality as a paraphilia, or "an abnormal sexual desire." Most academic articles analyzed the prevalence of bestiality in other centuries and eras by relying on court documents. Studies in psychology or sexology were based on an insane or a criminal cohort.

He also experimented sexually. While it was technically a public barn, it was rare for strangers to show up, and on the odd occasion that Russell walked in on him, the two men didn't discuss it. Paul was especially drawn to a horse named Britney. He says he didn't love her, but he felt as if their connection was strong, and it was with Britney that he learned how much he enjoyed giving oral pleasure.

When Paul talks about this, he's matter-of-fact, as if challenging you to judge him. In our interview for "What It's Like," he put it this way: "When I first gave a horse oral sex . . . one of the things I had to overcome was the thought that it's disgusting . . . much like the way some men feel about women. But as I discovered, mares taste very, very nice, like mown grass or fresh hay, and they really enjoy oral stimulation. I've always made sure, except for the first few times when I was a neophyte, that my partner has an orgasm, whether it's a human or a horse, and oral is something she almost always enjoys."[57]

After he'd been on the farm for about a year, Juno developed an illness called Cushing's disease, which usually afflicts horses when they get old. Its symptoms, which include excessive urination and thirst, are similar to diabetes. Paul sat with her when she appeared to be in pain. He felt as if he were giving back to the horse who had confirmed his zoosexual identity; perhaps this even made up for the lack of connection during their first time.

One spring afternoon, Paul came back to the farm from a day at college. He made his way through the hay up a hill to his trailer, where he found Juno dead on her side. He later learned that the vet had euthanized her while he was in class. Paul respected that the decision was Russell's to make—he owned Juno after all—but he would have appreciated a warning. He knew it was her time to go, but the shock of the passing was rough. Maybe the vet saw her and made a quick decision, he reasoned, as he lay beside the dead horse in the sun.

In 2009, it was Fran who suggested that Paul finally get his own horse. Ms. C., an Arabian mare, was destined for a slaughterhouse when Paul paid one hundred dollars to save her. When Ms. C. came into his life, his marriage to Fran became a "poly V," or a "single-ended triad." He's the point in the V, Ms. C. is on one side, and Fran is on the other. While his connections with Juno and Britney were strong, he says his chemistry with Ms. C. is unique: "I have never had a relationship with a horse that is so in depth." When she came into his life, he started riding lessons again; he'd hardly been on the back of a horse since that humiliating childhood lesson. They galloped together through the windy forest, just behind the highway, and it seemed as if their bodies worked together seamlessly. "I have the bounciness and exuberance of a young child," he said, "but more than once she's moved to stop me falling off; she moves to do things for me and with me." He found that he had to force himself to talk about her to Fran, and then me, in the first person as a lover: "The silence is so ingrained in my soul." She had been in his life for about a year before they were intimate for the first time.

In our original interview he described the logistics of sex with Ms. C. in detail, using their first sexual encounter as an example. "So I'd had her for about a year. I had her in the barn. I'd given her food. I'd brushed her, cleaned her under her tail, and cleaned her face . . . We were in a barn with all the lights out and a nice warm heater; it was lovely. So, she was settling in for the night, and I went to the stall and I just sat in the corner. I let her come to me, and that's one of the things I am very adamant about: I never use a halter or any kind of restraint. So, she chooses to come with me, and I leave her food and she puts her head on my chest and we snuggle and I whisper sweet nothings in her ear and rub her cheeks—what she likes. By this stage, she knows I'll rub her thighs. She really loves the area between the back of her legs touched. So, she turned around and she actually backed into me while I'm sitting down. I slip my hands up a little further up and play with her genitals." Her clitoris? I'd asked, to clarify the nature of the intimacy. He described standing on a bucket to manage the height difference: "I was sitting with my back to the wall, and she had actually pressed into my face hard enough that I was pinned there performing oral sex."[58]

The encounter went on. "We did that for about 20 or 30 minutes. Mares aren't easy to satisfy. They need a lot of stimulation. This leads me to the penetrative sex. I was about 38 at the time, and I was about 10 to 15 pounds too heavy for the bucket. So we have this plastic bucket upside down, and I'm standing on it and my drawers are dropped. I'm in the corner of the stall, and my mare friend has turned around and is looking at me strangely, and she comes over and sniffs and rubs and snuffles me. Because horses love biting things I was a little bit concerned; I kept my hand in a way that I could save myself if I needed to. But the really interesting thing is that after having oral sex she turned away from me, lifted her tail, and walked backward into me and actually onto me. Unfortunately, the bucket was buckling, and I fell off. So while there was penetrative sex, that was my first big time with my mare friend: having to catch myself after falling off a bucket backward."[59]

We went deep on the issue of consent, which is always held against zoophiles: "I believe that question is asked because there is no answer to it and so it proves the point that zoos are bad ... Why are people concerned about consent when my sexuality is involved but not when it comes to drinking milk or eating steak, both of which require artificial insemination and semen collection, which are very sexual acts? You put your arm inside the cow, and you masturbate the bull ... I'd argue you aren't worried about consent; you're worried about where my penis is."[60] As Joanna Bourke notes in her history of bestiality, when Washington State was drafting the legislation to criminalize bestiality that was passed in 2006, there were complications while lawmakers worked to distinguish bestiality from sexual acts that occur during animal husbandry. It was agreed that the difference was motivation: libidinal versus economic.[61]

Paul was armed with examples: "Consent is *very* important to me . . . If someone is mute and can't write or give you a verbal response, are you allowed to have sex with them? Even if they are an adult and mentally sound? Are words the only way to get consent . . . ? Do you go up to a strange dog and automatically pat him on the head without looking him in the eye to make sure he's okay with it? No smart person does that because the dog could bite your hand. If he's perky and happy, you go in for the pet; if he's not, you don't want to interfere with him. So for me that's a good way to make people understand that an animal doesn't need words to consent to being touched."[62] Paul says that Ms. C. would often initiate sex; her nonverbal cues are very clear. Like humans who do not always use language to indicate their comfort with a sex act, her consent is indicated by "enthusiastic participation." "She is often forcefully putting her butt into my space. What other signs? Watching me, ears focused on me, backing and pressing on me, my hand, my face, and my hips. Giving me easy access to her body. It would be very simple to prevent me from touching her, and even a little sign she wasn't willing to have me touch her in that way I would listen to."

It was the way he made me think about consent that was a turning point when I got to know Paul—as if that were the moment I finally held my hands up and surrendered, thinking, you're right, assuming I trust that he doesn't restrain, drug, or otherwise force animals to have sex with him, this is not really about consent at all. Justin Lehmiller agrees that consent might not really be behind people's disgust, given that most of us actively harm or torture animals in our food and lifestyle choices and do not ask animals for verbal consent for anything. He thinks it's visceral: "They think it's wrong in some way, and they are looking for a justification of that, and the consent angle is one that they cling to." When I'd talked to Nussbaum, who had commissioned Peter Singer's piece, she did not want to comment on zoophilia at all, but she did say she was worried about consent. I got defensive, and we lapsed into a surreal conversation about her cat ("did your cat verbally consent to living with you?" I asked).

Singer pointed out that when it comes to animals, consent may actually be very simple to establish: if an animal is allowed to walk away and they don't, they are saying yes. "I find it interesting that people who stand up for animals in general are actually running down their capacities to consent. Of course you could say it's not the same fully informed consent that normal adults give when they consent to have sexual relationships, and it's not, but that doesn't mean that there's not sufficient consent to say this is not harming the animal, this is not something the animal dislikes, this may in fact be something positive for the animal, a special kind of closeness with a human companion, who knows?" When I discussed consent with Hani Miletski, she was also pretty clear that animals can give nonverbal consent: "Animals do communicate with us, even though they can't talk, and give consent, even if it's not verbal. They know how to express when they want something and when they don't . . . I actually really like animals and I have learned from discussions with a lot of zoophiles they really, really love their animals. They treat them better than humans. They really care if the animal enjoys what's happening or not, and they can tell."

When Ms. C. came into Paul's life, his paranoia got louder. He's terrified that if they're caught and reported, she'll be taken from him and put down. He has a series of Google alerts, and he'll obsess over reports of "perverts" who have been caught with animals during sex. He never hears the outcomes, but the endless electronic stream of doomy headlines that pop up on his phone or laptop make him feel as if his sexuality were under constant attack. Despite their open marriage, Paul hasn't had sex with anyone but Ms. C. or Fran for the last twenty-one years, and when we met, it had been more than four years since he'd done anything sexual with Ms. C.

That's not by choice, though. At first, he got lucky with a good rate at a private barn, but when that stable owner decided to sell, the rent went up so high that Paul had to move her. Her new stable is communal and is surrounded by houses on all four sides, so Paul has self-imposed a ban on sexual intimacy until he can guarantee privacy (Hammer's shower curtains wouldn't be sufficient). There's just too much risk. It all boils down to money. Private stables are expensive, and because Ms. C.'s well-being comes first, Paul has to be sure he can trust anyone who has access to her when he's not around (to find her current home, he studiously inspected and interviewed each facility). Fran has offered to stand guard, but Paul wouldn't be able to relax. He hates that the concern and legality have had this impact on him: "It's a very sad thing how paranoid zoophiles are."

Perhaps the biggest problem with Ms. C.'s inability to communicate verbally is Paul's fear that she'll die. He fastidiously monitors her health and well-being for any signs of Cushing's, colic, or strangles—a very common upper respiratory infection that in rare cases leads to death. He's had her immunized for eastern and western equine influenza, and makes sure she's regularly tested for EIA, equine infectious anemia, which has been called "HIV's country cousin"—an autoimmune disease for which there is no vaccine or cure.[63]

After he'd been with her for about three years, Ms. C. developed colic. The vet had been over a few times, and Paul didn't think they were taking her condition seriously. He was sure Ms. C. was gone. She was sweating and lethargic; all she could do was lie down. Paul stayed with her in the barn and whispered goodbye. She came over, sidled up to him, and put her hip beside his head with her belly against his shoulder; she seemed to move until he found the right spot. He patiently pressed, massaged, and rubbed, easing her off on her journey. Sick with preemptive grief, he called the vet again the following morning, determined to save her. This time the doctor treated her with a gallon and a half of mineral oil, which helps horses pass the impacted mass. By six o'clock that night she was back to her old self. That brush with death was terrifying, Paul hates thinking about it: "I can't imagine what I would have done to get over that."

Ms. C. stood on a plate of frozen paddock with the sun shining on her copper hair. "I just don't know how anyone could *not* find that attractive," Paul said as we approached the Arabian mare whose head, neck, and torso were covered by an insulated plaid blanket. "I know it's supposed to be the opposite, but I just don't understand," he continued, sighing. Her jet-black mane hung neatly as if parted on the side just covering her eyes—an equine hipster with killer bangs. Her eyes, endless inky wells powered by that famous peripheral vision, were glossy, as if she'd been interrupted watching a sad movie. The pair hadn't seen each other for about four days. Paul kissed her nose, cradled her jaw, and stage whispered in baby voice into her ear: "Let's take that off you, eh?"

When Paul released Ms. C.'s blanket, he turned to me and, as if anticipating judgment about her less than perfect winter coat, said, "I don't like putting them on her, but the hair rubs off on her chest, so you have to so she doesn't get cold." In winter the temperature can dip as low as minus forty. "You are probably seeing her at her worst right now," he said as he led Ms. C. from the pasture into the stable for her grooming routine. "At the end of winter she'll shed all that hair out, and she will look slick and beautiful." I hadn't been around too many horses, but she looked just fine to me. Anyway, I was too busy being intimidated by her size and scale and those omnipresent monitoring eyes, which seemed to clock my every move.

I peered in the bucket at a set of combs, brushes, some files, and a small hoof knife. "Cold weather is not kind to anyone's body!" I defended Ms. C. on his behalf, aware how concerned he was to give a good impression. He didn't hear, though. If we were at a bar, I'd say it was as if they were the only two in the room. He let her sniff each tool before he set to work. "It's a respect thing so she knows what they are. I want her to know what I will use on her body," he said. I watched the pair, shifting my feet, which were becoming numb, digging my hands into my pockets, amazed at Paul's stamina; it was so cold. He used a pick to dig into the hoof to remove stones, as if he were shucking oysters. Then he trimmed them with a file, flakes of hoof shard billowing into the air like a cloud of pixelated smoke before settling on the icy ground and curling up.

When I talked to Dr. Miletski, I asked her directly: Does she think something causes someone to be a zoophile, like trauma or childhood abuse? She admitted that when she began her research, she was looking for origin stories like that but her findings proved otherwise, and in her experience as a therapist most people—zoophile or otherwise—have experienced some kind of trauma.

Paul stood directly behind Ms. C., brushing her tail. "I would never stand behind a horse I didn't know and trust," he said. Then he poured water on the pellets and carrots he'd mixed for her so it wouldn't swell in her stomach. Ms. C. busily looked up wearing a thick food mustache. "I see what you mean about privacy," I said, looking around at all the houses with direct view out to the barn and field. He sighed and said he feels bad that it's been so long since they were intimate. He's established a routine so he can visit her once during the week and then again at the weekend, but it's been tough. "I can see in the way she responds to me that she doesn't have much of a connection with me, and I don't have the connection that I want with her." It's not just the absence of sex that gets him down; he wishes they could be together more: "If I never had sex with her again, that wouldn't change anything. I would keep her and love her and hold her. Just like I could never stop loving my wife . . . Sex is secondary."

"Is she okay around strangers? Is my presence weird for her?" I asked. "She's actually one of the best behaved horses I have ever met," he cooed, rubbing her nose. "She's good for the vet; she's good for everybody." I stared into Ms. C.'s eyes, which reflected back a tiny image of my body, like a convex traffic mirror. I gazed at her for a while, wishing somewhere there was an archive of photos taken by her eyes. "How do you feel being here with her?" The question I'd asked so many times felt more urgent in her presence. "I would never characterize it like, oh, I'm going to visit a girlfriend . . . it's like, I'm going to visit Ms. C. I never did a lot of dating, so maybe I don't have the language? I guess it's like visiting an old friend? I'm really happy to see her, but because of the facilities and the fact that I'm not riding at the moment, we don't really have anything to do together. A lot of people would argue that riding is not very nice, but it would be good to do *something* with her." Like many long-term relationships, you end up just functioning together, I thought. "I take her for walks in the forest, and it's nice, but there's no what's next? Where are we going from here?"

On the drive home we had one of those multi-topic conversations where it feels as if you need to pause and write minutes and an agenda—like the talks I have with close friends when I haven't seen them for a while. He told me about a bestiality case that would soon be heard by the Supreme Court of Canada, which he was concerned might close a loophole where non-penetrative sex acts with animals weren't prohibited (and in 2019 a bill was

passed that tightened the criminal code making all sexual activities with animals illegal and deeming that anyone convicted
of bestiality would be listed on the sex offender database). We
shared our reaction to the internet comments his interview had
attracted, and he filled me in on the latest Canadian political gossip. As we neared my hotel, he became emotional. "I wish I could
be this open every day," he said, staring straight ahead, avoiding
eye contact, apologizing for all the secrecy. "I wish I could come
out." Later he wrote by email, "I guess thinking about it, you are
the first completely 'straight' person to ever see me kiss a horse
and know what I was."

That night Fran, Paul, and I retired to a local coffee chain.
Paul took out his iPad and scrolled through his photos, proudly
showing me pictures of Ms. C. and a selection of Fran's handcrafts. When Fran spilled her cup of hot chamomile tea all over
his iPad, he moved quickly, noting that he cares more about his
wife's well-being than the current version of the technology that
brought them together. He checked that she wasn't burned and
handed her a mountain of napkins, whistling merrily, trying to
keep the mood upbeat while he wiped the table dry. "Fran needs
some aspirin, anyway," he said, smiling, before ducking out into
the cold night to get his laptop so we could continue the photo
show. "He's so devoted to you," I said, and Fran agreed. "That's
why instead of letting shit break us apart, I went to therapy,"
she explained. "When you go through years of bad relationships
with men, when you find something good, you kinda wanna
stick with it."

When Paul returned, he sat down and scrolled through his
photos—Ms. C. lying on her side sleeping, Ms. C. in the paddock,
Paul bolt upright (on Ms. C.'s back), smiling and wearing an
adult male helmet. He flicked through an album and paused on
an image of a poster for a 1970s film called *Equus* that is based
on a play by Peter Shaffer, about a psychiatrist who wants to fix a

kid who has a fascination with horses. "You should watch that," he said to me. Fran jumped in and said, "I found it brutal." "Well, it's a nasty story, but the kid is confused," Paul timidly protested. "He ends up blinding a whole lot of horses. The story is told by his psychologist, who is debating whether he should make this boy normal because his moments of passion are so intense." When they started dating, Fran went online and visited a few zoosexual forums so she could learn more about his world. The first thing she saw was an anonymous post from someone boasting about the terrible things they liked to do to cats. Fran lowered her voice and stared directly at Paul: "It was torture, and I'm sorry but I really have issues with torture."

Paul sighed, scrolling aimlessly through his photo album. "I'm not arguing with you at all," he said, but Fran didn't let him finish: "That image will stick with me for the rest of my life. And you know, the roommate that I met Paul through told me about another person who took kittens from . . ." This time Paul interrupted her: "He was only saying that to get a rise out of you." Fran folded her arms across her chest and said, "Well, he did." "I've tried a couple of different times to get on different forums, and I always come across people . . . the last forum I was on it wasn't torture but it also wasn't pleasant. And they also had some serious issues of *prove it to me by providing photos, and tell me where you live, I'm coming to your country. Invite me over for your dog.* Since then I told Paul, you know what? This is the last time. I know he's had completely different experiences with these people, but I get very angry at people who have that attitude."

It's an argument they often have, a staple in the roster of repetitious couple-fights. Paul tried a different angle: "I know, but there are bad people everywhere. If you go on Tinder, you get the same." Fran promptly shut that shit down: "You will notice I'm not on Tinder, and I wouldn't go on any sort of dating app."

Paul was torn. He has his own issues with abusive bestialists who he thinks give zoosexuals a bad name, but he's protective of all zoosexuals. "Look," he said, "a lot of zoos don't learn any better. They aren't talking to anyone, because they *can't* talk to anyone, and then they do join these communities, and the first people they talk to are . . . not always the best." Like when you move to a new job, or a new country, I offered, trying to ease the tension. "Exactly," Paul agreed. "Do they represent the entire country or job? Of course, I'd argue that the only way to make it better is to give kids information about zoosexuality as they grow up." I tried my hardest to be diplomatic, knowing how unlikely it is that scenario will ever occur. "But in the U.S.A. many adults don't even believe in telling kids about sex with humans," I said.

By the time I got back to my hotel, it was almost midnight. I said goodbye from the backseat, and when neither Fran nor Paul got out of the car for a farewell, I figured it was because they were worried about being seen. When I got to my room, I ran a bath. My feet still felt cold from hours standing outside much earlier that day. I undressed and examined my pale winter body in the mirror as if I were an aging horse. A weird squishy lump on my leg that materialized in my twenties; a scallop-shaped scar on my knee earned as a kid throwing a supermarket parking-lot tantrum; faded mosquito bites on my ankles; purple marks from years of waxing. I was crying when I stepped into the water. I'd been alone, cut off from my communication networks while I absorbed the weight of Paul's secret life and sadness about not being able to be intimate with Ms. C., which, I guess, needed to get out. I felt the weight of Paul's situation: that he will never be able to live in the open, that his sexuality will never be accepted or understood.

The next day I killed time at a shopping center while I waited for the train. I was in line at a pharmacy when a man cut in front of me. "Am I fucking invisible?" I yelled, startling the young female cashier, the man, his female companion, and probably the whole sense of Canadian social order. "Keep a low profile," I reminded myself while the young woman avoided eye contact and gingerly scanned my items. I walked to the train station and checked my email on my burner phone. Paul had replied to a message I sent early in the morning asking how he'd found the weekend. He dwelled on my departure: "The only thing I regret is not giving you a hug goodbye . . . I really, really should have. It surprised me a little bit that you hugged me at first sight. I mean, even if *I* don't believe it, having the whole disgusting hillbilly stereotype upon you can make you expect people to treat you differently. I guess that is something always at the back of my mind."

It had been almost five years since my very first phone call with Paul when we met again. He had some time off from work for the summer, and I was visiting Canada, so he drove to spend the day with me in the city. He set out early and updated me from the road. I was pottering around getting ready when I realized the nerves that dominated the buildup to our first meeting had been replaced with a new set of emotions. Paul and I hadn't communicated much by phone or email over the last year. I'd been less persistent. I made up excuses, and even canceled a few scheduled conversations. Sometimes I'd contact him, then put off replying to his emails or messages. I'd become so apprehensive about the prospect of publishing a book that included a chapter about his sexuality that I avoided him and internalized the suspicion, disgust, fear, and ridicule that was projected onto me when I talked about him to "outsiders." That's who I'd divided the world into, those who "understood" and those who didn't. Those who screwed their faces up or made any other sign that they didn't want to hear about Paul were filed away as "outsiders."

I knew they just didn't get it, and I was sick of the suspicion that fell upon me when I tried to explain what I'd learned from Paul.

But during that time avoiding Paul, his familiarity, his humanity, his normality had given way to that darkness and suspicion that was usually projected onto his sexuality. This time while I was preparing to meet him, I wasn't so much worried about what he would think of me, or what state I would find him in. Instead, I was craving connection with him as someone who understood.

We met on the street outside my rental apartment. "You're looking good!" I complimented him as I slid in the front passenger seat. And he was—tan and refreshed from summer and a long weekend he'd just spent with Fran. He rubbed his soft cheeks, which had that vulnerable look as if he'd just shaved. "That's just my winter weight," he said with a laugh, "and also I cleaned up my face for the occasion." We set off for the day—Fran had asked him to get some CBD oil for sleep—so we stopped by a dispensary ("we are buying drugs from a wholesome grandma," Paul joked when I commented on the unorthodox drug dealer attire: spectacles and an apron). Then we turned to Siri to find a Thai or sushi restaurant (his favorite cuisines are not strong in his less-than-cosmopolitan local area). When we sat down to eat lunch, I thought of his inaugural meeting at that sushi restaurant with that zoophile almost thirty years ago, when he was just a teenager, and how much the experience of traveling to a distant place in search of physical human connection with a like mind had shaped his entire life.

After lunch, he suggested we find a park so we could talk more openly. His GPS was acting up, so instead of googling, we weaved around the streets that were unfamiliar to both of us searching for a clearing. As if he had a sonar, Paul looked up into the distance and spotted a misty fluff of green on the horizon and continued to drive toward the comforting organic anchor, his version of those golden arches showing a McDonald's on a barren stretch of highway. We sat on a bench and watched young men and women in yoga pants and tank tops stretched out in the sun with thick textbooks and mobile phones, and I filled him in on the research I'd done since we last met. He listened keenly, jealous that I could access these people and ask questions without fear.

Then the conversation returned to the questions that always hung in the air when I was with Paul: Why did I put myself in this position? Why was I interested in his sexuality, in his world? Why voluntarily open myself up to the attack and abuse that come with even talking about it? Why did I care? Why did I believe that he wasn't cruel or abusive? They're never easy questions to answer, but I tried: I told him that it's so nuanced, and I'm worried as a culture we are losing the ability to take our time and think through how something makes us feel. Why do we have to have an instant opinion about everyone and everything? I'd learned about his world out of curiosity, and once I got to know him, I found it difficult to judge him: Why should I be prevented from writing about that? I told him I think the repulsion that is projected onto his sexuality reveals how contradictory humans are. We don't ask for verbal consent from animals for anything, ever. So to me, that logic just doesn't make sense. I also told him that regardless of what I think about zoophilia, the way that he used the internet to come of age as a zoosexual says something important about its power as a tool for how people can discover who they are in the world today: he went online and came of age as a man attracted to horses, and I think that story needs to be told.

He can't ever be visible and he's been intimately dealing with this for his whole life, and he knows how unforgiving the backlash will be. Zoos learn by observation the risks of going public and becoming the face of zoosexuality. It's not worth it. But as he'd pointed out when we spoke for the very first time, he was so tired of the self-fulfilling loop. Nothing changes because everyone stays hidden. Paul was at a point where he'd gladly make that leap; he'd wear the social stigma. But the risk of losing Ms. C. isn't worth it. "If I had nothing to protect, I'd be open," he said. Instead, he's given up on trying to convince people that his sexuality isn't abusive or a joke; that was the same way I'd felt. He plans to shut down all his social media and retreat from the conversation completely. "They have already made up their minds. There's nothing I can say to convince them that I'm a good person. They would have to know me, and even then that might not be enough."

On the way home we made a few wrong turns. Paul wasn't used to driving in the city anymore. I told him I was getting ready to leave New York. The pace was getting too much, it was too expensive to live alone, my family were far away in New Zealand: the anonymity I'd craved when I was younger had slowly turned into isolation. "If I stay there, I worry I'll end up like one of those people you see alone at the supermarket muttering to themselves while they look for the smallest portion of frozen meat, talking to pigeons in the park." Paul laughed. "I can see there's a lot of appeal to living like that, though, without any dependents. You can be yourself, authentically," he said. "I guess you always have to trade something when it comes to your lifestyle," I said, feeling guilty complaining about any difficulty I may have in life while I was in the company of a man whose entire identity was bundled up in so much secrecy and compromise. Paul agreed. "I put up with a lot of bullshit at work I wish I never had to," he said, "but I have a secure job for life and a guaranteed pension. I made that choice. When I get frustrated with corporate or when someone screws up, I remind myself: you made a trade-off."

This time when we parted, I leaned in and gave him a hug. I made my way up the stairs to my apartment thinking about how much lighter I felt—lighter than I had after my first physical encounter with Paul but also lighter than I had felt that morning, lighter than I had in months, maybe even years. It felt so good to talk without judgment, to be open. To have the comfort of someone who knew, intimately, the anxiety and isolation I'd been living with, a version of the way that he'd felt after that first time we met. I was there as an outsider who had been able to peer through the iron wall that prevents his identity from ever being normal.

# Acknowledgments

I am extremely grateful to my agent, Elias Altman, and to Tim Bartlett and Alice Pfeifer at St. Martin's Press.

So many friends and family in so many cities and countries gave me advice, support, accommodation, and encouragement during the years I spent reporting and writing and I am so grateful to all of them, especially Athina, Barry, Kristina, Amanda, Aaron, Ashley, Daniel, Katie, Mary Jane, Michael, and Molly. My colleagues at *New York* also offered tremendous support, and I'm very grateful to all my editors there (at the magazine, *The Cut*, and *Science of Us*). I am indebted to everyone who read drafts, provided honest feedback, and brainstormed ideas with me.

Thanks to Katherine Barner and Elissa Sanci for their thorough transcribing and reporting; Matthew Giles for his intrepid research, reporting, and fact-checking; and the staff at the Kinsey Institute's Library for helping me access archival material used in chapter 1. The New York Mills Regional Cultural Center's residency program gave me valuable time to write, as did Katie and Ryan's perpetual (unofficial) Chicago-based writer's retreat.

This book represents countless phone calls, emails, and encounters with a range of very open, patient, and trusting people.

There are so many conversations, meetings, adventures (and misadventures) that didn't make it into the final version of *Finding Normal,* and I'm indebted to all of those who shared their time and life experiences with me, and welcomed me into their world. Thank you to everyone who hosted me during reporting trips, introduced me to friends and family, and tolerated my endless stream of questions. My heartfelt appreciation goes to Shelly and Paul for risking so much by talking to me, and to everyone else who so generously trusted me with their story.

# Notes

### Introduction

1. Double Dick Dude, "I Am the Guy with Two Penises. AMA," Reddit, Jan. 2, 2014, www.reddit.com/r/WTF/comments/1u3rj2/man_with_2_penises/.

2. Alexa Tsoulis-Reay, "What It's Like to Date a Horse," *Cut*, Nov. 20, 2014, www.thecut.com/2014/11/what-its-like-to-date-a-horse.html.

3. Saddle, "What It's Like to Date a Horse—New York Magazine Has Gone Too Far," Filly Girl, Nov. 24, 2014, fillygirl.com/what-its-like-to-date-a-horse-new-york-magazine-has-gone-too-far/.

4. Peter Cryle and Elizabeth Stephens, introduction to *Normality: A Critical Genealogy*, ed. Peter Cryle and Elizabeth Stephens (Chicago: University of Chicago Press, 2017), 2, where they also cite Ian Hacking, *The Taming of Chance* (Cambridge, U.K.: Cambridge University Press, 1990), 160, 169.

5. Peter Kurth, "'The Trouble with Normal' by Michael Warner," *Salon*, Dec. 8, 1999, www.salon.com/1999/12/08/warner_7/. See also Michael Warner, *The Trouble with Normal: Sex, Politics, and the Ethics of Queer Life* (Cambridge, MA: Harvard University Press, 1999).

### 1: Ken, Russ, Emily, and Kathy

1. Dan Savage, "Savage Love: Meet the Monogamish," *Stranger*, Jan. 4, 2012, www.thestranger.com/seattle/SavageLove?oid=11412386.

2. James R. Fleckenstein, "Polyamory and Alternative Non-monogamy," in *The Continuum Complete International Encyclopedia of Sexuality*, ed. Robert Francoeur and Raymond Noonan (New York: Continuum International, 2004), 1205.

3. Wesp, interview by Haslam, 2008.

4. Dossie Easton and Catherine A. Liszt, *The Ethical Slut: A Practical Guide to Polyamory, Open Relationships, and Other Adventures* (San Francisco: Greenery Press, 1997), 21.

5. Ibid., 40.

6. Ibid., 15.

7. Ibid., 34.

8. Fleckenstein, "Polyamory and Alternative Non-monogamy," 1206.

9. Deborah Anapol, *Love Without Limits: The Quest for Sustainable Intimate Relationships* (San Rafael, CA: IntiNet Resource Center, 1992).

10. *Glamour*, June 1990.

11. *Cosmopolitan*, Jan. 1992.

12. *The Joan Rivers Show*, July 13, 1992.

13. *Donahue*, April 22, 1992.

14. Rick and Jan Ross to Anapol, April 28, 1992, Kenneth R. Haslam Collection on Polyamory, Kinsey Institute.

15. Robert G. Lucas to Anapol, April 27, 1992, Haslam Collection on Polyamory.

16. Larry S. Plemn to Anapol, May 29, 1992, Haslam Collection on Polyamory.

17. David Southcomb to Anapol, April 23, 1992, Haslam Collection on Polyamory.

18. Larry Jones to Anapol, Aug. 17, 1992, Haslam Collection on Polyamory.

19. Jim and Pat Kyro to Anapol, May 21, 1993, Haslam Collection on Polyamory.

20. Barbara Passerelle to Anapol, Sept. 12, 1993, Haslam Collection on Polyamory.

21. See Susan Dominus, "Is an Open Marriage a Happier Marriage?," *New York Times Magazine*, May 11, 2017, www.nytimes.com/2017/05/11 /magazine/is-an-open-marriage-a-happier-marriage.html; Alex Morris, "Tales from the Millennials' Sexual Revolution," *Rolling Stone*,

March 31, 2014, www.rollingstone.com/interactive/feature-millennial
-sexual-revolution-relationships-marriage/; Editors, "The Next Sexual Revolution? A Look at the Estimated Millions of People Exploring Open Marriages," *Marie Claire*, Dec. 14, 2015, www.marieclaire
.com/sex-love/a17341/the-next-sexual-revolution-open-marriage/;
Whitney Joiner, "My Boyfriend's Married, and His Wife's on Board,"
*Elle*, Sept. 14, 2016, www.elle.com/life-love/sex-relationships/news
/a39126/open-marriage-secondary-partners/.

22. Alexa Tsoulis-Reay, "5 People on Coming Out as Poly to Their
Families," *The Cut*, July 13, 2018, www.thecut.com/article/what-is
-polyamorous-relationship.html.

23. Morris, "Tales from the Millennials' Sexual Revolution."

24. Kim Parker and Renee Stepler, "As U.S. Marriage Rate Hovers at
50%, Educational Gap in Marital Status Widens," Pew Research
Center, Sept. 14, 2017, www.pewresearch.org/fact-tank/2017/09/14
/as-u-s-marriage-rate-hovers-at-50-education-gap-in-marital-status
-widens/.

25. A. W. Geiger and Gretchen Livingston, "8 Facts About Love and
Marriage in America," Pew Research Center, Feb. 13, 2019, www
.pewresearch.org/fact-tank/2019/02/13/8-facts-about-love-and
-marriage/.

26. Cunning Minx, PW: 427 "Poly Geezers with Ken Haslam," *Polyamory Weekly*, podcast, April 6, 2015, polyweekly.com/pw-427-poly
-geezers-with-ken-haslam/.

27. K. Saad, letter to the editor, *Delaware Valley Synergy*, date unknown.

28. "Saturday June 02-Prudes Night Out: 7:30PM Non Permissive," *Delaware Valley Synergy*, May 2001.

29. Dominus, "Is an Open Marriage a Happier Marriage?"

30. Claire Kimberly and Robert McGinley, "Changes in the Swinging
Lifestyle: A US National and Historical Comparison," *Culture, Health,
and Sexuality* 21, no. 2 (2019): 220, doi.org/10.1080/13691058.2018
.1460692.

31. Terry Gould, *The Lifestyle: A Look at the Erotic Rites of Swingers*
(Toronto: Random House Canada, 1999), 4.

32. Kasidie, accessed Nov. 16, 2020, www.kasidie.com/.

33. Kenneth Haslam, "Foreword," Mark A. Michaels and Patricia Johnson,

*Designer Relationships: A Guide to Happy Monogamy, Positive Poly-amory, and Optimistic Open Relationships* (San Francisco, CA: Cleis Press, 2015).

## 2: Julia and Eileen, Andrew and Jane

1. Rebecca Flood, "Woman, 24, with Girlfriend, 61, Says 37-Year Age Gap Doesn't Affect Relationship," *Sun*, Jan. 6, 2019, www.thesun.co .uk/fabulous/8132275/lesbian-couple-age-gap-love-relationship -marriage.

2. Julia Zelg, "Trip to Rio with My Fiancee," YouTube, Feb. 1, 2019, www.youtube.com/watch?v=0qLENFV-TYg.

3. Julia Zelg, "Weekend Away with My Girlfriend (Lesbian Age Gap Couple)," YouTube, Sept. 19, 2018, www.youtube.com/watch?v=jGAEsu 2hCDo.

4. Julia Zelg, "Our Morning Routine/Lesbian Couple," YouTube, Jan. 22, 2019, www.youtube.com/watch?v=Tm_B1A1Ycbk.

5. Julia Zelg, "Moving In with My Girlfriend VLOG," YouTube, Oct. 12, 2018, www.youtube.com/watch?v=1xYwdN-6l88&t=107s.

6. Rosemary-Claire Collard, "Cougar Figures, Gender, and the Performances of Predation," *Gender, Place, and Culture* 19, no. 4 (2012): 527–28, doi.org/10.1080/0966369X.2011.610179.

7. Collette A. Banks and Dr. Paul Arnold, "Opinions Towards Sexual Partners with a Large Age Difference," *Marriage and Family Review* 33, no. 4 (2001): 5–18, www.tandfonline.com/doi/abs/10.1300 /J002v33n04_02.

8. "Table FG3 Married Couple Family Groups, by Presence of Own Children Under 18, and Age, Earnings, Education, and Race and Hispanic Origin of Both Spouses: 2017," *U.S. Census Bureau, Current Population Survey, 2017 Annual Social and Economic Supplement*, www.census.gov/data/tables/2017/demo/families/cps-2017.html. May 2, 2021.

9. Shannon Keating, "What It's Like to Be a Lesbian Couple with a 20-Plus-Year Age Difference," *BuzzFeed*, Dec. 14, 2015, www.buzzfeed .com/shannonkeating/lesbian-age-differences.

10. Butch Wonders, "Mind the (Age) Gap: How to Do a May/December

Lesbian Relationship," *Autostraddle,* Feb. 8, 2012, www.autostraddle .com/mind-the-age-gap-how-to-deal-with-may-december-lesbian -relationships-131564/.

11. Jill Pitkeathley and David Emerson, *Age Gap Relationships: The Attractions and Drawbacks of Choosing a Partner Much Older or Younger Than Yourself* (London: Thorsons, 1995), 1.

12. Ibid., 8.

13. Jill, "Got Married on My 52nd Birthday at Instant Marriage, Encino, CA 11–24–18," May December Society, Dec. 1, 2018, maydecem-bersociety.com/post/7799088/got-married-on-my-52nd-birthday-at -instant-marriage-encino-ca-11.

14. "Jane Beckman," May December Society, accessed Nov. 19, 2020, maydecembersociety.com/jancb.

15. Jane Beckman, "Crazy Generations—My Age Gap Family," May December Society, May 13, 2016, maydecembersociety.com/post/5314383 /crazy-generations-my-age-gap-family.

16. "Ailene & Taylor," May December Society, accessed Nov. 19, 2020, maydecembersociety.com/profile/263247.

17. Ailene & Taylor, "After 9 Long Months of Waiting," May December Society, March 12, 2018, maydecembersociety.com/post/7125911 /after-9-long-months-of-waiting.

18. Julia Zelg, "Reading Hate Comments with My Older Girlfriend," YouTube, Oct. 28, 2018, www.youtube.com/watch?v=lDNB-fhBMGo.

19. Julia Zelg, "We're Moving In Together! (Lesbian Age Gap Couple)," You-Tube, Sept. 26, 2018, www.youtube.com/watch?v=AiCFYPVLRDU&t =296s.

20. Julia Zelg, "Proposing to My Girlfriend on Stage (Lesbian Couple)," You-Tube, Dec. 13, 2018, www.youtube.com/watch?v=CMichfphACY&t =462s.

21. Julia Zelg, "My Coming Out Story," YouTube, Oct. 18, 2016, www .youtube.com/watch?v=hosxmIqtdcQ.

22. Eileen De Freest, "Coming Out in the 80s," YouTube, Feb. 18, 2019, www.youtube.com/watch?v=cHuQlpG3cww.

23. Julia Zelg, "Julia and Eileen's WEDDING Video/Lesbian Wedding," YouTube, June 29, 2019, www.youtube.com/watch?v=oJ2hiP4C1Wg.

24. *Extreme Cougar Wives,* season 1, episode 3, "This Cougar Is Very Dangerous," TLC, Aug. 22, 2013; *Age Gap Love,* season 1, episode 2, Channel 5, Sept. 22, 2014.

**3: Maddy**

1. Alfred C. Kinsey et al., *Sexual Behavior in the Human Male* (Philadelphia: W. B. Saunders, 1948), 654.

2. Zoe O'Reilly, "My Life as an Amoeba," *StarNet Dispatches,* May 30, 1997, web.archive.org/web/20030210212218/http:/dispatches .azstarnet.com/zoe/amoeba.htm.

3. Gary, comment on O'Reilly, "My Life as an Amoeba," https://web .archive.org/web/20030305150007/http://dispatches.azstarnet.com /zoe/amoeba2.htm.

4. Dani, comment on O'Reilly, "My Life as an Amoeba," web.archive .org/web/20030305150007/http://dispatches.azstarnet.com/zoe /amoeba2.htm.

5. Amy, comment on O'Reilly, "My Life as an Amoeba," web.archive .org/web/20030305150007/http://dispatches.azstarnet.com/zoe /amoeba2.htm.

6. "Overview," Asexual Visibility & Education Network, accessed Nov. 9, 2020, www.asexuality.org/?q=overview.html.

7. David Jay, AVEN Media Team Guidebook.

8. Anthony F. Bogaert, "Asexuality: Prevalence and Associated Factors in a National Probability Sample," *Journal of Sex Research* 41, no. 3 (2004): 279–87, doi:10.1080/00224490409552235.

9. Sylvia Pagan Westphal, "Glad to Be Asexual," *New Scientist,* Oct. 14, 2004, www.newscientist.com/article/dn6533-feature-glad-to-be -asexual/.

10. *The View,* ABC, Jan. 15, 2006.

11. *The Situation with Tucker Carlson,* MSNBC, March 28, 2006.

12. *The Montel Williams Show,* "Asexuality: The Joy of Sex," Jan. 4, 2007.

13. See Anthony F. Bogaert, *Understanding Asexuality* (Lanham, MD: Rowman & Littlefield, 2012); Karli June Cerankowski and Megan Milks, eds., *Asexualities: Feminist and Queer Perspectives* (New York: Routledge, 2014); Angela Chen, *Ace: What Asexuality Reveals About Desire, Society, and the Meaning of Sex* (Boston: Beacon Press, 2020);

Ela Przybylo, *Asexual Erotics: Intimate Readings of Compulsory Sexuality* (Columbus: Ohio State University Press, 2019).

14. See *AZE*, azejournal.com; Sandra Bellamy, *Asexual Perspectives: 47 Asexual Stories* (Truro, U.K.: Quirky Books, 2017); Julie Sondra Decker, *The Invisible Orientation: An Introduction to Asexuality* (New York: Skyhorse, 2015).

15. *Sex Education*, season 2, episode 4, directed by Alice Seabright, written by Laurie Nunn, Netflix, Jan. 17, 2020.

16. Quacks, Reply to Jules.2P, "Ace Representation in the Series 'Sex Education,'" Asexual Visibility & Education Network, Jan. 18, 2020, www.asexuality.org/en/topic/193518-ace-representation-in-the -series-sex-education.

17. *House*, season 8, episode 9, "Better Half," directed by Greg Yaitanes, written by David Shore and Kath Lingenfelter, Fox, Jan. 23, 2012.

18. Lori A. Brotto et al., "Asexuality: A Mixed Methods Approach," *Archives of Sexual Behavior* 39, no. 3 (2010): 599–618; Lori A. Brotto and Morag A. Yule, "Asexuality: Sexual Orientation, Paraphilia, Sexual Dysfunction, or None of the Above?," *Archives of Sexual Behavior* 46, no. 3 (2017): 619–27; Lori A. Brotto and Morag A. Yule, "Physiological and Subjective Sexual Arousal in Self-Identified Asexual Women," *Archives of Sexual Behavior* 40, no. 4 (2011): 699–712; Lori A. Brotto, Morag A. Yule, and Boris B. Gorzalka, "Asexuality: An Extreme Variant of Sexual Desire Disorder?," *Journal of Sexual Medicine* 12, no. 3 (2015): 646–60.

19. Amy N. Antonsen et al., "Ace and Aro: Understanding Differences in Romantic Attractions Among Persons Identifying as Asexual," *Archives of Sexual Behavior* 49, no. 5 (2020):1615–30.

20. Frances Chapman, "Talking It Out in New York City: Is the Sexual Political?," *Off Our Backs* 3, no. 5 (1973): 6.

21. Ibid.

22. Ibid.

23. Margot Adler, "An Excerpt from Heretic's Heart," hourwolf.com /heretic/index.htm.

24. "Quick Facts: New Orleans City, Louisiana," U.S. Census Bureau, accessed Nov. 9, 2020, www.census.gov/quickfacts/neworleanscitylouisiana.

25. Lisa Orlando, "The Asexual Manifesto" (1972), 1.

26. Siggy, "Lisa Orlando, Author of the Asexual Manifesto (1972),"
The Asexual Agenda, July 19, 2019, accessed March 1, 2021,
asexualagenda.wordpress.com/2019/08/01/lisa-orlando-author-of
-the-asexual-manifesto-1972/.

## 4: Shelly

1. Judy, "My GSA Story," GSA Forum, Oct. 13, 2013, thegsaforum.com
/topic/985-my-gsa-story/.
2. Dale, Reply to "What Does GSA Feel LIKE," Lost Sister, GSA Forum, Aug. 20, 2013, thegsaforum.com/topic/948-what-does-gsa-feel
-like/.
3. Barbara Gonyo, "Genetic Sexual Attraction: Is It Bonding?," in *I'm
His Mother but He's Not My Son* (Barbara Gonyo, 1991), loc. 1576,
Kindle.
4. Andrew M. Colman, *Oxford Dictionary of Psychology* (Oxford: Oxford University Press, 2006), www.oxfordreference.com/view/10
.1093/oi/authority.20110803095847705.
5. Kindred Spirits Forum, accessed Nov. 12, 2020, ks2016.forumactif.fr/.
6. John, "Secretly Struggling with GSA with Half Sister Without Her
Knowing," GSA Forum, March 30, 2016, thegsaforum.com/topic
/1362-secretly-struggling-with-gsa-with-half-sister-without-her
-knowing/.
7. Serena, Reply to "Secretly Struggling with GSA with Half Sister Without Her Knowing," GSA Forum, March 31, 2016, thegsaforum.com
/topic/1362-secretly-struggling-with-gsa-with-half-sister-without
-her-knowing/.
8. Keith Pullman, *Full Marriage Equality* (blog), accessed Nov. 12,
2020, marriage-equality.blogspot.com.
9. Keith Pullman, "Case Studies," *Full Marriage Equality* (blog), accessed
Nov. 12, 2020, marriage-equality.blogspot.com/p/case-studies.html.
10. Diane Rinella, *Love's Forbidden Flower* (Midnight to Six, 1992).
11. Cristina Shy, "History," *Friends of Lily*, accessed Nov. 15, 2019,
www.lilysgardener.com/history.html.
12. Michelle Ann Owens, "Cristina Shy on Genetic Sexual Attraction,"
*Nothing Off Limits*, podcast, March 13, 2017, www.breaker.audio/
nothing-off-limits/e/16293598.

13. Alexa Tsoulis-Reay, "What It's Like to Date Your Dad," *Cut*, Jan. 15, 2015, www.thecut.com/2015/01/what-its-like-to-date-your-dad.html.

14. Ibid.

15. Gonyo, "Discovery of Pregnancy," in *I'm His Mother but He's Not My Son*, loc. 2942.

16. Ibid., loc. 177.

17. Ibid., loc. 190.

18. Ibid.

19. Ibid., loc. 213.

20. "Adoptee/Birth Parent FAQs on Changes to Vital Records Law," State of New Jersey Department of Health, accessed Nov. 20, 2020, www.state.nj.us/health/vital/adoption/vital-record-law-changes-faqs/.

21. Gonyo, "Maternity Home," in *I'm His Mother but He's Not My Son*, loc. 264.

22. Ibid., loc. 276.

23. Ibid., loc. 264.

24. Ibid., loc. 432.

25. Ibid., loc. 313.

26. Gonyo, "Birth," in *I'm His Mother but He's Not My Son*, loc. 595.

27. Gonyo, "Maternity Home," loc. 383.

28. Gonyo, "Birth," loc. 475.

29. Ibid., loc. 506.

30. Gonyo, "May 1979: Recollections of the First Meeting," in *I'm His Mother but He's Not My Son*, loc. 53.

31. Gonyo, "Birth," loc. 533.

32. Tsoulis-Reay, "What It's Like to Date Your Dad."

33. Kathryn Harrison, *The Kiss* (New York: Random House, 1997).

34. Cumbria County Council, *Genetic Sexual Attraction*, accessed Nov. 20, 2020, www.cumbria.gov.uk/eLibrary/Content/Internet/327/857/6802/42109163456.pdf.

35. Edvard Westermarck, *The History of Human Marriage* (London: Macmillan, 1891).

36. Betty Jean Lifton, *Journey of the Adopted Self: A Quest for Wholeness* (New York: Basic Books, 1994), 226.

37. Ibid., 227.

38. Maurice Greenberg and Ronald Littlewood, "Post-adoption Incest

and Phenotypic Matching: Experience, Personal Meanings, and Bio-social Implications," *British Journal of Medical Psychology* 68, no. 1 (1995): 37, bpspsychub.onlinelibrary.wiley.com/doi/abs/10.1111/j .2044–8341.1995.tb01811.x.

39. Tsoulis-Reay, "What It's Like to Date Your Dad."

40. Cosmo Frank, "This Woman Lost Her Virginity . . . to Her Dad and Now They're Getting Married," *Cosmopolitan*, Jan. 16, 2015, www .cosmopolitan.com/sex-love/news/a35384/this-woman-is-getting -married-to-her-dad/; Tracy Moore, "This Interview with a Woman Dating Her Father Will Haunt You Forever," *Jezebel*, Jan. 15, 2015, jezebel.com/this-interview-with-a-woman-dating-her-father-will -haun-1679768194; Emma Cueto, "What It's Like to Date . . . Your Dad," *Bustle*, Jan. 17, 2015, www.bustle.com/articles/59074-nymags -what-its-like-to-date-your-dad-interview-raises-a-bunch-of-red -flagsbesides-the.

41. Siam Goorwich, "This Interview with an 18 Year Old in a Relation-ship with Her Own Father Blows the Lid on Incest," *Metro*, Jan. 16, 2015, metro.co.uk/2015/01/16/this-interview-with-an-18-year -old-in-a-relationship-with-her-own-father-blows-the-lid-on-incest -5024888; Shari Puterman, "Incestuous 'Love Affair' Is Absolutely Horrific," *Asbury Park Press*, Jan. 22, 2015, www.app.com/story/life /family/parenting/shari-puterman/2015/01/22/incestual-love -affair-absolutely-horrific/22160189/; Elizabeth Armstrong Moore, "18-Year-Old Plans to Marry Her Long-Lost Father," *USA Today*, Jan. 16, 2015, www.usatoday.com/story/news/nation/2015/01/16 /daughter-plans-to-marry-long-lost-father/21859547/; Nina Gol-gowski, "Great Lakes Teen Says She Plans to Marry Father in New Jersey After Recently Reuniting, Losing Virginity to Him," *New York Daily News*, Jan. 19, 2015, www.nydailynews.com/news/national /teen-plans-marry-dad-romantic-reunion-article-1.2084306.

42. Samantha Allen, "'Consensual Incest' Is Rape," *Daily Beast*, Jan. 17, 2015, www.thedailybeast.com/consensual-incest-is-rape.

43. Louis C. Hochman, "Incest 'Is Totally Offensive,' Likely to Get on N.J. Legislature's Radar, Republican Leader Says," NJ.com, Jan. 20, 2015, www.nj.com/news/2015/01/incest_is_totally_offensive_likely_to _get_on_nj_le.html.

44. Brian Connolly, "Incest's History," *Los Angeles Review of Books*, Feb. 11, 2015, https://lareviewofbooks.org/article/incests-history/.

45. Che_Is_Dead, comment on Tsoulis-Reay, "What It's Like to Date Your Dad."

46. Mama.Maria, comment on Tsoulis-Reay, "What It's Like to Date Your Dad."

47. Moore, "18-Year-Old Plans to Marry Her Long-Lost Father."

48. Leslie Mann, "Mount Prospect Invites Families," *Chicago Tribune,* March 19, 2010, www.chicagotribune.com/ct-home-0319-mt -prospect-chomes-20100319-story.html.

49. *Dr. Drew*, CNN, Feb. 16, 2015.

50. Gonyo, "First Search," in *I'm His Mother but He's Not My Son*, loc. 616.

51. Gonyo, "Search," in *I'm His Mother but He's Not My Son*, loc. 785.

52. Gonyo, "Reunion," in *I'm His Mother but He's Not My Son*, loc. 1979.

53. Ibid., loc. 853.

54. Ibid., loc. 1017.

55. Ibid., loc. 1029.

## 5: Paul

1. SWDThrowaway453, "[NSFW] I'm Emotionally Dependent on My Partner and I Don't Know if I'll Be Handle Her Dying," Reddit, Oct. 27, 2014, archived online at zooish.net/r/zoophilia/post_2kfekd .html.

2. TheEthicalZoo, "Feminist/Social Justice Zoos, Where Are You?," Reddit, Nov. 24, 2014, archived online at zooish.net/r/zoophilia/post _2n7ojf.html.

3. Danpetman, comment on Crazy_ManMan, "How Do You Feel About the Term Zoophile," Reddit, Sept. 26, 2014, archived online at zooish .net/r/zoophilia/post_2hhv4d.html.

4. Pawwsies, comment on Furvert_Tail, "Should We Fight, or Should We Hide?," Reddit, Oct. 16, 2014, archived online at zooish.net/r /zoophilia/post_2jfzdr.html.

5. Jackdempsey8083, "Going Through Some Times with Accepting Myself," Reddit, March 28, 2015, archived online at zooish.net/r /zoophilia/post_30m7g0.html.

6. AliasTheReindeerPone, "Going Through Some Times with Accepting Myself."

7. BTWIAMAzoophile, "Going Through Some Times With Accepting Myself."

8. PeculiarParable, "Should We Fight, or Should We Hide?"

9. M. Jenny Edwards, "Arrest and Prosecution of Animal Sex Abuse (Bestiality) Offenders in the United States, 1975–2015," *Journal of the American Academy of Psychiatry and the Law* (47) no. 3 (2019), jaapl.org/content/early/2019/05/16/JAAPL.003836–19.

10. Danpetman, comment on zoozooz, "Consent Consent Consent Consent Consent," Reddit, Dec. 23, 2014, archived online https://zooish .net/r/zoophilia/post_2q5u2b.html.

11. Ursusem, "I Wonder Why Society Thinks It Is Okay for People to Pet Animals and to Keep Animals as Pets Without the Explicit Consent of the Animals but the Act of a Human Having Sex with an Animal Is Considered Not Okay," Reddit, March 30, 2015, archived online at zooish.net/r/zoophilia/post_30s6j5.html.

12. Omochanoshi, "I Wonder Why Society Thinks It Is Okay."

13. Zoozooz, "I Wonder Why Society Thinks It Is Okay."

14. Kynophile, "I Wonder Why Society Thinks It Is Okay."

15. Sapphire_seam, "I Wonder Why Society Thinks It Is Okay."

16. Hani Miletski, "Understanding Bestiality and Zoophilia (the Book)," Hani Miletski, PhD, MSW, LLC, accessed Nov. 13, 2020, www .drmiletski.com/prolog.html.

17. Mark Matthews, *The Horseman: Obsessions of a Zoophile* (Amherst, NY: Prometheus Books, 1994).

18. Hani Miletski, *Understanding Bestiality and Zoophilia* (Bethesda, MD: East-West, 2002), 1.

19. Ibid., 85.

20. Ibid., 70.

21. Joanna Bourke, *Loving Animals: On Bestiality, Zoophilia, and Post-human Love* (London: Reaktion Books, 2020), 103.

22. Bourke, *Loving Animals,* 105.

23. Ibid., 107.

24. Battlecrops, "Zoophilia/Zoosexuality Survey RESULTS," *Battle-*

*crops' Zoo Survey* (blog), March 23, 2015, battlecrops.wordpress.com /2015/03/23/zoophiliazoosexuality-survey-results/.

25. Alfred C. Kinsey et al., *Sexual Behavior in the Human Female* (Philadelphia: W. B. Saunders, 1953), 509; Alfred C. Kinsey et al., *Sexual Behavior in the Human Male* (Philadelphia: W. B. Saunders, 1948), 671.

26. Battlecrops, "Zoophilia/Zoosexuality Survey RESULTS."

27. Ibid.

28. See Carreen Maloney, *Uniquely Dangerous: A True Story* (Manitoba: Carreen Maloney, 2018).

29. Malcolm Brenner, *Wet Goddess: Recollections of a Dolphin Lover* (Punta Gorda, FL: Eyes Open Media, 2009).

30. *Broad City*, season 3, episode 3, "Game Over," directed by Lucia Aniello, written by Naomi Ekperigin et al., Comedy Central, March 2, 2016.

31. *The Jerry Springer Show*, "I Married a Horse," 1998.

32. Yearningmice, comment on jennif990, "I (F24) Had Sex with a Dog for the first time . . . very conflicted," Reddit, Sept. 18, 2014, archived online at zooish.net/r/zoophilia/post_2grkz2.html#t1_cklu15u.

33. Alexa Tsoulis-Reay, "What It's Like to Date a Horse," *Cut*, Nov. 20, 2014, www.thecut.com/2014/11/what-its-like-to-date a-horse.html.

34. Ibid.

35. Ibid.

36. Ibid.

37. Maril.elle, comment on Tsoulis-Reay, "What It's Like to Date a Horse."

38. Eyoo90, comment on Tsoulis-Reay, "What It's Like to Date a Horse."

39. WWM, comment on Tsoulis-Reay, "What It's Like to Date a Horse."

40. Maril.elle, comment on Tsoulis-Reay, "What It's Like to Date a Horse."

41. Alexa Tsoulis-Reay, "Atypical," *New York*, Feb. 23, 2015.

42. Ibid.

43. *New York*, Feb. 23, 2015.

44. Post Staff Report, "Have Men's Mags Turned the Other Cheek?," *New York Post*, Feb. 22, 2015, nypost.com/2015/02/22/have-mens -mags-turned-the-other-cheek/.

45. BRosen, comment on Tsoulis-Reay, "What It's Like to Date a Horse."

46. RushBabe, comment on Tsoulis-Reay, "What It's Like to Date a Horse."

47. Santorum, quoted in John Corvino, "Homosexuality and the PIB Argument," *Ethics* 115, no. 3 (2005): 501.

48. Corvino, "Homosexuality and the PIB Argument," 501–34.

49. Justin Lehmiller, *Tell Me What You Want: The Science of Sexual Desire and How It Can Improve Your Sex Life* (New York: Da Capo Press, 2018); Justin Lehmiller, "Things That Make You Go Hmmm: Uncommon Sexual Desires and the Psychology Behind Them" (bonus chapter to *Tell Me What You Want*), Sex and Psychology by Dr. Justin Lehmiller, accessed Feb. 28, 2021, www.lehmiller.com/tmwyw-bonus-chapter.

50. Peter Singer, "Heavy Petting," *Nerve*, March 2001.

51. Feral, quoted in Brian Carnell, "Animal Rights Activist Attack Peter Singer over Bestiality Stance," Brian.Carnell.Com, March 28, 2001, brian.carnell.com/articles/2001/animal-rights-activist-attack-peter-singer-over-bestiality-stance/.

52. "Animal Husbandry?," *Washington Times*, March 24, 2001, www.washingtontimes.com/news/2001/mar/24/20010324–021733–1042r/.

53. Sarah Boxer, "Think Tank; Yes, but Did Anyone Ask the Animals' Opinion?," *New York Times*, June 9, 2001, www.nytimes.com/2001/06/09/books/think-tank-yes-but-did-anyone-ask-the-animals-opinion.html.

54. "Animal Husbandry?," *Washington Times*.

55. Ingrid E. Newkirk, "Letter to the Editor," Canada Free Press, July 21, 2005, https://canadafreepress.com/2005/rubin072105.htm.

56. "PETA's Statement on Bestiality," PETA, June 21, 2016, www.peta.org/media/news-releases/petas-statement-bestiality/.

57. Tsoulis-Reay, "What It's Like to Date a Horse."

58. Ibid.

59. Ibid.

60. Ibid.

61. Bourke, *Loving Animals*, 31–32.

62. Tsoulis-Reay, "What It's Like to Date a Horse."

63. Caroline Leroux, Jean-Luc Cadore, and Ronald C. Montelaro, "Equine Infectious Anemia Virus (EIAV): What Has HIV's Country Cousin Got to Tell Us?," *Vet Res* 35, no. 4 (2004): 485–512.

# Index

*Game of Thrones* (series), 115

genetic sexual attraction. *See* GSA

Getz, Barbara (a.k.a. B. Junahli
    Hunter), 124–25, 132–36, 142

*Glamour* magazine, 6

Gonyo, Barbara
    age-gap advocacy, 149, 157,
        183–84, 190–93
    childhood, 156
    in-person interview with, 178–79
    marriages and family, 179, 191
    online support created by, 150,
        169, 183
    pregnancy and adoption
        experience, 149, 156–60,
        179–80, 184, 190
    relationship with John (Mitch),
        180–82
    teen pregnancy, 156–57, 158–59

Gould, Terry, 31

GSA (genetic sexual attraction)
    anonymity and, 150–51, 154, 164
    as developmental disruption, 167,
        184
    empathy for, 148, 154, 188–89, 202
    *vs.* "genetic attraction," 184
    as illness/affliction, 147–48, 150,
        165
    intense/addictive nature of, 148–
        49, 150, 153, 164, 165, 167, 168
    interviewees, 164–67, 172 (*see also*
        Gonyo, Barbara; Jimmy; Shelly)
    mainstream media coverage of,
        149, 157, 169–72, 176, 183–84,
        190–93
    online communities for, 147–48,
        149–50, 152, 166
    as sexual orientation, 150, 151,
        202
    term origin, 149

GSA Forum, 150, 166, 183

GSA relationships
    advocacy for normalization of,
        150–52, 154, 166–67, 188
    childbearing risks in, 152
    concerns about normalizing, 148,
        153–54, 169–70, 185, 188–89,
        193
    consent issues in, 151, 154, 163,
        169, 176, 187
    disgust for, 167, 191
    legality and prosecution of,
        169–70, 176, 177, 178
    moral objections to, 147–48, 150,
        153, 154, 188, 189
    power issues in, 154, 163, 169,
        184–85, 187–88
    psychological disruption and, 153,
        185, 187
    *vs.* sexual abuse, 171

guilt, 208

Hacking, Ian, xviii

Hammer, 41–42

Hardy, Janet, 5

Harrison, Kathryn, 163

Haslam, Ken
    demisexuality of, 111
    on "designer relationships," 22
    discovery of polyamory, 13–14
    on faked orgasms, 21–22
    friendships and emotional
        relationships, 26, 33
    on internet, 29
    Kinsey polyamory archives
        curated by, 4, 13
    openness about polyamory, 28, 29
    on "permissive" events, 19
    polyamory advocacy, 4–5, 13, 29
    sexual philosophy of, 24, 27, 30, 33